W9-DCZ-158

THE BUSINESS MENTOR:
Elevate your Management IQ

A series of fireside chats on business philosophy, market growth strategy, brand development, and common sense

Ira Bernard Teich

THE BUSINESS MENTOR:

Elevate your Management IQ

A series of fireside chats on business philosophy, market growth strategy, brand development, and common sense

---

First published 2017

Copyright © 2017 by Ira Bernard Teich

All rights reserved. No part of this book may be reprinted or reproduced or utilized in any form or by any electronic, mechanical, or any other means, now known or hereafter invented, including photocopying or recording, or in any information storage or retrieval system, without permission in writing from the author.

Trademark notice: Product or corporate names may be trademarks or registered trademarks, and are used for identification and explanation without intent to infringe.

This book may contain copyrighted materials. In some cases, the copyright is owned by third parties, and this book is making the third-party content available to you by permission or under the fair use /fair dealing doctrines. The Content is made available only for your personal, non-commercial, educational and scholarly use. You may not use the Content for any other purpose, or distribute or make the Content available to others, unless you obtain any required permission from the copyright holder.

First Printing June 2017

Electronic Book Format ISBN: 978-0-9959442-4-4

Paperback Book Format ISBN: 978-0-9959442-2-0

To Janet, Sarah, Jonah, Miriam, and Avi
for providing the higher purpose to my life

PERSONAL COMMENTS

As I approach the intellectual prime of my life at seventy years, I reflect on the diverse experiences that have contributed to my becoming a passionate advisor to organizations. I use the word passion because I could only write a book on a subject about which I am passionate. My study of Science taught me the discipline of the scientific method in pursuit of evidence-based truths. My experience as a combat soldier brought me face-to-face with the near-magical capabilities of a committed team with a common mission, and where failure was not an option. My financial and business training made me appreciate the insights that arise when details form patterns, and patterns form understanding of root causes and their consequences. I have enjoyed a career in the management of one of the largest, most sophisticated, multi-national corporations in the world, working in staff and operating positions; and I learned that complexity is not intimidating when one understands how everything inter-connects into one elegant, integrated, framework. I have also enjoyed building and leading a marketing and creative agency to world-class recognition and commercial success because we learned how to understand consumers, and connect them to the organizations that strive to serve them. And my pastime as a visual artist opened my heart and hands to the healthy catharsis of self-expression. Finally, in these last twenty-five years, I have been privileged to advise large consumer-product and service organizations, manufacturers, start-ups, NGOs, and foreign governments, on developing business concepts, ideas, market growth strategies, and brands - in dozens of countries around the world. It continues to be a thrill. In all that time, I have used technologies that continue to evolve with incredible speed, from comptometers and 16 Kb computers, to terabyte pocket drives, and soon, I'm sure, to atomic memory. Terminology has also evolved, and much thinking and decision-making has been automated; but I have not seen changes in the basic principles and needs of businesses: the understanding around people and markets. The people who manage and work, the people who represent the market, and the people who are the constituency groups of stakeholders. Accordingly, my book deals mostly with the only really critical resource, an understanding of which, often eludes us, and that is, of course: the human factor inside and outside of the organization. It is an understanding about the way we must think, and manage, and market - to prosper in any endeavor or enterprise. I hope you will enjoy this material as much as I have enjoyed gathering it up from the recesses of my mind.

I.B.T

FOREWORD

I have written this book because 30% of all new businesses will not survive 24 months; 50% of all new businesses will not survive 5 years, but 70% of all mentored businesses survive more than 5 years[1].

THE BUSINESS MENTOR: Elevate your Management IQ - is written as a series of fireside chats about business philosophy, market growth strategy, brand development, and common sense.

We do learn from our failures, but many failures are costly, not only in terms of money, but in time, health, and emotional well-being. Some failures do not allow for recovery. My sense is that many failures are preventable.

In addition to a degree of self-indulgence - this book is essentially my attempt to mentor you. If you have bought or borrowed this book, we are in a way, connected now. Read these pages thoughtfully - and ignore, adopt or adapt, any of my comments as you see fit. If you have a question or the need for clarification, email me. I will respond as best I can. I hope that you will find value in these pages.

But *hope* is not a strategy. The five key root causes[2] of business failure or of sub-optimal business performance are:

- They don't identify and understand the customer, and the optimum channels of distribution to the customer. As a result, the customer doesn't know, understand and value them.

- Absent or weak value proposition. Failure to communicate the value proposition; can **you,** in 10 words or less, as the elevator doors close?

- Lack of leadership and expertise; lack of an effective, motivating, profitable, focused, and actionable business model, shared-mission, strategy, and road map.

- Short runway, over-spending, *(or spending on the wrong things)*; running out of time, money, enthusiasm, energy; expanding prematurely.

- Overly patient; tepid sense of urgency; waiting instead of passionately pursuing success.

Some of the best people were mentored: Alexander the Great by Aristotle; Plato by Socrates; Albert Einstein by Max Talmey; Bill Gates by Warren Buffet; and for the Science Fiction buffs: Luke Skywalker by Obi-wan Kenobi.

Mentoring is not only to move people from a failing state to a passing one. It is most effective in moving people up from a state of excellence to higher states of highest potential, self-actualization, and perhaps even joy. I expect this book will be most useful for managers in small to medium sized companies, up to approximately 500 employees. However, all managers in every department of every company are also the CEOs of their own businesses, and should behave as such – naturally with profound consideration given to the resources and synergies available, and the common, shared-mission of their organization. Accordingly, this book ought to be useful for managers in large organizations as well.

You will notice that I've chosen to insert quite a few endnotes, 205 to be exact. So, you are immediately able to drill into a bit of extra detail where appropriate. You may also notice some repetition in these pages. I suggest that you generously choose to think of this as my emphasis, rather than my age.

My wish for you: May you feel inspired and enabled to operate at the highest levels, to trust your common sense, and to achieve stunning successes.

TABLE OF CONTENTS

INTRODUCTION

There are hundreds of thousands of Business Books available, and each year 11,000 more are published[3]. A few gain a degree of recognition, become "Flavor of the Month", and recede into oblivion. Most never make it at all. A rare few deliver lasting value and even become classics. What many have in common is that they review examples of highly successful companies, and look for common attributes that can be characterized as the "secret sauce", or formulae for success. I have a hard time accepting this hypothesis. Many companies do the same things and have different levels of success.

The old adage, "I have learned more from my failures than from my successes", suggests an opportunity to study organizational performance; so, I spent a little space here on post-mortem business analyses within companies; a good thing. Personally, I mostly stopped reading business books years back; I couldn't keep up with the number of books being thrown into the market; and that was before the proliferation of e-books[4], online, and self- publishing. Then as a CEO, I subscribed to a *posh* monthly service that delivered to my desk - synopses of every notable business book published each month. That way, if a client mentioned a new, popular book, I would, at least, have an inkling about the main messages. On occasion, those summaries would lead me to read a book or two. But how many times can one read a re-hashing of the same ideas? Transcending all, this book attempts to deal with critical components of any business. These are my experiences with hundreds of clients over many years, and not a product of a research project. The genius of business lies not only in the understanding of the principles, but in their implementation; so, I do focus on how to approach, apply, and benefit - from business and market growth principles. Many of you are aware of these. For the most part, these are simple concepts, and will confirm and reinforce well-imbedded principles for many seasoned executives. For other readers, they should deliver useful insights. And for all: my hope and expectation is that it will provide a bridge between concepts and their execution, and a sense for prioritization.

Businesses today over-complicate things, often confusing themselves and more importantly, their customers and strategic partners. This is not necessary nor desirable. The truth lies in simplicity. Simplicity isn't always that simple to incorporate into an organization, but it's possible.

You will read in my book, basic truths about appreciating the needs of customers and consumers, and how you can solve their problems and deliver ideas and suggestions that they will value. I describe how creativity can and must be nourished in the workplace and I argue that creativity and intuition thrive well with, and complement - the rigor of a disciplined planning methodology. Both are essential.

I show how great long-term planning can be flexible and can generate returns from the very beginning. Disruptive strategies are explained as actions that many adopt to adjust to and leverage profound changes - without using that term that intimidates smaller business owners. Strategy is explained and demonstrated, as a program paving a continuous path forward; and it always begins with an insightful understanding of your current situation as well as your crisp future vision. I explain how to develop core values and unambiguous unique visions and missions - that are valuable to your markets and are an essential tool for the organization to screen all important decisions. I talk about branding a lot, and how a well-managed brand will deliver the necessary bond between your customers and your company - resulting in loyalty, equity, and earnings. I often use the retail and manufacturing models as effective ways to explain brands and the relationships that they build between the creator of the brand, and the consumers of the brand.

In the section on organization effectiveness, you will find advice on harnessing the collective intelligence of groups, harvesting their creative powers, generating high levels of motivation, and earning their trust, confidence, and loyalty. I also write about turning perceived disadvantages into advantages, and about the learnings and positive actions that can emerge from our understanding of failures, both our own, and those of others. My passion is the seeking of simplicity within complexity. I can get a bit preachy. Sorry, but I am convinced that there are only a few things you need to get right, to be successful. The noise in the business world, and the proverbial large number of moving parts – are illusions, and sometimes excuses. I try to relieve some of the intimidation around this.

The book concludes with chapters that address the value and techniques around selling and presenting ideas, products, and services, consultatively and with authority. Mostly, I deal with effective communications, honesty in communications, simplicity in getting the messages across to the right audiences, at the right time, and using the very low-cost and profound effectiveness of current communications technologies - to hear our audiences, understand them, have them understand you, respond to their needs, influence, and share.

The book also covers some of the risks and rewards of partnerships and alliances. I have a small section on NGOs and charities. These are the least understood of the business models and we can learn from these. In addition, I am motivated to encourage a subset of my readers to get involved, volunteer, and contribute their skills for a higher purpose. My last chapter deals with the future. Everything will continue to change dramatically and with ever-increasing velocity, but some things will never change.

If you can integrate some of these principles and styles and techniques into your workplace– then the result should be a happy, productive, cohesive team, working in a smart, creative organization – that is connected with its customers, defined by them, driven by them, and valued by them. If you achieve that, financial prosperity is automatic.

Enjoy!

CHAPTER 1
BUSINESS PRINCIPLES

It doesn't much matter if it's a large corporation, an NGO, a start-up, or a government – or if the sector is financial, automotive, manufacturing, retailing, food, service, or hospitality. Business principles are mostly all the same. When you identify and strip away the idiosyncratic differences and calibrate lexicons – all businesses follow a common business model and generally respond to similar sets of inputs. This connecting-of-the-dots, and of integrating principles is my realization from over 40 years of management, and from advising diverse organizations in dozens of countries around the world.

All organizations desire profits, and profits are always only the tiny difference between two very large (sets of) numbers. All organizations include only three basic components: 1) some kind of raw material; aka, the *Supply*, 2) some process that is inputted and applied to the system (whether it's physical or intellectual, or organizational or logistical) whereby *Added Value* is created, and 3) the resulting end product or service is made available to the consumer or customer in the market. I have challenged numerous business groups over the years and even offered a cash prize to anyone who can propose any kind of enterprise where this model is not applicable or relevant. They have tried. Some have been creative, suggesting ideas that range from criminal activities to prayer councils. All have failed.

THE SIMPLE BUSINESS MODEL THAT APPLIES TO ALL BUSINESSES AND ENTERPRISES

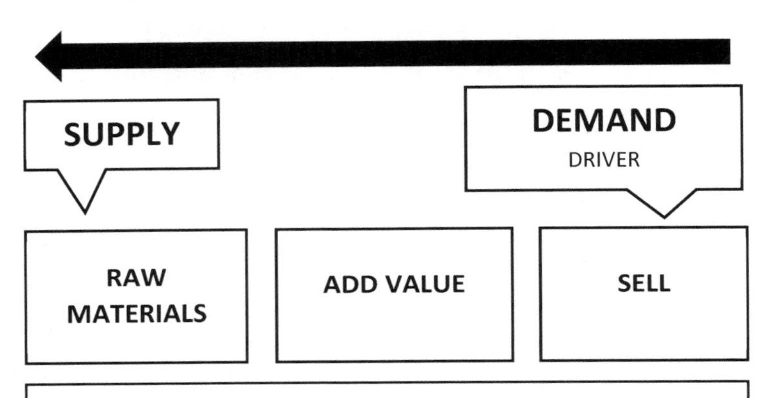

Despite my description of this simple business model as proceeding from supply, through value-add, and finally to market - in reality, the actual dynamic flow is in the opposite direction. This is one of the most critical insights necessary to successfully survive and prosper. By that I mean, that all organizations must be defined and driven by the market, aka, by the demand side. This may seem elementary to many readers, but we shall see that it is not so obvious nor easy when planning and operationalizing the organization; and not so straightforward when defining and enforcing the way the organization must behave in their marketplaces.

Some of you may challenge the market/demand driven assertion by pointing to innovators like Apple or Dyson or Tesla. After all, no consumer group demanded the breakthrough products that these companies developed. Did not therefore Apple create the demand? In a way, yes they did. But in a more fundamental way, they did not. Instead, they correctly interpreted the consumers' demand for products that worked better, saved time, delivered security and comfort, provided aesthetics in their lives, provided products to impress friends, and massaged their egos. Consumer behaviourists and marketing psychologists are busy understanding what motivates consumers. They understand, for example, that one's appreciation with their motor vehicle can transcend functionality. Some people even name their cars, like pets. They attribute personalities to them. Most of us are drawn to the beauty of motor vehicles and at an extreme, consider them a sculptural art form of sorts. Product design connects to the consumer at a higher emotional level, a level where brand loyalty resides. Think the look and feel of the Apple iPhone.

Understanding what consumers want and need is an evolving field and imperfect. The first wheel on an axle bearing was invented around 5,000 B.C., and it took 7,000 years until Macy's first offered the wheeled suitcase in

1970. How many suitcases do you see today, without wheels?

New economics of the past twenty years or so have introduced new concepts in market-driven operations (not just in the articulation of philosophy and mission). The older, supply-driven model implied *produce, inventory,* and *sell,* whereas the newer demand model implies: *sell,* then *produce.*

More on this later, but as a general observation, most management types will vigorously nod their heads up and down enthusiastically, approving the many "feel-good" textbook-esque business principles, and then they are shocked when faced with the pragmatic implications and ramifications on the business - of applying these principles every day in the reality of their operations. This is a failure to translate, understand, and incorporate principles into the planning process - a challenge that can be remedied by following some fairly basic business planning principles included in this book.

CHAPTER 1 TAKE-AWAYS BUSINESS PRINCIPLES	
1	Regardless of business sector or model, business principles are mostly all the same.
2	Organizations must be defined and driven by the market, their customers.
3	Demand models imply: sell, (then) produce.
4	There is often failure to translate and incorporate principles into the planning process.
5	Executives almost always agree on the principles but do not appreciate their ramifications on policy and operations.

CHAPTER 2
IDEAS AND PLANNING

Organizations need creative ideas. Albert Einstein, referring to himself as an artist, was flawless when he said *that imagination is more important than knowledge*[5]. I choose to adapt Einstein in the following manner: because imagination in business-educated adults who manage organizations is often rarer or undervalued versus their business knowledge, it is therefore mission-critical to recognize the value of imagination and nurture it in every enterprise. Organizations need to believe in and commit to creative idea-generation, and we need to formalize that process in every part of the organization. To position and characterize idea generation as a process and a methodology may seem antithetical. However, to deliver real, measurable and sustainable value, the business plan must be fuelled with creativity as well as with cold, deliberate, focused, laser-guided, operational discipline. These two macro-ingredients need not be in conflict.

The dichotomy of creativity and methodological rigor also makes for a "fun" component, a necessary ingredient for motivation and success. For a plan to work, it will need to include all the people with diverse and complementary interests and talents, will need to empower all the people with appropriate skills, with motivation, with rewards, with clarity of mission and purpose, and with a real sense of ownership and team. Nothing energizes like success. And success hardly ever happens (consistently and predictably) by accident. Hope is not a strategy.

So, a non-plan approach that wings it, that relies on loose, "free wheeling" albeit talented, and even high-creative people, and that depends on the spirit and goodwill and camaraderie of the group: that *non-plan* plan will likely eventually fail, or will deliver sub-optimal results. Sub-optimal results in a competitive environment is equivalent to failure. Oscar Wilde once said that "bankruptcy happens very slowly, then quickly"[6]. Great ideas that drive great plans that drive great execution that drive great, measurable outcomes are what it is all about. And the process must be imaginative, bold, passionate, energizing, cold, objective, precise, professional, engineered (all of those) – in order to generate a spectacular sense of common purpose, successful outcomes, and wonderful fun. Fun is normally absent if you are not successful.

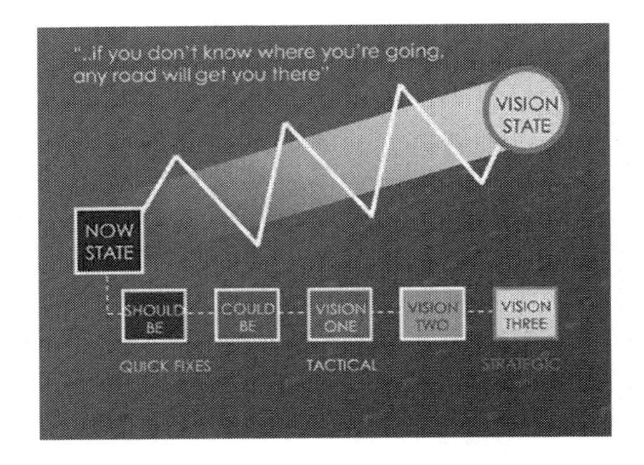

Like any planned road trip, you need a roadmap; and you require at least two coordinates: first, where you are starting from (the NOW state), and second, where you are intending to go (the destination, or for purposes of my illustration, the VISION state). The Vision may be a moving target over time but must be crystal clear at each snapshot point. You have many passengers in your car (perhaps then, let's call it a bus), and there will probably be a number of drivers. Regardless of who's driving at the moment, you all have to agree on the vision state, and have good reasons to commit to and own that destination.

In real life, many managers when surveyed, will articulate subtle and sometimes dramatic differences in their understanding of their company's vision and mission. The existence of multiple (often competing or contradictory) visions in an organization can be even worse that the lack of any vision whatsoever. The requirement for a single, commonly-shared vision is paramount. Unless all management speaks with one unified and powerful voice, their organization will flounder. After all, without one vision to bind all parts of the organization, how can one expect to see an aligned mission, a strong strategic consensus, team cohesion, and ultimately, cooperation. An army whose soldiers march in different directions will never arrive at their destination and never complete their mission. This phenomenon of multiple visions is easy to test. Ask anyone in the organization to repeat their vision and mission. You will not consistently hear the same thing. Yet this should be a fundamental expectation, because without that common purpose, much of the accumulated talent, failing to walk in lock-step all in the same direction toward a defined end state: wastes energy, becomes distracted, and confused by the absence of a strong foundation on which to build.

One sees a reliance on *hope* in business everywhere to some extent, and more so among religious peoples, especially in countries of the developing world. This sense of hope and faith seems connected to a degree of acceptance and fatalism which may well be a survival and coping mechanism. I am not a social scientist, but as a business consultant with experience in developing world economies, I can see a social value in the attitude of *hope*. After all, hope helps to deal with natural calamities and feelings of helplessness. This is understandable given an often-discouraging quality of life and the absence of many basic necessities - a condition that sadly affects many hundreds of millions of people. This attitude however, when embedded into culture and imported into business and planning behaviour – can be extremely counter-productive. I sometimes tell the following story to client groups in religious

Asian and African countries who are hope-driven, in my attempt to offer them perspective:

A great rainfall came to the village, and the pathways and countryside were becoming flooded. The mayor of the municipality ordered buses and trucks to circulate throughout the neighborhoods and he asked the residents to evacuate their homes. One man stood at the doorway of his 2-story house, ankle-deep in water, and waved-off the bus, shouting: "I will not leave my home, for I put my faith in the Lord." The waters rose up to the windows of the homes, and the man was forced to climb up to the 2nd storey. The local police rescue teams sent in a rubber dinghy boat and called out to the man: "Come into the boat and we will evacuate you to safety". The man called back from his 2nd floor window: "I will not leave my home; I put my faith in the Lord". The boat left as they could not force anyone to leave their own property. The water, however, continued to rise. The man was forced to climb out onto his roof, and from there he could see all the fields around were covered with water and all that was visible were the peaks of the roofs poking out of the water. He sat there with the water now chest-high when the regional air rescue arrived and hovered overhead in a helicopter. They lowered a rope ladder and shouted through a megaphone: "climb up and we shall save you; the waters are continuing to rise!". The man responded as before, that he would prefer to put his faith in the Almighty and that he would not leave his home. They could not persuade him, and so the helicopter drifted away, leaving him stranded there on his roof. As they had predicted, the waters rose even further; to the point that he was almost being floated away, off his roof. He would surely die without anything to hold on to, and he could not even swim. He raised his head and voice skywards to the heavens and loudly lamented: "Oh God, Lord: why hath thou forsaken me?" In response, the heavens opened and the voice of the Lord came bellowing down from the heavens, saying: "Forsaken you? What do you mean "" forsaken you?"". I sent to you, a bus; I sent to you, a boat; I sent to you, a helicopter!!!"

The learning that I express to these groups goes something like this: If you are inclined toward religious sentiments that guide your behaviours in life and in business, consider that God has given you a great gift that no other species has received: the gift and capacity to be creative, to be intelligent, to be capable of forward-oriented thinking and planning. Waiting for divine assistance, for fate, for luck, or for any help that is outside your control, is a waste of those gifts and is most likely to result in failures that could have been avoided.

From my personal perspective, for every flood, hurricane or other disaster victim whom we see interviewed on CNN extolling the grace of God for having saved (ergo "blessed") his family and his house – there are dozens who were not so "blessed" and had their loved ones perish and their homes destroyed. Were they then *cursed?* I somehow doubt it.

PATH TO VISION: NOT A STRAIGHT LINE

"Everyone has a plan 'till they get punched in the mouth"
- Mike Tyson

Referring back to the business model, we normally do not reach our destination by driving in a straight line; hence the wavy line. But the trajectory of the line must be true to vision state. The value of defining the trajectory includes some level of insurance that prevents us from being seduced by a perceived valuable distraction. For example, if one of your managers argues in favor of a diversion off the line to capture some calculated benefit with an attractive return on investment – then with the plan as your baseline (and as a screen for decision-making), you will be able to deduct from that argued benefit, the true cost involved to return to the plan after that singular benefit has been harvested. I would propose that this cost will often negate the benefit calculation. Many companies do not follow this discipline and regret not doing so.

IMMEDIATE ROI[7] FOR GREAT PLANNING

Correct planning methodologies will include a situation analysis, an understanding of the NOW state. Unfortunately, the perceptions of many senior managers (especially in larger corporations) are founded on what the official operations manuals and other related policies have to say about how things work. This may not reflect reality accurately (that is an understatement). Their perception of the NOW state is what I refer to as the "Should Be" state of affairs. In my consulting practice, instead of exclusively talking with senior management, I would always wander over (e.g., in a manufacturing facility) to the shipping and receiving area, and talk with the workers there to get the real dope on the state of affairs – from the perspective of their day-to-day experiences. I usually call *that* the "IS" (or now) state. So, what the executives often consider as the IS state, is in reality the SHOULD BE state; aka, what they think the current reality is, is only the "intended" reality based on policies, operations manuals, high-level stewardship reports, etc. The delta between what IS and what SHOULD BE: can become *Quick Fixes*. This is a potential benefit harvested from a methodology to planning - that exposes the opportunities for quick fixes, even though they are harvested from within a process designed for longer-term strategic planning. Quick fixes, according to my definition, are fixes that can be made within days and weeks (not months), and sometimes they are so profitable, that they can help finance the (longer-term) plan. Quick fixes that arise from strategic planning motivate the folks involved in planning - by demonstrating immediate, positive benefits, associated with the strategic planning methodology. This is worth stressing. *Success energizes people and organizations*. Typically, a long-term plan is seen as an investment in the future. This is sometimes a difficult "sell" inside organizations that face budgetary constraints and shareowner demand for short-term, measurable returns.

Long-term plans also tend to be complex. It is challenging to maintain employee motivation to work everyday in new ways, in order to experience results three years down the road. However, if the strategic plan is staged in a way such that it returns tangible benefits immediately, and in chunks throughout the process - the motivation to continue the implementation is significant and positive.

The second set of motivations deal with the psychology and management of change. Resistance to change is real and not to be underestimated. The comfort of the "status quo", even for an under-potentialized status-quo, is also real. As in physics, energy is required to alter the course of an established trajectory. To continue the physics metaphor, the law of entropy equally applies to business. Even if the existing plan/trajectory seems appropriate in a particular business, that trajectory, if left alone, will naturally degrade over time and break down – without the injection of fresh energy to maintain it.

Implementing strategic changes are often best done in bite-sized chunks, lest the organization choke. There is a big difference and degrees of difficulty - between concept and implementation. The totality of the change parameters may be complex in concept, but implementable when introducible in digestible chunks. This is often appropriate for very large organizations. It takes a super tanker two kilometers to turn 180 degrees in open seas. But more than that, change requires a mental attitude.

Progress is impossible without change, and those who cannot change their minds cannot change anything – George Bernard Shaw

---

Strategy itself is nothing less than an organization's response to change in their environment. These changes may deliver opportunity or threat; in either case, the response, by definition, is strategic, and lays out the "how" of the response. Those who correctly respond, win.

"It is not the strongest of the species that survive, nor the most intelligent, but the one most responsive to change"- Charles Darwin

---

There are also situations where revolutionary (versus evolutionary) change is required or desirable. This disruptive approach may be necessary to take a set of changes and revolutionize the way an organization, for example, recognizes a new market segment, and goes to market in a totally different way than previously. In these cases, where speed-to-market is a competitive imperative, the risks inherent in forcing an organization to absorb change quickly will have to managed very carefully. Many organizations, though well-intended, overestimate their capacity for dramatic change. JC Penney and HP are good examples of organizations that attempted overly fast turnarounds and suffered as a result. The "too fast - too slow" dilemma is a tough one, but the organization's capacity for change, their customers' willingness to respond to dramatic change, the penalties for not changing fast enough, and the patience of board directors and capital markets – all must be factored into the algorithm that will drive a decision on pace. The take-away here is that all decisions must be well-considered and deliberate. Taking action, and not taking action, and the timing of both – must be the result of conscious decision-making with neither course of action being a default scenario.

DISRUPTIVE STRATEGIES

"If you won't disrupt your own business, someone else will do it for you" - Shane Parrish[8]

Just a bit more on the subject of "disruptive" thinking. Why disruptive strategies must usually be implemented in almost violent ways in an organization - is because they often require fundamental shifts in infrastructure, including organization structure. The new disruptive strategy itself may be technology-based or market-target-based, or both.

On the technology front, disruptive models often displace existing market strategy, with for example: new functionality, mobility-portability, and miniaturization. Think: cell phones, smart watches, LCD/LED TV, e-books, e-cigarettes, social media platforms. Disruptions also often break the rules around the traditional trade-off between cheaper and better. They also replace and integrate. Consider the smart phone that replaces and displaces many stand-alone products: cameras and video, eBooks and email readers, gaming technology, alarm clocks, wrist watches, calculators, organizers, and even laptop computers. At the same time, these technologies, as well as other disruptive innovations, including services – often require a new form of (disruptive) marketing. An example may be Apple's iTunes that delivered music in a mass-customized way and created a market demand that did not exist before. It is true that customer demand must define and drive business. However, this core principle does not conflict with the notion that sometimes the customer has not yet been able to articulate their specific demand. This allows inventive organizations to create a demand that did not exist before. Apple is a great example.

SHAKING THINGS UP

Market disruption is a specific technical term and does not necessarily include less profound behaviours that are more popularly understood as "shaking things up". There are usually lots more opportunities to shake things up inside an organization. Sometimes "shaking things up" leads to "shaking things *out*", like cost savings, and more important, new ways of thinking. A small, personal example comes to mind. Very early in my career, as a fairly new Chartered Accountant, I become the commercial comptroller of Esso Petroleum in Toronto. It was my first day on the job and I walked into my new office to find that the corridors outside of it were lined with rows of computer printouts stacked high. These were early days in computing. Some readers may remember these.

I asked about the situation and was told that part of my department's tasks was to print these massive reports each month and distribute them to the appropriate departments throughout the company. This was a lot of work, involved many hands, and was costly. The information reported every transaction by every operating unit in the company. I looked at some of the information, and for the life of me, could not comprehend how it would be of much value to the receiving departments. My first instruction of my new job was to delay the distribution of those printouts by a week. My staff was flabbergasted and thought I was crazy. Here was their new "boss", who didn't know anything (they were correct), and immediately I was giving orders that upset their comfortable world and risked the goodwill of our internal customers. They had become accustomed to treating the distribution of these computer printouts as a priority, and speed was paramount. Enter new boy, me, and in one fell swoop I told them to ignore their duties. But my calculus was: if these reports were important, the receiving departments would "miss them", and tell us so. I guessed that if asked in advance, they would all just want things to continue as they always had. These heavy stacks of paper also made good doorstops. I had seen that before.

It turned out that almost nobody missed these reports, and the next month, we cut their production down to about 1% of the previous month's production. That's not exactly what I would call a disruptive strategy, but it is an example of the value of "shaking things up".

More important than that small event was the mega-message behind it. Do not accept the status quo. Think about the reason behind everything and experiment.

.

SITUATION ANALYSIS

It's useful to briefly reinforce the often-neglected "now state". The business strategy and roadmap is like taking any road trip. You need to understand what and where your destination is, i.e. what your goal is – but you must also know where you are starting from. In life and in business, theoretically, if you are happy with where you are, then you would not necessarily embark on a trip, staying instead where you are now. And so, in the context of business planning, a situation analysis in important. In other words, an understanding of where you are - is critical information. God is in the details. Even small changes, small negative changes that may be occurring, become important to understand. Many of these changes may be under the proverbial radar. It can be challenging to detect, recognize, and measure these radar blips for what they are.

Ernest Hemmingway's answer to "How did you go bankrupt?" was: *"Two ways. Gradually, then suddenly."* An analogy depicting the phenomenon of unrecognized changes that become recognized only when they are too late to fix, is the story about the frog and the boiling water. It goes something like this:

When a frog is placed in a pot of very hot water, the sudden change in its environment and the resulting shock of the hot water to its neural network – triggers an immediate response. The frog jumps out instantly and reflexively. But when a frog is placed in a pot of cool water that is then heated gradually - by the time the water becomes fatally hot, the frog has become debilitated and cannot save itself. This biological phenomenon is a metaphor for business. Some human resource practitioners have (ironically) used this principle to argue that change needs to be introduced gradually in order for it to be accepted – a principle that is generally true, but as I have discussed, sometimes not advisable. Certainly, there are techniques to introduce change quickly, if it represents positive change whose value is shared and understood by those who must exhibit the changes - but that is another conversation.

My preferred take-away from the frog metaphor is that organizations must fine-tune their distant-early-warning system and recognize subtle hints of change before these become overwhelming. Complacency, false confidence, denial - are human traits that must be resisted in the objective environment of business or government or any organization.

As for recognizing issues in the present, this is where a passion (and courage) for honesty can be a huge advantage for an organization. Problems that are ignored do not usually disappear. They grow. We all know the metaphor about the annoying monkey we find in our desk inbox. Instead of dealing with it, we sometimes just open our desk drawer and shove it in there, slamming the drawer behind it. Next time we open that darn drawer, we find that our annoying monkey has become a serious 500-pound Gorilla. This is what happens with issues we *wish* would go away. They only get worse.

Honesty, which I deal with specifically later in this book, is almost the kind of quality you could go full-throttle with, wrapping yourself in an honesty flag of sorts, and celebrating the notion of it. Why? Because we live in an increasingly cynical world. If you can invest in a culture of honesty, this will result in a positive differentiation strategy with the outcome that your stakeholders will reward your organization. Permit me to provide an extreme human example. You probably have quite a few people whom you trust. You probably have fewer people that you trust absolutely, unconditionally, unreservedly.

Now, let us imagine that you have won the lottery, a prize of 100 million dollars. That small, unsigned, unnamed lottery ticket is simply a "pay to the bearer" document worth $100 million. Now let us pretend that you have sprained your ankle and you would like someone to go to the lottery offices with your ticket and pick up the money, all the money – on your behalf. How many people would you trust to do this (little) errand for you – without you having any concern whatsoever?

That, my friends, is the stretch target: the level of honesty and resulting trust that every organization should pursue and aspire to earn in the minds and hearts of their stakeholders.

If you think that I am being idealistic, I assure you that I am not. The truth does set you free[9]. It feels good, but morality aside, it makes great business sense. Customers look for and respond well to "wow" factors, to positive extremes. And in the extreme, such as in the example that I have described, the brand value would be astronomical.

In 2000, Malcolm Gladwell wrote his "The Tipping Point: How Little Things Can Make a Big Difference". To be somewhat simplistic, it explains how small changes can start off, and then with increasing mass, take on a kind of life of their own, making a significant difference, ergo "tipping point". He explained that "ideas and products and messages and behaviors spread like viruses."[10]

There are a few things that have the inherent potential and capacity to be tipping point triggers for profound competitive advantage. I personally believe that pure, unadulterated honesty is one of these. Humans are social animals; we crave legitimate excuses to be loyal to something, anything. In an increasingly cynical world, a truly honest organization can be an attractive object of the human need for loyalty. Loyalty goes both ways.

Not everyone will agree with the practicality of my (enthusiastic) "honesty" assertion. It is useful to distinguish between *honesty* and *disclosure. Honesty* in the business context deals with the truth of what is being communicated; think of "quality of the communications". *Disclosure* on the other hand may deal with the volume, or the quantum of what is communicated; aka, how much is being said; the quantity versus the quality. This is a paradox of sorts that McKinsey called "the Dark Side of Transparency[11]" when they summarized the issue as follows:

"Executives need to get smarter about when to open up and when to withhold information so they can enjoy the benefits of organizational transparency while mitigating its unintended consequences. Excessive sharing of information creates problems of information overload and can legitimize endless debate and second-guessing of senior executive decisions. High levels of visibility can reduce creativity as people fear the watchful eye of their superiors. And the open sharing of information on individual performance and pay levels, often invoked as a way of promoting trust and collective responsibility, can backfire[12]."

That rings true. I have stressed throughout that managing a business is mostly about managing its most mission-critical resource, the human resource. There are no perfect cookie-cutter solutions. One size does not fit all. The balance to be pursued between transparency and secrecy, between honesty and secrecy – will depend on the organizational culture and the quality of the commitment and dedication and sense of fairness and firmness that the organization is able to generate in its overall mission.

The bottom line is that honesty and transparency – quite aside from the morality of it – can be a low-cost brand differentiator and brand pillar, providing it is sincere and authentic.

According to a study by Food Revolution in 2016[13], "94% of consumers say food product transparency from brands and manufacturers is important and impacts purchase[14]."

Southwest Airlines uses honesty as a brand differentiator as seen in their recent campaign, "Low fares. Nothing to hide. That's Transfarency." Southwest's "Transfarency" is their positioning and philosophy designed to foster trust. Being both a low-cost supplier of air travel and an open and transparent business, is the combination required to be believed, and therefore trusted.[15]

The Tylenol scandal (1982) saw seven people die in Chicago after being poisoned by taking pills from tampered Tylenol bottles. Tylenol's lack of defensiveness, full transparency and honesty, and immediate development of the now famous tamperproof bottles - was an example of the level of honesty to which their consumers responded positively. They rewarded the company and Tylenol fully recovered. In 2008, some Canadians were poisoned by listeria contamination in Maple Leaf Food products. Instead of mobilizing their PR teams for damage control, their president, McCain, refused to meet with company lawyers. Instead, he admitted the mistake, apologized unreservedly, opened his manufacturing plant to the media, and effected massive changes in food safety protocols. There was no defensiveness and no artful side-stepping. Maple Leaf initiated a new "gold standard" in honesty in Canada. The market rewarded that behaviour. A number of surveys, including a Wirthlin survey reported by MIT Sloan, assert that the majority of consumers are influenced by the business' honesty - in their decision to purchase goods or services from that business. Likewise, the majority of investors permit their perceptions of the honesty of an organization to influence their decision about whether or not to acquire that company's stock.

In my experience, many consumers believe that branding and marketing are automatically and inherently dishonest and certainly not sincere, nor authentic. Companies therefore, start with that disadvantage from which they must earn their way out. This is a challenge worth embracing.

As for the situation analysis, this understanding of where the organization stands at their present moment (in their authenticity rating as well as in all aspects of their current status) is critical to be able to map a way forward. Throughout my career, over and over, I observed that there are managements who believe that the current situation that best describes their organization is articulated in the printed material located in binders and manuals, all collecting dust on their office shelves. These records purport to detail the principles, policies, standards, and procedures by which the company thinks and operates. This is usually quite far from the truth and is merely a management perception and the illusion of *what is.* The reality is that often these materials only describe what the organization "Should be", as described in the previous section.

"COULD BE"

Some people think of the "could be" state as a kind of *standing in the possibility* of some benefit that is remote but worthy of attainment. Not me. I think of it as a more immediate prize. The difference between the "Should Be" and the next step in enhancement can be the "Could Be".

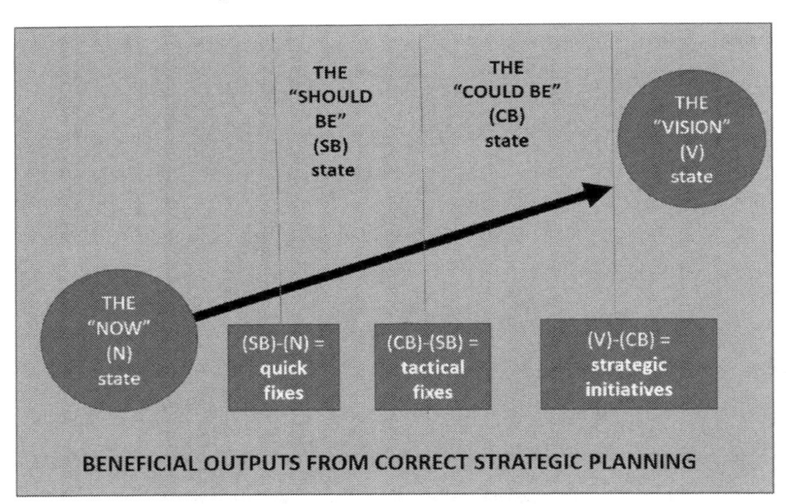

Those words suggest a state that is possible *now* or *soon*. It suggests a positive feasibility. It does not imply that the organization is lacking any core competencies, funds, time, equipment, or other enabling resources to make that

"Could Be" state happen. And so, I define that state as *tactical* with benefits being attainable in weeks or months but no longer than 12 months. Longer than 12 months, and I would call that longer-term or strategic.

HIERARCHY OF PLANNING

One piece of advice I can confidently give: to gain insight, walk around and talk with regular people.

There is a rigour to planning. It must be creative and imaginative but also must be facilitated and implemented with a disciplined methodology. As the flow diagram at the end of this section suggests, *Values & Beliefs*, then *Vision*, and then *Mission* – are the influencers and drivers that define the organization and that inform and enable the development of the organization's strategic objectives and goals. In turn, the way in which these objectives can be addressed and satisfied become the strategies (the "hows") of the organization; aka, how the organization plans to deliver upon their objectives.

There must be an internal consistency and referential integrity within the whole system of planning. These components are inter-dependent. For example, every contemplated strategy must be able to successfully pass the screen test for how they support the objectives, mission, vision, and values of the organization. If they do not, then either the strategy needs to be changed or the foundational mission and vision and objectives need re-examination for fundamental flaws. This can legitimately happen when the environment changes in profound and unexpected ways. However, it is more common that the linkages and inter-relationships among mission, objectives, and strategy are weak or overlooked and therefore not well managed.

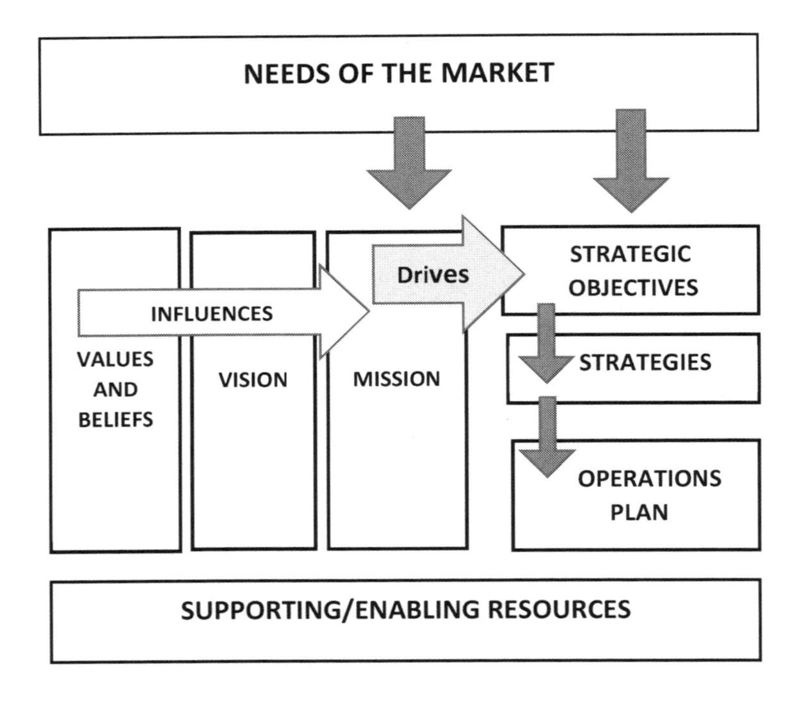

The principles of planning described here are not rocket science. They are exceedingly simple to understand and to business professionals and business academics, quite obvious. Why then do many organizations fail in this regard? In my experience, there are five main causes:

1. *Fuzzy Vision and Mission*

Unclear or fuzzy Vision and Mission. The organization has a flawed mission, or multiple visions/missions, or a meaningless boiler-plate vision/mission. Its people do not understand it, it is not shared or agreed-upon, it's not committed to, nor owned.

2. *Sloppy Planning*

Sloppy planning with market and other assumptions that are not defensible, not measured, or overly optimistic. Sometimes this takes the form of over-confidence which also can lead to an organization "biting off more than it can chew", or becoming a victim of its own propaganda. False confidence can lead to the organization deluding itself that it can be great at (too) many things. Taking on too many initiatives often results in a loss of focus, an inability to achieve excellence in any one aspect of the business, and in over-stretched and inadequate resources. Limiting the number of areas of focus should not be interpreted as my suggesting that the company rely on only one revenue model or source, or indeed that the business should expose themselves by being dependent on a very few customers for the majority of their revenue.

3. *Limited Outward Orientation*

A lack of outward perspective and intelligence. When an organization blindsides itself by not rigorously scanning its external environment and not appreciating the competitive landscape in which it operates and in which it plans to grow and win. This blindness also causes an organization to fail at developing appropriate benchmarks that describe the "best in breed". The company must understand to what levels of standards and operational goals they must reach and surpass.

4. *Lack of Skill, Discipline, and Oversight*

This failure is sometimes a failure of the necessary training to plan, measure, and continuously refine the process. Planning is iterative and must be enhanced within a continuous feedback loop system. In a sense, a plan incrementally loses its validity and relevance as soon as it is published. Therefore, planning is a program of work and not a project to be initiated every 3 to 5 years or even annually. It is a continuous process. Furthermore, there should not be a separate planning function except for coordination and consolidation purposes. Planning is a mission-critical strategic skill for each and every part of the organization, a function never to be outsourced. And the planning skills must be honed and practiced at every level of the organization.

5. *Lack of Clear, Relevant Principles, Policies, Standards, and Guidelines*

These ingredients for a healthy organization are part of the set of enabling resources. It is imperative that a healthy organization must be flexible in order to be responsive to an ever-changing and dynamic environment. Employees at every level should be free to make decisions that are correct in the circumstances and to take initiatives that best represent their organization to the myriad of its stakeholders. Accordingly, every effort should be made to limit the numbers of policies, standards, and guidelines to the absolute minimum that deliver core effective guidance in decision-making and behaviours.

First, let us calibrate lexicons. In my experience - policies, standards, and guidelines – are often confused terms and are unfortunately used interchangeably. To simplify and clarify this assertion using an everyday life example that most parents can relate to: consider how we instruct our children. We may say to them: "our family is committed to the safety of its children". This is a "principle" dealing with the subject of safety.

Then we might say (to a teenage son or daughter): "we expect you to be back home at a reasonable hour and by that we mean *not too late*". That statement is a statement of "policy" dealing with one aspect of the safety principle. It is noteworthy that there may be more than one *policy* that supports a single *principle*. The policy of being home early is one policy that supports the principle of maintaining a safe environment for the family, but there may be several policies that support that same principle.

Then we might continue and tell our teenage children: "we expect, in fact, we *demand* that you be home by 10 PM on weekdays, and by 1 AM on weekends". These statements are "standards" that support the policy of being home early. And again, there may be several *standards* that support a single *policy*. Of course, this is only an example. Many parents will have different standards appropriate to specific circumstances and their personal parenting philosophies. But the unique characteristic of a standard is that it is binary; that is to say, that there should not be any confusion about whether the standard was complied with or not. The child was either home by 10 PM or was not home by 10 PM. There is no interpretation required.

Finally, we might advise our children that it would be useful to always have emergency cash on their person so that if they are running late or if there is a disruption or other delay in the public transportation system, then having enough cash for a taxi ride home will enable them to comply with the standard. These are *guidelines,* and are designed to assist in complying with *standards,* but essentially these are helpful suggestions and not standards.

I have spent some space on this subject because I have observed over many years and across many organizations that it is not uncommon to see a confused jumble of principles, policies, standards, and guidelines that are mislabelled and used interchangeably. This generates uncertainty, and in some cases a kind of paralysis in decision-making and creativity. This is one of those simpler opportunities to correct, and to clarify what the organization's expectations are for the behaviours of its employees and to clearly spell out where compliance is expected and where creativity and innovation and skunk-works activities is encouraged. This is the challenge of the "tight-loose" balance so critical for the success of any organization.

CHAPTER 2 TAKE-AWAYS IDEAS AND PLANNING	
1	High creativity and methodological rigor are compatible and essential to nurture inside organizations.
2	Hope is not a strategy.
3	Planning requires a clear end-state goal and a profound understanding of the current now-state starting point.
4	Absent common purpose, the organization's talent is at best, wasted; at worse, self-sabotaging.
5	The path to vision is never a straight line.
6	Done right, long-term strategy can spin off immediate economic returns that can also energize and motivate the planning process.
7	Strategy should be implemented in bite-sized chunks to avoid the organization choking.
8	Do not be intimidated by terms like "disruptive strategies". It's just another word for what you have probably be doing.
9	Not taking action is also a decision. It may be the correct one but must not be a default scenario. All decisions must be thoughtful and deliberate and based on defensible assumptions.
10	Company radar must be calibrated to pick up more subtle clues in the competitive landscape and other external and internal changes.
11	Small things can make huge differences.

CHAPTER 2 TAKE-AWAYS IDEAS AND PLANNING	
12	Elevate honesty to be part of the company culture.
13	Corporate failures are mostly due to fuzzy visions, sloppy planning, limited outward orientation, lack of skill and discipline, and unclear policies and standards.
14	Be sure you recognize all of the enablers in your organization. Some are less obvious than others.

CHAPTER 3
VALUES AND BELIEFS

The sequencing of strategic planning follows a descending order from broad concepts to detail. It all starts with values and beliefs. These answer the question: what behaviours do we desire and which are we going to reinforce and enforce, and why? Values and beliefs are solid; in other words, they are perhaps the only articulation of an organization's position that does not change. The words describing values and beliefs are sometimes also referred to as *Core Values* and they can be engraved in a pillar of stone at the front gate of your factory or office. If they need revising from time to time, other than in very exceptional circumstances, then they are probably not true values and beliefs.

Sadly, many companies choose core values that are cliché and predictable, what we could call *motherhood* statements. However, this isn't always the case. Companies may also have negative core values. Companies exclusively driven by a profit motive, like tobacco companies, mislead their customers about the dangers of smoking. These core values suggest an exclusivity of self-interest. Investors with this same exclusivity of values have no issue investing in these industries.

PHILIP MORRIS CORE VALUES

The United States Surgeon General (on cigarette smoking) noted that "the brands most successful with teenagers seem to be those that offer adult imagery rich with connotations of independence, freedom, and authority, and or self-reliance" (USDHHS, 1994, p.176). Marlboro, the most popular brand among adolescents, epitomizes the stereotype of American independence.

As the Surgeon General noted, the "Marlboro Man" is usually depicted alone, he interacts with no one, he is strikingly free of interference from authority figures such as parents, older brothers, bosses, and bullies. Indeed, the Marlboro man "is burdened by no one whose authority he must respect or even consider" (USDHHS, 1994, p.177)[16]. Philip Morris International[17], which owns Marlboro and other brands, with $90 million in revenues (2015) and about 15% of the international tobacco market, is still growing. They've identified and targeted Eastern Europe, Africa and the Middle East as emerging smoking markets. By the way, they do not publish core values on their website.

VW GROUP CORE VALUES

More recently (2015), Volkswagen Group suffered their emissions scandal ("emissiongate"). They had intentionally programmed turbocharged diesel engines to activate certain emission controls only during lab emission testing. So, the cars met US standards when being tested but emitted up to 40 times more pollution in real-world driving. This affected 11 million cars around the world, a half-million of which were in America. This wasn't a one-year crime. It endured from 2009 until they were "caught" in 2015. The share price dropped by (only) a third. Their CEO after some reluctance, resigned, and others were suspended. The company announced they would spend about $18 billion USD to rectify the situation.

Why did they do this? Simple. Their emission system did not deliver good fuel economy by complying with the standards so they defeated the system when being tested. Students who cheat on exams get expelled. Volkswagen, to be sure, was embarrassed greatly and in their 2015 Annual Report, the Chair of the board, Matthew Muller announced on the first page: "Everyone at VW is working most diligently and with great commitment to rebuild the high esteem this Group rightly enjoyed for so long".

In the fine print of his letter in that same Annual Report, he was more conciliatory, saying: "as a result of the irregularities relating to diesel engines which contradict the very essence of what Volkswagen stands for, we find ourselves in the midst of what is probably *the greatest* challenge in the history of our company. On behalf of the Volkswagen Group, I would like to apologize to you, our shareholders, that the trust you placed in Volkswagen has been broken".

I could be picky and point out that the passive form is kinder than the active form, aka "we broke your trust" would have been stronger than "the trust has been broken". I could even be soberer and challenge the Chairman's remarks when he said that "we find ourselves in the midst of what is probably the greatest challenge in the *history* of our company". In my opinion, Muller didn't mean *scandal.* He meant a financial and marketing *challenge.* For me, this was not the most horrible event in their *history*. The VW scandal and core value-deficit of greater note was about the 12,000 slaves borrowed from Hitler's concentration camps whom VW terribly abused in their Wolfsburg plant during WWII[18]. VW has admitted to the use of slave labor[19]. Core value issues are not new to VW.

Why am I focused on this? Because if the organization is serious and wise, they can engineer their environment to ensure that core values are not only respected but loved. Not every employee may be able to comply with core value behaviour. Absent any legislation to the contrary, new employee candidates should be tested to ensure that they have the right personality for the job. For example, if your food service business is based on a uniquely personable approach to customer, we all know that you need to engage employees in those roles who are "naturally" friendly, enthusiastic, happy, smiley, optimistic, polite, etc. There are certain traits that you simply cannot train for. I would not wish to hire a corporate risk manager who is a natural optimist.

So, depending on the organization's choice of core values, they can successfully seek to gain control over the core value environment if they have the strategic will to do so. As for different kinds of values beyond the standard ones such as honesty, etc – there are choices such as humor, optimism, even fun-loving. If the organization is a toy manufacturer or an adventure tourism agency, then a fun-loving nature and curiosity might be valuable and relevant core values to behave by. If the organization is a bank – well, I want the folks protecting my money to be dead serious, responsible, obsessed with accuracy and security - and yes, I'll pass on the fun-loving piece.

For GM, they have articulated core values as follows: "Our Code of Conduct, Winning with Integrity, sets forth our fundamental commitment to conducting business ethically and honestly. We are committed to our core values: customers, relationships, and excellence. We must always act with integrity, take accountability for results, and do the right thing, even when the right thing is hard to do. Quality and safety – both customer and workplace – are foundational commitments, never compromised."

Typically, these descriptions should not take long to articulate but they drive the internal culture of an organization and are an important ingredient in the set of guiding principles of conduct that are commonly known as and referred to as the Values and Beliefs, and to a large extent, these drive parts of the Vision and the Mission.

CHAPTER 3 TAKE-AWAYS VALUES AND BELIEFS	
1	Strategic planning begins with values and beliefs (core values) and works down from there.
2	Core values must not be motherhood statements. They must be about specific behaviors you demand from your people as a condition of their employment.
3	There are certain personality traits which an organization needs, that are intrinsic to a person's nature. You cannot train these into people. Select people who already have them.

CHAPTER 4
THE VISION

Let's move on to Vision. If core values are designed to guide attitude and conduct, then Vision is something else entirely. I think of Vision as a kind of picture that the organization paints. It is a picture of the world as they would like to see it and experience it, and have a role in building. There are those who would disagree with my definition of a Vision (vision statement). They would argue that the vision should be a clear direction that the organization should take in the middle and long term timeframes and then they (usually) use the word mission within that definition.

The Vision should answer the question "why?". It should suggest the raison d'etre of an organization. Because of this, the vision and mission are very much related and often appear as two statements on the same page. One follows from the other.

"The ultimate test of an organization that really knows itself is when "there is a clear articulation of what the world would miss if that organization did not exist"" – Peter Senge[20]

Organizations ought to be obsessive about achieving clarity. Achieve clarity by developing clear, bite-sized, chunks of information that both stand-alone and are relatable to previous and subsequent chunks – to create a continuum of thinking that all ties together. Therefore, I recommend that the vision statement deal with the ideal world - related to and in the context of your business or organization. The mission statement will then describe your specific role in enabling the vision to become reality. And by the way, I think it's ok to develop one short document that describes both vision and mission on the same page, as long as each of those is clearly delineated.

THE DISNEY VISION

"To make people happy". With four words, one of the shortest vision statement to be sure. As an aside, Nike's vision in the 1960s was: "Crush Adidas". This could legitimately be criticized but it is certainly clear and directing of behaviour. Back to Disney: I like their four-word vision but I don't think it goes far enough. I can imagine the company team and their agency being quite happy with the punch and brevity of four words that capture the core essence of why Disney exists. On the other hand, I am not clear from that vision, whether they are in the hamburger business (burgers make ME happy) or in the transportation business (getting to my destination on time and safely makes me happy also) or they might be a gardening maintenance contracting company (I am happy not to see weeds in my garden).

So, Robert Iger[21], if you are reading this – may I suggest including the idea of "*storytelling*" in the Disney vision. It speaks to both entertaining and an educational dimension and the powerful way (including technology and innovation) that content is delivered. My invoice is in the mail.

THE TESLA VISION

What is an example of a really good vision statement? Let us look at a modern company I greatly admire: Tesla Motors Inc. Their vision statement states: "to create the most compelling car company of the 21st century by driving the world's transition to electric vehicles." I think that this is close to being a very good vision statement. I might change it, if I could, to:

A very cool 21st century where the world has transitioned to electric vehicles, and as a result, has become cleaner, healthier, quieter, energy efficient, and environmentally responsible.

Ok, so maybe, I wouldn't use the word "cool", but do you get the difference between them and me? I want the vision to be less about the organization and more about its aspiration and vision for the world at this point. For me, the vision statement should be able to answer the question:

Why? (and not what?). It ought to imply the raison-etre for the organization. It should therefore be both inspirational and aspirational. My version above of what Tesla's vision might have been, explains to the reader why it's so important that the world should transition to electric vehicles. After that "softening up" as it were – the reader might be readier to read about the mission; aka, the role that Tesla is committing to play in leading to bringing about that huge vision.

THE FACEBOOK VISION

Let's look at one more Company's vision, Facebook. They totally confuse me. Here's their vision statement: "People use Facebook to stay connected with friends and family, to discover what's going on in the world, and to share and express what matters to them."

And their Mission statement is: "to give people the power to share and make the world more open and connected."

To my mind, both statements have elements of both vision and mission. And that's what I meant before when I wrote about clarity chunks. What is Facebook really saying (or should be saying)? This is what I would advise them:

Vision: We want to see a world where people have the power to share and to make a more open and connected world. This capability will allow all people everywhere to stay connected with friends and family, make new friends, to discover what's going on in the world, and to express what matters to them to anyone at anytime".

That statement, though unwieldy (I'm not actually going to craft a refined, finished, fictitious vision statement for Facebook) actually contains the answer to the question *why?* Why it's important for the world, what benefit it delivers for the world, how our lives will be better, and why it is a worthwhile ambition to have a world look like and behave in this way in the future.

The mission, then, will expound on how the organization Facebook will work to bring about this wonderful future world that we have just bought into after having read the vision.

CHAPTER 4 TAKE-AWAYS THE VISION	
1	Think of a vision statement as a kind of picture that the organization paints of the world that they would like to see and experience and have a significant part in building.
2	The vision should answer the question: *why*? It should suggest the raison etre for the existence of the organization.
3	Organizations should be obsessive about being clear. Disney's vision "to make people happy" is too vague. Hamburgers make me happy, but Disney is not a hamburger company. They should be talking about story-telling and imagination as a powerful force for educating, entertaining, and expanding minds.
4	The Tesla vision is one of the best I've seen.
5	The vision and mission statements flow from one another; they should probably be combined or on the same document.

CHAPTER 5

THE MISSION STATEMENT

The Mission informs and guides the organization's strategic decisions. It is a critical document, perhaps one of the most critical. It embodies the organization's role. If it's done right it should be quite unique to the particular organization and avoid boilerplate phrases. Ideally, it should be usable as a screen through which decisions and deliberations can be filtered to determine if the path you are intending to pursue is in alignment with your organization's mission and consistent with the promises made to its stakeholders.

Whereas the vision statement tends to answer the question *why*; aka, why do we as an organization exist, the mission statement should be capable of implying the answer to why, and more completely answering the questions: what? where? when? and who? (note: the question *how* – is answered by the strategy). In other words, to fabricate a mission statement: "we at ABC corporation are committed to profitably dominate the South American market by 2025 with a full assortment of our skin health and wellness products offered in over 50% of supermarkets, pharmacies, and hypermarkets…etc."

MISSION STATEMENTS: THE GOOD, THE BAD, AND THE UGLY

The failing of most mission statements is that they do not contain strategic (broad) macro-objectives. To be a valid mission, objectives must be quantifiable. If they are not measurable, you will never know if you ever got there or not. This does not necessarily mean that the mission statement needs to be long and convoluted. It can be crisp and still enlightening.

It cannot be emphasized enough that the mission be detailed and clear enough such that subsequent strategies (strategies that arose from that mission) should not come as a surprise. Many times, I have sat through mission development deliberations and have observed management nod their heads in (enthusiastic) approval of the "motherhood" mission statements of principle – only to scratch their heads later on, once they began to recognize the real and sobering ramifications and implications of what they had previously agreed upon.

What this suggests is that the mission was inadequate and unclear and incomplete. It is imperative that missions say what they mean and means what they say without ambiguity. Before mission statements are finalized and approved, real life (current and potential) scenarios should be developed and tested against the developing mission statements. The bottom line for me is that if the organization doesn't get this part right, what will follow is largely a waste of time. Further, if not done correctly, the mission risks becoming misleading and misused, resulting in potentially confused and inappropriate actions.

SIMPLICITY IS ELEGANT

A pizza chain whose business model was about efficient home delivery might develop a mission that says: "Pizza in 30 minutes". Believe it or not, that's a mission statement. What it doesn't say is important. It does say that if your friends are coming over and the Superbowl is coming on TV in 40 minutes, you will have the pizza in time for the kick-off. Presumably, the beer is already in the fridge. What is intuitively understood by its absence is: do not expect gourmet pizza. This business model caters to a certain target segment that has certain needs to satisfy. And it's a promise that triggers an expectation in its audience. In this pizza mission statement example, it does not directly answer the question who, or where. These may or not be implied depending on the audience. What is clear about that very brief statement is that in order to guarantee a 30-minute pizza delivery, the organization must be referring to sophisticated systems with computerized call centres and fulfilment logistics, fuelled by partners (franchisees, associates, or some other network of stakeholders) that can satisfy that promise.

One of the dominant pizza chains in Canada is Pizza Pizza with 750 restaurants in their royalty pool[22] and serving 30 million customers a year. Their mission is "best food made especially for you". In my view, that doesn't even come close to being an appropriate mission. First, no offence intended, but pizza in 30 minutes probably cannot be "best food". It may be *best in class*, in which case the mission could read: "what we can make for you in 30 minutes is amazing. Taste it to believe it". But most observers will agree that their success mostly stems from a reasonably good pizza with guaranteed delivery to your home in 30 minutes and we Canadians all know their number by heart! 967.11.11. This number has been drummed into our heads for years; it was a brilliant recognition and marketing strategy. Now, of course I order with my iPhone app but I will remember that phone number forever.

THE FORD MISSION

With some mission statements, it is unclear who the mission is designed to talk to. Ford's mission statement is "One Team. One Plan. One Goal." This is certainly short and punchy. Their consultants probably charged five figures to come up with it. And it's ok - but it clearly talks to their employees and other stakeholders and not to customers. Then again, we would have to understand who their customer is. As a consumer of automobiles, that mission statement means little to me. And so, it is safe to assume that it is directed mostly *inward* and not *outwards*. This mission likely deals with Ford's response to challenges that they face as a company, it encourages mostly employees and dealers, advising them that the company is aware of these challenges and they have the strategic desire (one plan) that will actively deal with those challenges. The general audience, customers, potential customers, and small, non-engaged shareowners – will basically not know what Ford is talking about. This begs the questions: to whom should the mission statement speak? Does a company need two mission statements: an externally-directed mission statement *and* an internal mission statement?

As for the Ford example, it is beyond the scope of this book to delve deeply into the special business model that characterizes the North American automobile industry where automotive manufacturers do not (and by law, must not) sell directly to consumers. There are significant advantages and disadvantages to this model. As for me, not being in control of one's own brand is a major weakness. But there are compensating benefits that deal with cash flow, capital, local need fulfilment and local market vagaries, and of course the simple focusing on core business. Therefore, it is not surprising that Ford's mission seems to be directed to its independent franchise dealership audience and not to its end-user driving audiences. In my opinion, it is a mistake for Ford not to address and seek to fill this gap. My guess is that due to the complexity of reaching shared consensus around the ideal Ford consumer experience and the promises required to achieve this, Ford has practiced avoidance. It feels like: *If it ain't broke, don't fix it.* Nevertheless, I do feel that a more courageous and ambitious mindset might deliver a measure of competitive advantage in a rather confusing industry. And certainly one might argue that it *is* "broken". Ford pulled out of Japan's closed market in 2016, citing "Japan is the most closed, developed auto economy in the world, with all imported brands accounting for less than 6% of Japan's annual new car market[23]". Then again, the popularity of the Apple iPhone in Japan soared to 72% of the smartphone market there in 2010[24]. While Apple's sales in Japan slipped in 2015, they remain the dominant marketer of smartphones there[25]. I realize that there is a bit of an apples-oranges comparison between the automotive and smartphone markets, but the fact remains that Apple was genius in its Japanese market strategy and in its obsession with undisputed quality. But that's another conversation.

To bring my former question forward: Does a company need two mission statements: an externally-directed mission and an internal one? - the answer I think, is the same answer that all competent consultants give: "it depends". Different stakeholder groups have both common interests and they also have very different interests. It would be a very long mission statement that attempts to address all of these segments and any attempt to be all things to all people never quite seems to work that well. At a minimum, the mission becomes so diluted and abbreviated that it risks becoming confusing and incomprehensible. It almost sounds like a company needs a large reservoir of segment-specific mission (sub-) statements from which it can hoist, emphasize, and communicate sections that are relevant to specific groups.

This is not a novel idea. Most larger companies will have divisional mission statements and other mission statements targeted right down to unit working levels. This is proper. Each team should be motivated. Each team leader, however small the team, should consider himself or herself as the CEO of that team with a proper mission. Thinking up through the planning hierarchy, a departmental mission will sound like a unit's operational plan, to the head office.

There are ways of creating a short but meaningful mission that guides the behaviour of an organization in interesting ways. Back in the late 1980s, I had occasion to advise the executive team of Bell Mobility. In one of our first group meetings, we discussed issues facing their customers and how the company might respond with operational changes that better satisfied, and even delighted the customer. I mentioned somewhat off-the-cuff, that it should be as easy to become a Bell Mobility subscriber and customer, as it is *to call for a pizza*. Sounds like I am somewhat obsessed with pizza, but that single notion which enjoys a fairly common association (almost everyone has called for a pizza delivery) – drove much of the discussion and resulted in some dramatic changes in the way that Bell Mobility management started to think about their service model. That little metaphor never made it verbatim into any formal mission statement but it influenced the organization and possibly made a difference in the subsequent growth of that organization in Canada. It was outwardly focused but it carried significant implications on how the company must operate to satisfy that goal of making it easy and painless for customers to engage.

TIME FOR A MISSION PARABLE?

There was a group of three bricklayers, laying their bricks. The local news van pulled up to the construction site and the reporter, armed with a tape recorder, stepped out to interview the workers. She asked the first bricklayer: "what are you doing?", and he answered: "Can't you see? I'm laying bricks". She asked bricklayer number two: "What are you doing? He responded: "I'm working to support my family". Finally, she asked the last bricklayer: "What are you doing? He motioned up to the soaring infrastructure and announced: "I'm building a cathedral".

The third bricklayer, you see, had a sense not only of his specific role, but also how his role fits into the overall mission; how his contribution is mission-critical to the whole. Which one of those three bricklayers would you like on your team?

SOME MISSIONS ARE SELF-EVIDENT

"Nothing astonishes men so much as common sense and plain dealing." - Ralph Waldo Emerson[26]

There are some industries that are inherently better understood than others. Many of these are the service industries, both food service and hospitality – and of course the two are related.

In mid-2016, I was in the Philippines advising their Ministry of Trade and Industry. I stayed at a local hotel during the low season. In fact, at times it appeared as if I was the solitary guest, and as such, I often took my early-morning breakfast with the hotel manager. He was lamenting the high cost and effort of formal, professional staff training for hospitality behaviours and he was shocked to hear my off-the-cuff assertion that much of it was probably unnecessary if he hired his people after filtering for the right personality traits that excel in this kind of work. I emphasized to him that some behaviours that are simply human in nature just come naturally with little formal instruction. This is what I told him: Most of us have relatives whom we love and appreciate dearly. And the reality is that most of us have one or two relatives whom we would probably not have as friends, if they had not been relatives in the first place, with the familial obligation that that implies. Here's the thing: when we have the relatives that we love and they visit us from another town, we inherently know exactly what behaviours are required to make them feel welcome and comfortable. If we really and truly desire that they should extend their stay with us or at least to have them come back and visit us again soon, we know how to conduct ourselves in order to achieve that goal. We would anticipate every need, and over-deliver to the point of delighting them. We would try to be creative in entertaining them, making suggestions, asking them what would make them happy and then striving to make them happy. It's a natural skill that most of us humans possess and use when we genuinely wish to have them visit again soon. On the other hand, when we are dealing with relatives that we like less, we also know very well indeed what the minimum respectful conduct is - usually delivered with a polite coolness - to avoid offending but to still make it clear that our duty has been fulfilled and that they should take their time (preferably a long time) before they consider a return visit.

I encouraged the hotel manager to experiment with a hiring approach that includes up-front filtering for the appropriate natural personality traits. Of course, we are not talking about relatives whom we love but we *are* talking about (hotel) guests, without whom his staff would not have jobs and would not be able to have a family or support one. If his staff could be selected for the personalities and attitudes that were naturally warm, friendly and happy, plus if they could internalize this concept of adopting and practicing *behaviours that would bring our guests back to us,* that would be superior, in this writer's opinion, to most classroom training sessions on how best to hold a broom or fold napkins.

CHAPTER 5 TAKE-AWAYS MISSION STATEMENTS	
1	Mission statements, to be useful, must be specific and quantifiable and therefore usable as a screen by which critical business decisions and deliberations can be accepted or rejected.
2	Missions should generally be directed toward customers (external mission) but it may be useful to have a subset of the mission specific to your employees/management (internal mission).
3	Don't develop a mission through a democratic process. Senior management creates it (with inputs) because they are being held accountable for it. Then, employees can be inventive within the boundaries of the mission.
4	You don't need a mission to tell employees that they must find ways to delight customers in every possible and sensible way. That is self-evident and should be a condition of employment. Those who don't embrace this kind of common sense should have no place in your organization.

CHAPTER 6
CREATIVITY

Perhaps the easiest skills to cultivate and harvest, though it may be perceived by some to be the hardest, is creativity and imagination. I believe that there is an inner child in each of us just below the surface (and in some cases on the surface). This child-dimension is a valuable resource because it is not corruptible by the status-quo, because it can stand in the possibility of wonderful things happening, because it still believes in magic, and because it possesses creativity and spontaneity.

Some people can draw on their inner child on demand when imaginative creative ideas are required or desired. For others, there are ways in which their imaginative side can be coaxed out.

The notion that creativity exists in all of us is still surprisingly somewhat debated. The traditional view describes three categories of abilities that are required for (business) success. Most people display varying degrees of these abilities.

Abilities	Skill Attributes[27]
Analytical	analysis, evaluation, judgement, comparing and contrasting
Pragmatic	applying, utilization, implementation, activation
Creative	imagination, exploration, synthesis connecting, discovery, invention and adaptation

We still find in some quarters, a conventional wisdom that tends to treat these abilities as stand-alone attributes and skills. I prefer to believe that they are related. Consider a tax accountant that is so expert and knowledgeable with the details, the history, and the evolution of tax laws and regulations - that he or she is able to discover legal loopholes and other creative methods to avoid tax burdens (for their clients) without stepping over the line into tax evasion. That creativity arises from an expert and detailed understanding of the field. Consider a corporate lawyer so expert and experienced with the ins and outs of contract law - that he or she is able to construct a contract that is extremely inventive in the way that it anticipates potential future problems and protects the client. The creative dimension was available in those illustrations and was probably assisted by a well-articulated goal. My point is that a true expert with analytical ability is better positioned to be creative in analysing situations and coming up with creative solutions. Experts in pragmatic matters are more able to creatively apply knowledge and implement solutions.

Yet, there will be those who are more confident, more extroverted, and more socially adept than others. It is the responsibility of management and the members of every team - to coax out the participation of all employees and team members. The best ideas often come from the quiet folks who say little, know a lot, and think deeply.

THE POWER OF THE INTROVERT

"Altissima quaeque flumina minimo sono labi"
(the deepest rivers flow with least sound) — Ancient Roman proverb

---

In her book, "Quiet: The Power of Introverts in a World that Can't Stop Talking[28]", Susan Caine writes:

"But we make a grave mistake to embrace the Extrovert Ideal so unthinkingly. Some of our greatest ideas, art, and inventions – from the theory of evolution to van Gogh's sunflowers to the personal computer – came from quiet and cerebral people who knew how to tune in to their inner worlds and the treasures to be found there… and as the science journalist Winifred Gallagher writes: "the glory of the disposition that stops to consider stimuli rather than rushing to engage with them is its long association with intellectual and artistic achievement. Neither E=mc² nor Paradise Lost was dashed off by a party animal""

Caine[29] continues with a scathing critique of some organizational cultures that value "people skills" but distort the meaning and value of such. Employees are expected to promote themselves "unabashedly" to manage and advance their careers. Even authors, who were once thought of as a somewhat reclusive "breed" are now vetted by the publishers' publicists to determine if they are "talk-show-ready[30]".

This is an opportunity for the enlightened organization and every manager – to enable a fuller participation of all their human resources and harvest the resulting synergy that can be very powerful in generating creativity and the successes that come along with it. There are mechanisms and strategies available to coax out the creativity in organizations. I will illustrate.

POWER OF VISUALIZATION

"To bring anything into your life, imagine that it's already there" – Richard David Bach, *American writer, best known for best-seller, Jonathan Livingston Seagull (1970)*

In 2001, I was approached by Trizec Hahn Corporation, a real estate developer with assets of about two billion dollars and 10,000 employees. They were headquartered in Canada and California at that time but operating worldwide. Peter Munk was the founder, chairman and CEO of Trizec Properties and chairman and founder of Barrick Gold, the world's largest gold mining corporation. Trizec was suffering. Malls in America were in trouble having lost over the years, their main anchors such as supermarkets, electronics, and hardware retailers - which evolved to larger format offerings that became central to the then new Power Center retail locations that often featured large Best

Buy, Ace, and Home Depot type stores. This left Malls with a hodge podge of fashion/clothing, footwear, and cosmetics stores, department stores, and food courts. Trizec's shopping Mall investments in the United States were underperforming. They wanted me to advise their retail mall development executives on how they might think of and try a different approach to managing the business. Munk even faxed me an article entitled "The *Mauling* of America"! I arrived in their California board room to a group of executives down on themselves. My working hypothesis came down to this: Mall developers simply built the structure and then as leasing agents, leased out stores essentially to anyone who had the financial credit to pay the rent. The developer didn't manage the mix, weren't retail experts, and could not affect in any significant way the customer experience. After all, their customer was simply the lessee. But they did have a vested interest in the consumer/shopper because the rental revenue was (and still is) usually some combination of a base rent plus a percentage of store sales. The more successful the store, the higher was the mall developer's revenues. Very simple and straightforward.

It was a bit strange for these development executives when I asked them to close their eyes and imagine. Good thing I was wearing a suit and came recommended by "the man". So, they complied. I asked them to visualize a scenario not of the present real world. Instead, I asked them to imagine that the stores in their Mall were not a collection of many different stores, but rather one big store with many departments, a huge department store, if you will. I also asked them to think and visualize that they owned and operated this giant store themselves. And then I asked them that given this new imagined reality – what would they do that is different from what they are doing today.

After a few minutes, there was no stopping these folks. One said that since it was one huge store, the shopper could shop at all the departments and pay later only once for all their purchased items. Another suggested that each "department" could share their data and offer suggestions and discounts to customers who bought merchandise in one area to buy in another, as in coordinating wardrobes and accessories (promotional mechanics). And another talked about how shopper fatigue sets in after the weight of their purchases exceeded a certain poundage, and they could eliminate that by providing shopping carts that could be taken from "department to department". Yet another talked about rearranging all the departments so that the flow, the navigation, and the mix of products – all made more sense from the shoppers' perspective. We created quite a nice list. And then I woke them from their reverie and broke it to them that they had to withdraw from the imaginary world that I had conjured up for them; for indeed, the reality remained that they were (just) leasing agents. But my challenge to them was this: what ideas from this list can you adapt and import into the reality of today that can deliver value?

Visualization allowed this group to ignore and think past the operational constraints and free themselves to consider ideas that would normally not be available for them to consider. The next stage, once reality was again allowed to influence them, was to figure out how to adapt these ideas to fit and enhance their current operations. It can be a powerful tool for creative thinking and ideation. One of many.

STANDING IN THE POSSIBILITY

Creativity comes in many forms and a common element is the ability to *stand in the possibility.* This is more easily done for some than for others but all of us have the ability to tap into our inner child and activate the imaginative powers that we all had in our early years. This may not be easy to do *on demand.* Creativity and creative thoughts often come to us at unexpected and inopportune times. Carry a notebook and keep one on your bedside table! Years of living in the cold reality of our lives can push our creative powers deeper into our psyches; but in my experience, this does not diminish our creative power, it simply sometimes makes it harder to access. One challenge to overcome is the constant programming to be "rational" from the get-go. By that I mean that as a group of business people, we sometimes dismiss too early, those ideas that we feel are "crazy" instead of working on discovering the seeds of a brilliant idea often buried in a crazy one.

As for the awkwardness and psychological programming that we all undergo in life, try this little two-minute exercise (but not while driving):

Assuming that you are right-handed, take a suit jacket (or any kind of long-sleeved shirt) and put it on normally. This will normally involve right arm first into the right sleeve then some body maneuver to get the left arm in position, then slide your left arm into the left sleeve. That took about 2-3 seconds, right?

Now remove the jacket and hold it in front of you. Now put it on again except this time left arm first, then right arm. How long did that take? Was it a seamless operation? (forgive the unintended pun). Did it feel awkward? For most of us, this was a more awkward set of motions and required an adjustment of our programmed set of automatic, sequenced motions. *You were out of your comfort zone*. But you accomplished the goal. This little exercise is useful in demonstrating the comfort zone effect. Any activity outside of that zone and we tend to avoid it. When an idea is expressed that fits somewhere outside of our mental comfort zone, we tend to dismiss it. It demands an awkwardness in our normal mental processes or in our sense of logic that we are usually not willing to experiment with, because its not comfortable; because it doesn't *fit*.

"We can't solve problems by using the same kind of thinking we used when we created them" – Albert Einstein

The point here is that before one can solve a problem, one usually has to identify what that problem is.

Sometimes, the most brilliant solutions appear at first awkward and outside of the normal way of thinking. Some folks call that *counter-intuitive*. A somewhat more mundane but useful application of dealing head-on with comfort zones – is the ability of an organization to shed low-value work, that has become entrenched within the organizational pool of habits.

Therefore, I find it useful in the early *ideation* stages of strategic planning to accept and record all ideas and to challenge the group to find the potential nugget in each idea. The rough ideas as initially articulated may sound a bit weird, or funny, or just plain science fiction - but there may be a gem hiding there that can be coaxed out through group discussion. Indeed, there may be no gem to be found; but through simple lateral association, the group may stumble onto an idea with the initial crazy idea having been the trigger. The bottom line is: it may not have been possible to have arrived at that brilliant idea without having first massaged a few crazy ones. And do not worry: there will be plenty of time later - during the stage of rigorous analysis - to vet ideas on the basis of feasibility and other "rational" screens. They may well be rejected and most will but the point is not to dismiss too early, which is too often the case in business.

One last point on working outside of the "safe" comfort zone and the challenge for managers to reward this behaviour. If you have watched Olympic diving you will appreciate the dual-mode scoring system. One factor that determines the diver's score is how well the athlete technically executed the dive. The other factor recognizes the degree of difficulty associated with the specific dive that was selected by the diver. So, if you choose a simple forward dive in a tuck position and you cut into the water like a spear without as much as a ripple, that's great. But if you choose a reverse 4½ somersaults in pike position and actually make it albeit with a splash – you win. Applying this reward and recognition philosophy under appropriate circumstances should be the norm.

THE ACCIDENT OF **Post-It** NOTES

A classic business story comes to mind. It's a longer story than I am re-telling. 3M, in trying to develop a strong glue for the aerospace industry back in the 1960s – failed. One of its attempts resulted in a very weak adhesive. Not only was it weak, it was re-usable, yet its market appeal and value were not well considered. Instead it was chalked up to the many expected failures in the engineering lab before success is reached. The focus on goal sometimes suggests that any result not achieving that goal is a failure and to be ignored other than the usual post-mortem often performed to evaluate learnings. What every failure should trigger of course, is an evaluation as to its *alternative uses*. It turns out that at 3M there was one such champion

but was a voice crying in the wilderness for some years before 3M attempted a market launch of samples of Post-It notes to the executive secretaries of CEOs in many of America's largest corporations. The rest is history.

This may seem to the casual reader as an example of creative business and marketing thinking and surely it is. However, there is methodology behind it. The simple fact is that one needed (only) to ask the probing process questions: What, When, Where, Why, Who, How, etc. Faced with a weak but reusable adhesive that leaves behind no glue residue – one might have asked:

What is this product? What possible uses could be made of it? **When** would be those circumstances? When could it be used? During the work day? At home? At play? **Where** could it be used? Outside? Inside? In the car? At the dinner table? At conferences? At meetings? **Why** would we use such a product? Why would the market see it as interesting? **Who** might be the primary users? The secondary users? Who would wish to use it? Is it possible to segment the market into psychographic segments? Socio-economic segments? Ethnicities? Age groupings? Professional/work segments? Who are the possible users versus who may be the influencers of those possible users? **How** would they use it? Is it easy to learn? Is there education or training involved? Is it intuitively obvious? etc., etc., etc.

This may all sound obvious but it is astonishing how little, this simple market-investigative technique is used. Sitting here writing this section, it occurred to me that if I were using the 6 process questions with one of the contact lens drops companies,[31] for example, one might discover that of the 30 million Americans wearing contact lenses[32], 17%, or about 5 million wearers have blue eyes. Has anyone explored a market opportunity for eye/lens drops specifically designed for the more sensitive blue-eyed population? I have not seen any research nor any products targeting that 5 million+ market. Just an example of the kind of legitimate considerations that one gleans when asking process questions.

In my experience, asking and re-asking these probing basic questions can transcend symptomatic responses and more easily get at the possible root of a problem or an opportunity. Far too often, a senior manager stifles innovative thinking and therefore innovation by too quickly dismissing ideas – without at the very least – having the patience and the wisdom to have these process questions asked, answered and considered.

THINKING THROUGH CRITICAL READING

Another example of creative thinking requires people to reject assumptions and to avoid accepting so-called facts at face value. Some years ago we were faced with the challenge of coming up collaboratively with the "next act" for a company whose business involved after-market automotive parts and equipment. The company had evolved and matured over the years to other automotive-related businesses such as taxi fleets, rental cars, and trucks. One of the first things I normally request of a client is the opportunity to review the work of other consultants, both internal and external, that they may have engaged in the past few years. There is good reason for this. First, it is efficient. Material that may have been gathered may not have been analysed fully or creatively. Second, it's useful insight to understand what the client adopted versus what they may have rejected.

Recommendations are rejected for a multitude of reasons, and sometimes for no reason at all. Perhaps the implementation was too complex, perhaps they lacked internal competencies, perhaps the execution was not staged in logical steps, perhaps there were infeasibilities related to other factors. Perhaps the recommendation was never made or made with strength of conviction. Or a key decision maker may have been sick that particular day. There was indeed a massive amount of background material in this case. One of my pet peeves about the dysfunctionality of the consulting model is that many consultants sell their work by weight. The larger the report, the greater the fee. That is a two-fold problem. The client doesn't have the patience to read through all that stuff and the good stuff may be buried deep in the jungle of filler typically comprised of old historical data and other background, often courtesy of professor Google. Charts, maps, tables, graphs of various types and perspectives also are a good filler. They look professional, and complete. Much of it is useless.

"Managers often struggle to get the most essential information from a research report. Front-line supervisors are intimidated by the blather and complicated, convoluted, thick reports circulated by the young MBAs on the staff... report authors with MBAs fall prey to the seductive idea that the boss will be impressed that the authors had really done a lot of homework if they included sophisticated words in their reports, and made them look physically impressive" – Essentials of Business Research Methods[33]

But in perusing all of that automotive industry material, there was one nugget gleaned from an article and it stuck out. And it read (not verbatim): *Half of all Americans who cannot afford to buy a new car buy a new car.* If true, what can one reasonably conclude from that statement? First, it is necessary to ask why? And next, it is necessary to ask

what is wrong with the used car marketplace that forces buyers to buy a new car even when they cannot afford to do so? So, we toured a number of used car lots. They were basically all the same: 100 cars on a corner lot, tattered red and green triangular flags waving in the wind, rusted metal signage seeking to persuade that today was a special promotion day not to be ignored, salespeople wearing rumpled, brightly colored sports jackets that look like they had never been dry-cleaned and a sales style that most people respond to by checking that they still had their wallet or handbag before executing a hurried escape. Market strategists love these opportunities that offer up the possibility of developing a new business model that can kill and replace existing models in the product or service category. That's a category killer.

CREATE A CATEGORY KILLER

Our answer was to create a category killer[34], a new paradigm in used-car sales; and over sandwiches in our boardroom this is what the team came up with: instead of a corner lot: a campus-style area complete with a test track. Instead of 100 cars: 1,000 cars. Instead of fake, tired, tattered flags: fresh, clear and honest communications. A café so customers could sit over a latte and ponder their (large) purchase without being hassled. An indoor playground so children are happily occupied instead of pulling on their parent's hands pleading "can we go home now?" A service centre to implement a 100-point safety and mechanical check together with a warranty that the vehicle will not stop working 3 months after the customer hits the streets. Computer terminals, so the customers can check independent consumer reports on the year and model of the contemplated vehicle before purchasing. A test track to drive and experience the vehicle of their choice. A one-stop shop for car insurance, upgraded stereo system, financial services – so that the customer can buy and drive away satisfied and worry-free. The salespeople: to wear green golf shirts and clean, pressed khaki pants or skirts. Lastly, if the customer had come in needing a Ford compact and was pressured into buying an Audi A8, and if after 30 days the customer expressed remorse - the salesperson would not receive the commission. This was a customer-centric, customer-friendly, honest, and professional environment. We designed the first two prototype stores and they blew the competition out of the water. This was the birth of Wayne Huizenga's AutoNation in 1996 and it became America's largest retailer of pre-owned cars. It all began with creative insight gleaned from the survey results: *Half of all Americans who cannot afford to buy a new car, buy a new car.*

Finally, creativity and its executional counterpart sometimes called innovation – are worth pursuing systematically and ironically with rigor. There is an old-time expression: *better, faster, cheaper – pick any two.* I have always found this expression a bit disappointing. As an aside, I had the same feeling with respect to Einstein's theorem that concluded that the maximum theoretical velocity is the speed of light. While that velocity may seem huge at 186,000 miles per second, if true, the implications of a ceiling on speed in a galaxy where our nearest neighboring solar system is measured in light-years suggests we will likely never visit there even at maximum velocity technologies. Similarly, if we were limited by those three variables, namely, better (quality) faster (time to market), and cheaper (cost of research, development, production, and distribution) – this theoretical limitation would be unfortunate. Yet, with disruptive approaches to market and with paradigm changes in product and service development, and with advances in game-changing technologies (3-D printing comes to mind, for example) – I do not accept the *better, faster, cheaper -pick any two* limitation and assumption. Neither should you.

Having said that, it's probably useful to add that in business as in life there are many perceived truths that are subjective and relativistic. I am not proposing that in all businesses - better, faster, and cheaper become three core branded attributes. Nordstrom did not build its brand on cheaper - but on customer service. McDonald's did not build its brand on better - but on faster and consistent. The key here is *value* and value is a function of the market segment that is being targeted; it is a perception. What I am saying however, is that within any specific category all three: *better, faster, cheaper* – are legitimate and attainable goals. I want outstanding customer service and I would value it even more if it were delivered to me quickly.

FORCE FIELD ANALYSIS

To define this term: Force field analysis is based on a model for thinking about change as proposed by Kurt Lewin[35] who saw behavior in an institutional setting not as a static (motionless) habit or pattern but as a dynamic balance of forces working in opposite directions. According to this way of looking at patterned behavior, change takes place when an imbalance occurs between the sum of the forces against change (Restraining Forces) and the sum of the forces for change (Driving Forces). A force field analysis assumes that any social situation is a balance between these forces. An imbalance may occur through a change of magnitude or a change in direction in any one of the forces or through the addition of a new force.[36] This visual model[37] demonstrates driving forces that can support and accelerate the attaining of strategic goals and the restraining forces

FORCE FIELD ANALYSIS – KURT LEWIN

DRIVING FORCES
(Positive forces for change)

RESTRAINING FORCES
(obstacles to change)

Present
State
or
Desired
State

that can be an obstacle to attaining strategic advantage. The way I employ this very simple model is to work with my clients to creatively turn restraining forces into supporting forces. After all, a force is a force; it has energy. As in many martial arts styles where the kinetic energy of your opponent is turned to be used against him, I try to leverage the restraining forces for good. What I have used this for is to generate ideas that could promote the attainment of winning strategies.

The same can be said for other tools, such as the classic SWOT (Strengths, Weaknesses, Opportunities, Threats) analysis. Both force field and SWOT analyses tend to be under-employed by many organizations and are simply used to generate lists of phrases about strengths and weaknesses, etc. Again, the real trick, and what's re-quires to tap-in to creative thinking, is the consideration of how to turn weaknesses and threats into opportunities, and opportunities into real strengths. In fact, weaknesses that are not addressed become threats.

SMALL CAN BE BEAUTIFUL

To illustrate this point, in 2014 I had the opportunity to advise the Foundation for Investment and Development of Exports (FIDE)[38] in Honduras, in the context of the new Canada-Honduras Free Trade Agreement. I met with Honduran producers and manufacturers of wines, coffee, sugar, and related products to assist in improving their international marketing efforts to grow their export markets. In addition to major potential exporters, I also met with some small, niche, family-run producers - one of whom produced fortified wines. The family goes up into the hills and collects wild berries. The home-based winery produced a very small number of bottles, approximately 3,000 annually, and sold the wine at local markets for about 50 cents per bottle. Total annual revenues were $1,500, about half the annual minimum wage.

The wine was spectacular (I tasted it extensively!). On a SWOT[39] or on a force field analysis, the obvious weakness was the limitation of production capacity and the operation was not readily scalable. Stuck with these low production volumes, how was I to turn the disadvantage into an advantage?

First, the "story" was a romantic one: wild, naturally organic berries, handpicked in the hills. Wine is used to entertain and this story was potentially a very nice relatable story, waiting to be told. The wine itself was homemade in the Honduran countryside by a family. And it was astonishingly delicious. While a glass-half-empty person might view the limited production volumes as a fatal weakness, a glass-half-full[40] consultant might say that limited production renders it rare and precious. I thought of a high-end lithograph signed by the artist and numbered. And I visualized this beautiful wine signed and serialized, aka: 1/3,000, 2/3,000, etc. The 50-cent local market ticket price could become $30-$50 in the liqueur stores of Canada, United States and Europe. And the result could be a move upward from a $1,500 annual below-poverty-line income, to $150,000, an upward multiple of a hundred. This is an example of an inherent weakness potentially converted to an advantage. Would it take work to potentialize this wine in a market? Of course it would, and the effort could fail. But the potential is real. The point here is that the value of these strategic analysis tools is not simply to generate lists but to generate insights around the inter-relationships between perceived weaknesses, threats, and the opportunities to be harvested by thinking creatively. Stand in the possibility. And understand the category. A bottle of Legacy rum by Angostura is priced at $25,000 USD.

SIMPLY ELEGANT SOLUTIONS

Here's another example to illustrate how applied creativity can solve inherently difficult challenges. In 2016 I was consulting and helping to develop entrepreneurism mentoring programs for the Philippine Department of Trade and Industry (a DTI - CESO Canada partnership). In that context I met with several small enterprises being supported by DTI. One women's co-op was given a high-capacity roaster and bagger for processing and packaging locally-harvested coffee beans. Their small facility was located on the highway outside of a small town in the province of Batangas. They hoped to sell packaged coffee beans from that facility but hardly anyone stopped to buy coffee. Their sales were almost non-existent: only 200 kg. of coffee with a spare, unused production capacity of 70,000 Kg. I asked them if they had considered some basic questions about their product offering. I explained that simple process questions like: what, when, why, who, and where - needed to be asked and considered.

What are they selling? An expensive product (even for the Philippines) at a price that most customers might not be willing to pay given that they don't know that particular coffee or that particular brand. Would they have to somehow taste a cup, before deciding to invest in a whole (expensive) bag of beans? When are they selling the coffee? Is there a time-of-day factor or any cyclical demand pattern that could provide insight or opportunity?

Why would people buy this coffee? What would motivate people to stop their cars and buy this mysterious coffee? How much would they be likely to spend?

Who would most likely buy the coffee, and where would they most likely buy it? Is it feasible to convince food stores to carry the product, and promote it to their customers?

Ask questions. Listen carefully. Ask again and again until there are no more answers.

ASKING THE RIGHT QUESTIONS

A group of consultants went out for a day's recreation in a hot air balloon. It became very cloudy and the balloon was blown off course. When the sky cleared, they found themselves out in the country, floating over a large cornfield. They looked down and saw a farmer working in his field and they called down to him: "where are we?" The farmer shoutedback up to them: "you guys are over a cornfield"! The consultants, frustrated, grumbled:" a perfectly accurate answer, but totally useless"; at the same time the farmer chuckled to himself: "consultants, they don't even know which question to ask."

I left the coffee co-op ladies to discuss these questions among themselves and I walked to the roadside with my smartphone on stopwatch mode. I counted 37 cars passing by during a 5-minute period, which extrapolates to 3,000 cars in an 8-hour period. If 2% of those motorists (I assumed that car owners can afford a cup of coffee) can be encouraged to stop for coffee, that translates to 60 cups sold per day at 20 pesos/cup totalling 438,000 pesos annually. If one-in-ten coffee cup drinkers was impressed enough to also buy a bag to take home at 100 pesos/bag, this translates to an additional 220,000 pesos per year. The logic and marketing strategy is straightforward. The roadside location of the roaster facility is on a busy road where motorists pass frequently, including long trips to Manila. Motorist fatigue and the incentive to "caffeine up" to stay alert is an opportunity to market this delicious and strong coffee. This notion could answer our question: why would they stop?

I recommended an experiment: that they erect three signs: Two signs 100 meters down the road on each side from the location, saying: *"slow down; in 100 meters stop for a delicious cup of coffee, roasted on location. Drink our amazing coffee and stay alert and safe!"*; and one sign at the location saying: *"Park here and have a great cup of our freshly roasted Barako coffee. Love it and take a bag home!"*

The customer would not be asked to invest in a whole kilogram of coffee before tasting/sampling and discovering how good it really was. We estimated the cost of signage to be about 3,000 pesos. All other equipment / resources necessary were in place. They were ecstatic with the idea and committed to it.

And why would I present such a tiny example? I have advised large organizations like Bell Mobility, CBC,

Walmart, Safeway US, Deutsche Bank/DHL, Conagra, and dozens of others. Because the principles are all the same. This example, through its total simplicity, strips away the noise and perceived complexity to reveal that logic, common sense, and creativity, combined with research and a commitment to seek out the simplest solution – can yield interesting results. Basic principles were followed. How can we get folks to learn about the brand and then buy in quantities? What messaging would likely motivate the motoring customer to stop and sample? How can we use what we already have (existing facility) and keep costs and risks low? How do we ensure that the level of added complexity is well within our internal competencies? This was a simple solution that yielded potentially elegant results, and as a principle and business philosophy, it can scale almost indefinitely.

CREATIVITY IN LARGE ORGANIZATIONS

In large organizations, especially when decentralized, creativity has no official structured outlet. It is rare to have a meeting dedicated to the thinking up of great ideas. In fact, we often cannot produce creativity on demand. We have all experienced those eureka moments and they happen at the oddest times. For Archimedes, his "aha" moment happened in the bathtub – which is understandable since his epiphany dealt with the principle of the displacement of water.

We have all had great partial ideas, pieces of insight that are half-baked. Similarly, we have all heard someone in a meeting say something that is very cool but seems to be a solution without a problem to solve. Much high quality thinking and even revelation, happens in snippets and not in whole, structured, complete thoughts. And almost all of these thoughts - these genius-level snippets - happen when we are talking about something totally different and not in a meeting called for the purpose of idea generation. These ideas are hardly ever captured for later consideration. And in the remote possibility that they are captured, partial ideas don't normally end up going anywhere.

What organizations need to consider is to establish an idea repository, a database of sorts that stores and indexes idea fragments and then is able to relate these fragments on the basic of certain common or complimentary elements. Think of this concept like a large jigsaw puzzle. The fragments relate to each other by having similar colours, complimentary edge/perimeter configuration and a contiguous pattern. I would wager that a data base with a set of algorithms programmed to recognize and integrate idea fragments would come up with interesting and creative ideas. This would of course only work if every meeting recognized that there is a likelihood that idea segments will be generated, would encourage folks to articulate them, or input them into the "idea system" for integration with other segments.

SIMPLE WINNING IDEAS

"There are some ideas so wrong that only a very intelligent person could believe in them" – George Orwell

---

All businesses start with an idea. Some ideas are ill-conceived. Some are brilliant. Some companies outlive their one really good idea and then die. A few manage to evolve with other ideas, and build on their market foundation. Some say that the genius isn't the idea, it's the execution of the idea. That is only partially correct, or more precisely, only half right. You need both. The organization may be able to manufacture the highest quality and least costly buggy whip, but in 2017 that product may not have been the best idea. And yet there are exceptions (there always are) such as the coming-back-to-life of vinyl records; but that is a different conversation. It has also been said that the quality of being a visionary and also a pragmatist cannot exist in the same person. I don't believe that.

Walmart is a good example of having started with an innovative model. It wasn't as much a creative model as it was a creatively efficient one - a model that captured market growth and logistics innovation. They captured the rural model then they high-ended their stores into the suburban markets. With customer traffic in mind they introduced food under their own label in the centres of their stores. Walmart understood the value of being a *traffic generator;* the typical customer shops for general merchandise once a month and shops for food once a week.

As their sales volumes grew, they focused on cost of sales with significant sourcing, harmonization of vendor-partner systems, and high-volume purchases of limited assortment merchandise. The creativity was the thinking behind selecting products for each merchandise category. Simply stated: identify the highest velocity SKUs and buy and offer huge numbers of these items at a price point that competitors could not profitably match. The rest was innovation in systems and frankly some bullying on the purchasing side; let's call it leverage. The next piece of innovation was the decision to passionately embrace food retailing and offering this under a gold standard private label. The basis of Walmart's success included a third piece of thinking. Sam Walton came up with the idea that the stores must always price their merchandise consistently low all the time. The term "EDLP" (Every Day Low Pricing) was born. It was quite a creative notion. It basically said to the customer: you needn't shop around for the best deal or look for "sales". You needn't "cherry pick". You will always get our best price here for everything.

So, Walmart succeeded with three dimensions of market innovation and a profoundly significant logistics and inventory management innovation that leveraged its size and purchasing power.

In their heyday, many retailers' strategies were a direct response to Walmart's competitive threat in their trading area, but EDLP has not become ubiquitous in the marketplace. Even Walmart after Sam Walton's death appears to have wavered on their founder's passionate commitment to the EDLP philosophy. Their repositioning to *rollback pricing,* which some call a euphemism for promotion, is anathema to the original Walmart credo. EDLP carries with it a fairly high front-end investment both in the branding and repositioning of the retailer as well as their costs of implementation. High-low pricing strategy retailers prefer the advantages of frequent promotions - which a certain segment of shoppers also prefer, especially in the food and beverage category. This "cherry picker" shopper segment also shops more frequently which tends to increase the volume of impulse purchases. There is room for a multiplicity of models and formats in the market.

But nothing is forever. Walmart faces serious domestic competition that renders true, pure, competitive EDLP unrealistic. *Total Retail* magazine soberly explained it well: "Grocery channel rivals like Aldi currently offer as much as 30 percent in savings for similar items when compared to Walmart prices[41]".

Walmart is a phenomenon. They have also made enemies along the way but the consumers continue to vote at their checkouts. As their competitors "catch on" and the markets slow domestically, Walmart has expanded internationally into markets that did not know Walmart – so they could not anticipate and prepare for Walmart's expansion. Nor was Walmart an experienced global player and they have made some mis-steps in their foray into international spaces. More on some of that in subsequent chapters of this book.

Where Walmart and others fall short on maximizing their potentials is where people are involved. It is the most difficult challenge to hire, filter, and train people that will love their employer and want their company to succeed. Yes I said "love" even though that word will not normally be found in any business book.

MANAGING BUSINESS CYCLES

Organizations are normally pretty good at acquiring but not at disposing. Do not forget to weed out your garden. A useful example is the retail store. Normally all the shelves are filled or ought to be filled. Empty shelves in a store shouts out "mismanagement". How then can a retailer add new SKUs[42]? The answer is that something must be taken away, aka "de-listed", in order to make room for the new or replacement SKU. These decisions must be deliberate and based on criteria such as the difference between margins generated on the old SKU versus the projected margins of the new SKU which competes for shelf space. This is a concrete example about how businesses add and subtract. However, the principle is or should be the same for adding processes, objectives, and operational activities. Typically, businesses keep on adding these without considering the need to discard underperforming impaired assets, processes, and functions. All organization, over time, becomes burdened with excessive or redundant activities that consume resources and muddle the clarity of both objectives and operations.

This issue can be understood at a much deeper level. Many organizations of all kinds are mired in tradition despite the talk of the last 20+ years about flexible "boundary-less" organizations. As far back as 1992, Harvard Business Review[43] asserted that "The traditional organizational map describes a world that no longer exists". These "new-ish" mental models will not eliminate boundaries; they will create less official ones. They will not eliminate conflict, they will require new relationships to be formed that figure out issues of identity, containment, authority, leadership, recognition, and rewards. In today's reality or at least in my experience and perception of it, experimental organizational structures tend to be introduced piecemeal and in some cases in a manner which is designed to run parallel, simultaneously with old structures, "just in case". Just in case it doesn't work and we have to revert; just in case so we don't end up throwing out the proverbial "baby with the bath water". This risk-averse, trepidatious approach is understandable - but will likely result in half hearted attempts to make new things work. Having an easy fallback makes it too easy to fall back. I cannot help thinking of the Israeli general's answer to the question about how the dramatically outnumbered Israeli army prevailed in the 1967 six-day war. He simply replied: "we had no choice."

There is a time for everything, and a season for every activity under the heavens - Ecclesiastes

---

This suggests a deep issue. How does one get an individual or a team to perform as if his or her life depended on it? In the foreword to my book, I wrote that one of the root causes of business failure is a lack of a "sense of urgency". On the other hand, a problem with some managers is that everything becomes (equally) urgent. The backlash to that style tends to be the opposite of the desired result: that nothing is deemed urgent. In my management days I had a very simple code that I shared: 1, meant drop everything and get this done. I used this very sparingly; to abuse this would be disastrous. 2, signified important and to be fitted in with normal expected job function and it was justifiable to be challenged with the question about what could be taken off the plate in order to accommodate this task. 3, meant that when time permitted, this should be done, for example within 2-3 weeks.

The real urgencies were treated in a war-room crisis-centre type of environment. We deployed the right team and didn't stop until we had the answers. So how does one get a team to pull out all the stops? I have found that a team with a shared understanding of the urgency and the reward works better (than individuals) together to solve these kinds of issues. To continue the military metaphor, when soldiers are interviewed about their prime motivation in battle and for whom they are actually fighting, their usual response is not country, god, or ideals. In the heat of battle they are fighting for (and with) their comrades. This traditional wisdom has been validated over and over again over many years[44].

SKEWED PERCEPTIONS

Priorities, issues, organizational capabilities, and many other matters are items of perception in any organization and often differ at every level of the organization chart, whether it is a formal chart or an informal one.

I recall many instances where management often on a whim, asks for a study on this or that. Typically, the manager's mental model is that the employee needs only to step up to his or her computer, type in a few keystrokes, and presto – the desired information prints out and immediately satisfies the request. In reality however, the employee works overtime for 6 days - gathering, compiling, analysing, formatting – and may involve a team in order to satisfy the management demand. This phenomenon is both the fault of management and its employees. On the one hand, management must be more conscious of what exactly is involved (or they must ask) and how important is the information requested. A good manager must share with the employee the reason for the request, inquire about the effort and cost involved in obtaining it, and decide if it's worth that cost and effort. In some cases, a request is not even made but is perceived to have been made. Management should clarify after every transaction with employees, precisely what has just happened. Aka: whether a conversation was an exchange of information only or whether there was a request for (further) action. From the employee side, the employee must clarify and confirm what they thought they just heard and if it was an action request, that employee is obliged to inform the manager about exactly what is involved in complying with the request. Too often, employees insulate and isolate management from the true effort of complying with requests. It is perfectly appropriate for employees, to use the previous retail shelf-space example, to ask the manager what current activity should be suspended or stopped in order to comply with the new request. The principle being that like the store shelf analogy, the roster is almost always filled to capacity and before one can add anything, one must subtract something.

CHAPTER 6 TAKE-AWAYS CREATIVITY	
1	Imagination and creativity resides in every person and is one of the most valuable resources in every organization. Never discount its value. Nurture it.
2	Recognize the power and potential of the (often deep-thinking) introvert. Include them and gently coax out their participation.
3	Techniques like visualization and encouraging attitudes of standing in the possibilities will draw out the creative force in each of us.
4	Ask the right questions and then listen. Ask again, listen again, until all the drill-downs are exhausted. There are six key process questions that can deliver an understanding of root causes and insights.
5	Find and read or re-read previous consultants' reports (up to 5-years old). There are likely insights there to discover that were not picked up previously.
6	Think big. Ask yourself what would have to be done in order to become dominant in the market we are playing in. If I had all the money in the world, how would I capture 80% of my market – to become a category killer.
7	List what you consider to be natural disadvantages. How could you turn them upside down and reposition them as advantages? For example, can you position and market low production products as rare and precious?

CHAPTER 6 TAKE-AWAYS CREATIVITY	
8	Small can be beautiful. You don't need to create an empire if that is not your ambition. You can develop a very smart and profitable niche business and then try to make it impenetrable.
9	Among alternative solutions, look favorably at the simplest one. Distrust complexity. Complex models tend not to work well.
10	Create a sense of (quiet) urgency but don't drive your people crazy. Not everything is urgent, so prioritize.

CHAPTER 7
SELLING IDEAS

PROPOSALS and PRESENTATIONS

Many potential suppliers suffer from a common ailment: the need to talk about themselves instead of focusing on the needs and desires of the client. This reality can be used as an advantage for those who set themselves apart by behaving differently and deeply researching the potential client and their industry. It's important is to figure out what's keeping them up at night. Most winning consultancies, for example, will take a position and will have an opinion, i.e. *put a stake in the ground* about what the industry needs and what the target client specifically needs. This is not too much to ask. The investment in intellect and time is worth it, usually. This is the way the consultant establishes authority in their chosen area. The benefit of having advised a large number of diverse companies and organizations is that one is able to adapt winning strategies from one area and import them into another. Now of course, I am not (just) talking about consultants. I am referring to all employees and all managers in all organizations. Everyone sells. All of you sell your ideas and all compete for a portion of a very finite set of resources: for budget funds, for time and attention of senior management, and for advancement. Everyone is a competitor. My point is and my recommendation is that *consultative selling* is by far the superior way and the most satisfying. In the end, knowledge and insight will win out.

In the 1990s, when I was the CEO of a marketing and design consultancy, I read an interview in the business section of a Toronto newspaper. In it, the new CEO of a medium size supermarket chain was being interviewed. I was impressed. He was responding to questions in a thoughtful and intelligent manner. He was one of those leaders who had inherited the opportunity. His father was of the generation that visited the Central Food Terminal at 4 AM each morning to personally select and order produce for the chain. It was a grocer's culture. This young man of the second generation was sent away for an ivy league MBA and returned expected to lead. A very familiar generational business story. I called him up on the phone, couldn't get through to such a senior executive, but was able to talk to his assistant. I told her:

"Tell A. that he doesn't know me, that I was impressed with the newspaper interview and that he didn't mention it – but I think he should be concerned with the risk of his company being " middled" in the marketplace; and if he wants to know more about what I mean and how I would consider managing this risk – then it will cost him a café latte."

He returned my call admitting that he was intrigued and yes, he had been thinking of this market share challenge and about his being potentially trapped in a "squeeze play". We had our latte and over the course of the next several years, my company and his had a great and mutually profitable relationship. You see, I had an opinion. I was willing to put a stake in the ground. I was willing to win or lose on the basis of my opinion. If I lost then I deserved to lose. If I won then I will have established myself as an authority, as someone who could deliver value. Another benefit of this consultative selling approach is that one doesn't have to wait for a request for proposal (RFP), and then compete with many others. In a sense, having an informed opinion about filling a need that your client (customer, boss, etc) doesn't (yet) recognize – puts you soaring 30,000 feet above the competition, and above the noise.

On another occasion, we were invited to respond to an RFP from a 1,500-store retail chain. The proposal was to design their prototype – a new store of the future. RFPs were sent to the four largest retail design agencies and my agency had a retail design division in the top four. I have usually avoided these beauty contests. They're costly in two ways: they cost money to prepare for, of course, but mostly they cost in terms of reputational value. The potential client wants your best ideas up front as a basis to select you for the work. I was not prepared to erode the value of the idea phase, nor was I capable or willing to deliver the "best" ideas within the framework of a proposal. But some of my competitors were willing and sometimes they won and mostly they lost. Why? Because in my opinion, design is nothing more or less than the physical manifestation of a strategy. Many designers pursue subjective beauty, their own subjectivity. Indeed, some of the work is beautiful to look at. But commercial design is beautiful only if it generates revenues for the client, and its value is determined by their customers and measured at the checkout counters. All this is to say that before anything the strategy must be developed, and the design then follows. So I called the CEO and said (I paraphrase myself):

Thanks for including us on your short-list; I am not prepared to give you a design concept based on good looks and or an existing well-respected benchmarked store somewhere in the world. We are willing to explore a paradigm shift upwards in the way you could go-to-market and engage your customers, and it won't and cannot be free. But I am prepared to participate in this way: As a favor, I shall prepare six questions that you should ask your four (or three if it doesn't include my company) prospects when they present to you; these are strategic in nature and will indicate to you if they know enough about the market and your specific business, to be of value to you.

He accepted. It was obvious to me that he would accept. It was free, we were respected in the industry, and he was probably curious to see if there was anything new or insightful in my suggested questions that he and his team had not already thought of.

Many weeks later, he called me. They had conducted interviews with the three prospects. He used my questions. They failed to answer to his satisfaction. He said that there was no point inviting us to present as we had nothing to present except our track record and he assumed that if I had authored the six questions, then presumably, I would have the best answers. Of course he was correct. We got the job.

This is not to brag. It's to make a point. To be successful in business, in producing a product or in providing a service - one must develop with great effort and investment, an authority in something of recognized value. One must therefore as an authority, develop a position and a set of opinions that project that expertise. The opinions should represent solutions to problems that your target market is experiencing. Black and Decker used to say that they sell holes, not drills. This makes selling, relevant, easier, and enjoyable.

SELLING PRODUCTS, SERVICES, IDEAS

Products and services must solve a problem to be successful. Not your problem, the consumer' problem. The customer can be a buyer internal to your organization (when you are trying to win a budget allocation for your department), or a buyer external to your organization.

One of the most effective selling presentations that I have seen was back in the late 1970s when as a young member of its management and I attended certain meetings of the Imperial Oil executive committee and of the board of directors. It was budget time. Bob Peterson[45] (he later became CEO), a senior engineer who was in charge at the time of refinery operations, stood up to make his presentation. He had no notes and no presentation materials[46]. Without uttering a word, he took out a piece of fluffy material from his suit pocket together with a box of matches. He struck the match and touched it to the material and it ignited and burned. While burning down to his fingertips, he placed the remaining blazing material into an ashtray[47] beside him at the very long boardroom table. He waited while the material fizzled out consumed by the fire. All this without uttering a word. We were all mesmerized and curious. This was a story waiting to be told. And then he looked up and made his one-sentence speech: (paraphrased): *Gentlemen, this is the material we currently use as a flame retardant and insulator for our very flammable tank farm and fuel depots (gas storage towers).*

Bob got the funds to replace that material. It was the shortest presentation I had ever experienced. I learned a lot that day.

In addition to my larger clients, I also have the opportunity to assist governments in developing countries, one being the government of the Philippines. I have completed a number of assignments also as a volunteer with the Canadian Executive Service Organization (CESO[48]) working with the department of Trade and Industry (DTI) of the Philippines. One of the projects was to mentor small entrepreneurial groups[49] to whom DTI provides equipment and training with which to produce, at a quasi-commercial scale, whatever they have the skill and interest to produce. One particular group of women from small farming families had come together to produce and sell their delicious rice cakes (Bibingka[50]). They sold these cakes door to door in their rural communities but their new production capacity, made possible with new ovens provided by DTI, was not exploited. They didn't know how to market and sell; nor did they have the resources to do anything fancy. I suggested that they augment their sales and lower their costs of distribution by selling to a supermarket (SM[51]) in the nearest big town[52] .

Why am writing all of this? Because I want to demonstrate that the principles are the same whether you are selling home-made rice cakes in the north of the Philippines or whether you are manufacturing and selling into the baked goods category of Maison Kayser of Paris or New York City or into Tesco, Albertson, Loblaws, or Walmart. Common sense marketing research: I advised them to visit the SM supermarket and buy samples of every kind of Bibinka cake that SM carries on their shelves. They advised me that there were three such "competing" products. Then in the local outdoor market in the vicinity of the SM store, I suggested they set up a tasting survey table. The three competing products would be labelled as A, B, C, and *their* product would be labelled, D. They should have a CPA or lawyer from the community oversee this, or a Barangay captain[53] to attest and sign for the survey's authenticity. Without trying to teach them statistical formulae for calculating sample sizes, a sample size of about 300 will provide a confidence level of between 90%-95% for most scenarios. The idea was if these ladies can show that the population prefers their Bibingka cakes over the competitor Bibingka cakes, they can exploit this advantage. If unsuccessful, then they will know that they have some product development work to do[54].

I have to say that their Bibingka cakes were spectacular. I told them that if, for example, 80% of the taste respondents (80% of 300 respondents) prefer their Bibingka, then instead of approaching the SM buyer half-begging to take on their product, they now would have a better approach. I explained to them that the buyer is rewarded by volume/margin formulae[55]. The shelves are full, or should be – suggesting that the retailer usually must de-list (or likely reduce order/carry quantities) an existing supplier to make room for a new one. This action is not done lightly. However, the better argument (to the Buyer) might go something like this:

We the women of the rural improvement club make amazing Bibingka. We always thought so because our neighbours buy our cakes and love them. But we didn't want to risk becoming a victim to our own propaganda, so we conducted an independent taste survey, a blind taste test, and the results are that 80% of YOUR own customers prefer the taste of our Bibingka over the tastes of the three competing Bibingka that your stores now carry.

So we can make you a hero in the eyes of your customers. We're not asking for shelf space immediately. Why don't we do a 90-day trial. We could set up with a merchandiser, provide sampling, and sell the product in your store. If successful, we can negotiate a long-term supply arrangement.

And to add another dimension, SM can enjoy the bragging rights, that by supporting our product, they are supporting a poor, local, farming community trying to supplement family incomes. Consumers will feel good about their contribution and at the same time will enjoy a better, higher quality dessert.

This is not rocket science. It is the kind of approach that manufacturers do or should do on their budgets and the kind of approach that small entrepreneurs can achieve with almost zero investment.

The take-away point here is that regardless of the size of your business – *targeting your customer and delivering objective, evidence-based, consultative selling is the most effective way to market your product.* The buyer cannot easily ignore you when evidence is presented in this way.

The last point to be made here is that when facing a buyer or any potential customer, one must assume that though they may be intelligent and inventive, they most likely do not have the time nor the patience to imagine how your product or service could be re-sold (as in the case with suppliers/manufacturers selling to retailers). One might expect that the retailer would have the expertise to know exactly how your products should be merchandised and displayed in their stores. Do not assume this. They may have the potential skill but they likely will not have the time or patience to invest in the effort.

This suggests that the seller, to be successful, must do much of this work. So in our example of the Bibingka ladies, they would do well to understand who eats Bibingka, what do they eat with it, how it is purchased, when and how best to merchandise it. Armed with this and more knowledge, they might suggest to the food store's baked-goods category buyer that the product might do very well adjacent to a certain food, or on a stand-alone merchandiser with signage that communicates how it is made and by whom. If they could prepare in advance, a sample of such signage with a romancing story about it being home-made from farm fresh ingredients, hand-milled rice, with proceeds to help rural families, etc. - this may indeed open the buyer's mind to the possibilities.

GO WHERE YOUR CUSTOMER HANGS OUT

Part of understanding the customer is understanding where they congregate. This is especially crucial for online sales. A supplier of merchandise or services may have a spectacular website, but no one will show up unless they are invited. Blogs, Twitter, and other social media are all used for such invitations and to influence visits, but the supplier should understand where to find their target market. What better time to access that market than when they are already on their computers or smart phones, and online?

To connect with the teenage and young adult market, one of the large opportunity that has presented itself over the last 5-10 years and is still largely ignored - is the massively multiplayer online game[56] audience. There are many hundreds of online games that these potential customers play online. A popular game like *Runescape*[57] has 249,584,002 subscribers[58] with about 60,000 players playing at any given moment. This role-playing game like many hundreds like it, have many players hanging out (via self-designed avatars) in virtual worlds, many with their individual economies and currencies - playing, chatting, competing, and generally socializing. Some readers will recognize names like Eve, The Second Life, and World of Warcraft[59]. The latter game enjoys six million monthly subscribers who have spent $2.2 billion inside of the game. The company, Blizzard Entertainment, enjoyed revenues of $6 billion dollars in 2016 and 46 million online players in the USA alone. This is a market that we know how to connect to online in real time. Their purchasing power is astronomical. Looking at "youth" as a mega-segment (8 to 24-year-olds), they enjoy $211 billion USD in spending power[60]. They are sitting at their computers. Many are comfortable in the e-commerce world. Some may be too young; that's ok, most are not. Go, sell them stuff!

PRESENTATION MECHANICS

The presentation itself, when called upon to compete in that way, is the subject of many courses and articles that the reader can access outside of this book. It's not my intention to belabor this subject. However, a few important principles should be noted here. The three-part formula I've used and which has been attributed to the great Aristotle[61] is as follows: *First you tell them what you are going to tell them, then you tell them, then you tell them what you told them.* Telling what your presentation will be about takes away any surprises without going into the detail. The cardinal rule about senior management is that they do *not* appreciate surprises. Do not worry about revealing the mystery. Mystery is not a good thing outside of the movie theatre; and if your detail in the core of your presentation is boring, you are in trouble anyways. The last part - summarizing the presentation, is designed to reinforce what you have said and ensures that they will remember.

The core of the presentation should also be brief and the presentation slides (assuming PowerPoint) themselves should not be busy. White space is a good thing. Reading verbatim from your slides makes the audience wonder why they need you there in the first place. It also suggests that you must read because you really don't know your stuff at a deep enough, natural-enough level. Points on a slide should be enough to make sense to the audience and mostly serve to keep you on track and ensure the logical "build" of your argument. In theory, you really should not even need slides at all.

If you are given, say 15 minutes, it should not be 16 minutes. If you are not organized and disciplined enough to respect a timetable then your reliability is suspect. I would say generally that 15 minutes typically consumes 4 to 8 slides. Each slide should be able to be explained in three sentences. If you need an additional sentence, you probably need an additional slide. Never compliment yourself. The quality of your message should do that. Humor may be okay if its appropriate to the group but don't steal more than 10 seconds from your message. You probably have 15 seconds to make a stellar first impression. This does not happen by accident; work on it.

You must come across as an authority, as the *go-to* person, not through guile or showmanship, but through a genuinely deep understanding of the material and a natural and relaxed style of presenting it. My personal approach is to first research deeply about the industry even if the assignment may be mostly a process facilitation role.

Even in those cases, I feel obliged to study the industry, understand the issues, delve into global differences, and know who the current standard setters are. Your clients will undoubtedly benchmark best practices and if they do not, do it for them. If there are specific technologies and science underlying the business, do understand what these are and what the status of innovation is in the industry. Lastly, know the client company itself. Read the past 2 or 3 years of press releases, follow the dollars, read the investment analysts' evaluations, know what the company has spun off and why, what they acquired and why, what they've grown and why. Know who will attend the presentation and what their functions are, and where they were before. I do not go into that room without knowing these things; it's a waste of their time and therefore my time – because I do not deserve to win that proposal if I'm ignorant or lack insight about them and their business.

As to the presentation material itself, my personal policy is to review and rehearse beforehand every point on every slide and ask myself: what are the most likely questions (and even aggressive challenges; there's always one of those, in the room) that they could ask me on each of these points? And I make sure I can respond to all of those. Then I write my responses and ask myself a similar question: what are the possible follow-up (aka: drill-down) questions that they may ask me with respect to any of my responses? And I write those responses down. Then I repeat this cycle one more time so that I am comfortable in responding to two levels of drill-down questions. That prepares you for the conversation and shouts *authority*. Normally any further drill-down may either be responded to or you may even consider replying that in the interests of time, given the material yet to cover and the time you have been given in which to do so, getting to that level of granularity on any one issue may be best done outside of the formal meeting. That usually satisfies them; but never say that, as a substitute for not knowing. If you don't know, say so. Honesty is always best and most often acceptable. Fudging it is more detectable than you think and is never received well.

At the end of the presentation that relates to a proposal, remember to ask for the work. Be direct and tell them that you are confident about the positive impact that you can deliver and that you are asking for this assignment.

Some smart humor, relevant cartoons, images, imbedded video, appropriately wise parables – can be a good idea as long as they are used very sparingly. Even the most dour-looking group will respond to these. Be careful with stories that may be interpreted as racial, religious, divisive, making fun of the disadvantaged, socio-economic groups, etc. Sensitivities and sensibilities are difficult to predict and the most innocently intended story may backfire.

I'll provide an example – from when I was young and foolish. I was once trying to explain clearly what the difference was between *training* and *education.* I sensed that there was some confusion about these terms in the client environment. I explained as follows: *Think about the difference between training and education in the context of the difference between sex training and sex education: to which would you send your children and to which would you go yourself?* I figured that this clarified the semantical differences quite clearly and with a touch of humor. Indeed, I did receive a few chuckles but also some pretty negative body language. Note to self: avoid that in the future.

Stories and anecdotes can also become dated. What was acceptable in 2007 may not be acceptable in 2017. The same story may be acceptable in one environment and not in another. About 10+ years ago, I was asked to address a large group of Rotarians. Demographic: 60+ years old, all men, mostly traditional, and in that particular geography, mostly bible-toting. I was introduced with much fanfare and flattery and my CV was even embellished by the person introducing me. I actually felt a bit embarrassed (which is hard to do with me). So, I stood up at the podium, and said: *Now we have both sinned: you for exaggerating and me for enjoying it too much!*

It was clearly a hit; after all, this was as much a non-business social event as it was a business lecture, so I leveraged the momentum with a little story up front:

There is a bible story in Kings I, about King David when he was an old man. He probably had arthritis and there was likely no central heating in Jerusalem in those days. Anyways, the story in the bible goes something like this: He became old and couldn't keep warm in the cold mountain air of the Judean Hills. So, they brought him a young woman; a virgin – just to keep him warm at night (aka: no hanky panky). Her name was Abishag (1-Kings, 1-15). That's as far as the story goes in the bible, so I will extrapolate with my own extended version: So, in the morning the virgin left the king's bedchambers and all the servants and king's staff were so curious and they asked her: so how was it to sleep in the king's bed? And she answered: Now I know the difference between it is my ***honor*** *and it is my* ***pleasure.***

And of course, I continued by telling them that in this case it was both my *honor* and my *pleasure* to be addressing them and that my little story reminds us to be precise in our messaging to be fully understood in our markets. This was the subject at the core of my teachings to them on that particular evening, in the context of the Rotary International brand, and how it is understood or misunderstood among their various constituencies.

Why am I saying all this? Because one has to also be able to understand their audience and adjust behaviour and communication style to that which that specific audience digests. Would I tell that story today to a group of Rotarians or anyone else for that matter? I probably would not take the risk. After all, one or more of the audience might listen to my bible story and choose to focus on the abuse of the innocent by the powerful in biblical times - a decidedly negative and legitimate alternative spin on the story. But the bible story part is indeed from the bible and I was using humour to extrapolate and make a point and be remembered – albeit a risky way of doing it.

Aside from any technical protocols designed for effective presenting, the key need from any presentation is to be remembered and valued in a profoundly positive way. This is easier said than done. The audience will likely have been exposed to multiple presenters most of whom will be intelligent, will know their stuff, and will be articulate. How will you stand out?

I believe that the answers lay in your brand; aka what you stand for. How different you can be, how believable you are. How memorable your wit, insight, and stories are? In the book, Tipping Point[62], the idea of "stickiness" come up. What makes an idea interesting to an audience and likely to be remembered as a result? This challenge has been discussed by many thinkers over the years. "Made to Stick: Why Some Ideas Survive and Others Die[63]" describes a number of attributes that promotes this stickiness:

- Simplicity in exposing and describing the core of a concept or idea so that it can be easily understood and recalled at a later time.

- Impressing the audience and grabbing their attention.

- The idea must be believable, and also appeal to the audience at an emotional level.

- The power of storytelling and examples reinforcing the idea itself and its application and relevance to real life.

All reasonable points. The bottom line: keep it simple, use drama, connect emotionally, use narrative, make it real and believable. I would add: be personal, use your personal political capital, and share your experiences. This will create the believability/credibility, the drama, and the emotion to help to build rapport and a relationship.

A QUICK PERSONAL STORY

In 1998, I was asked to address Cuba's governmental agency and largest corporate conglomerate, CIMEX. It was responsible for all consumer and retail enterprises in that country. The project involved retail strategy and policy for the country. If my presentation was successful, a program of work would result in Cuba's first-ever western style, world class shopping Mall in Havana. My presentation began. The audience included senior officials, about 30 of them, including the President of CIMEX and the Chairman of the main bank of Cuba, Banco Financiere International. Fidel Castro was the honorary Chairman. The presentation went well, questions were asked, and answered; but at the end, the chairman remarked that they were grateful for my coming and sharing my expertise but they were not accustomed to engaging with non-Spanish consultants and were concerned that as a Canadian and northerner, I could not be expected to understand their culture, politics of socialism, and their social sensibilities.

This was for me, a not-so-delicate way of hearing "no thanks". I responded by saying that I understood their concern and I asked permission to tell them a funny and perhaps relevant anecdote, since we had a few minutes left on the agenda. They agreed, although they were puzzled. I told them my story:

There was an international agriculture conference and between speakers, groups of delegates gathered over coffee in the hallway. One such group included a Belgian dairy farmer, a Texas rancher, and an Israeli kibbutznik. (note: A kibbutz is a collective farm in Israel modelled after a socialist model of shared work and profits. Cuba had good rapport with Israel, which was quite socialist at that time). Anyways, the Texas rancher (as Texans tend to do) was bragging and said 'Why, back home, I have a ranch, that I can get into my vehicle in the morning and drive the whole darn day and still never reach the end of my property!". And to that comment, the Israeli Kibbutz farmer simply nodded his head and said: "yes, yes, I had a car like that once too!"

Not only did they laugh vigorously at my story, they understood that perhaps I appreciated their culture (and politics) more than they suspected and I got the job. This was the power of storytelling - when there is a message, a hook, a memorable punchline, and an authenticity/believability dimension. And of course, it demonstrated the power of humor. I truly believe that in that situation, this was the ideal solution and it worked.

NON-VERBAL COMMUNICATIONS

As for Body language – this is an area that every consultant or for that matter every person should try to master. Most researchers claim that body language makes up over half of all communications. People are constantly projecting non-verbal communications that are often worth reading and adjusting to. Your personal radar should always be turned on so that you can employ a feedback loop and adjust as necessary. We have all undoubtedly experienced a presenter going off on a tangent, making an inappropriate set of remarks, and we have seen the audience respond negatively – sparking our little wannabe telepathic voice to try to whisper to the presenter: *stop, you are digging that hole even deeper; get back on track, or change your style, etc.* – usually to no avail and then we watch them crash and burn.

To be sure, some body language can be misleading. Seeing someone cross their legs may not always signal that they are closing up and rejecting what we are saying; it simply may mean that their foot aches and they are changing position. Same with crossed arms, no eye contact *(masking emotions, fear of rejection, fear of engagement; usually the weaker member of the audience)*. So, it is usually best to look at body language as a group of signals rather than at individual, independent signals. Most of the time, we need not pursue any formal study of non-verbal communications. We usually, as a species, are able to "read each other" through a sense that we all possess but sometimes ignore (at our peril). We all know for example, that a frown or an eye-roll usually signals unhappiness, disagreement, or disapproval. It's what we do with that information that becomes important. There have been rare occasions where I have paused a presentation and disclosed that I am *reading some body language in the group* and that I would be interested in knowing whether my information is meeting their expectations or whether there are questions or concerns that perhaps should be shared before we continue.

On one such occasion, during a talk I was giving to the executive of The Canadian Broadcasting Corporation (CBC), I paused to ask such a question and discovered that the agenda they were given characterized my talk as being on a very different subject and they were understandably confused. One would think that someone would have stopped me (I would have) but they were being polite! Unbelievable really, but had I not paused to inquire in a sincere and honest way, it could have been a disaster.

PSYCHOLOGY OF MOTIVATION

"If you only have a hammer, you tend to see every problem as a nail"
- Abraham Maslow[64] (1908-1970)

A one-dimensional mindset focused on any problem is likely to lead to misleading observations and faulty problem identification. And a one-dimensional mindset focused on what triggers a response in a market is also likely to result in sub-optimal targeting. Marketing and branding considerations must embrace the multi-dimensional aspects of the human psyche and how and why we, as humans, respond to various stimuli.

Businesses struggle to understand their customer. They seek to segment the market into logical chunks and then further divide those segments into additional smaller chunks, or clusters. The effort to be as granular as we can be is driven by the marketers' appreciation of the value of recognizing and targeting audiences that have different needs and who digest information and respond in different ways. That being said, there are some characteristics that all audiences share, to a greater or lesser degree. There are some motivators, triggers to behaviours that are common across the totality of the human species. It's important to understand what these even to have a baseline concept from which to depart, as needed. Following is a model that describes one way of understanding a hierarchy of motivational triggers as it relates to the human psyche.

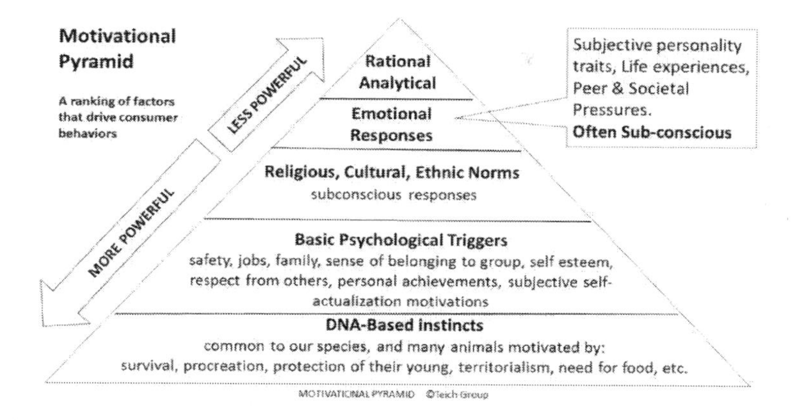

At the very bottom of my pyramid, lies the most basic instinctual responses. These are physiological (not psychological) in nature and intrinsic to our DNA. Almost all animals and certainly humans defend their young, for example. To be more accurate, that particular protective human drive is even more powerful in the mother. Mothers tend to be more highly bonded to their children than fathers, generally speaking. This is part of the mother's hardwiring[65]. We've all heard about how mama bears will stop at nothing to protect their offspring; it's true for the bears and it's true for the vast majority of human moms.

If a business offers a product or a service that legitimately leverages that instinct, it would likely be more effective than appealing for example, to a parent's intellect.

DECISION-MAKING @ TIP OF THE ICEBERG AND MOSTLY BELOW

As we proceed up the pyramid, the motivation and response becomes more conscious, more self- aware. It moves through Maslow-like factors to religious and cultural triggers that motivate only certain groups, and then to the classical emotional responses that individuals demonstrate under different stimuli. As the pyramid narrows, the responses become less powerful and less intense. Finally, at the top of the pyramid we find the small, rational, logical piece; essentially the responses that we are aware of. But in my view, that conscious response, the one we are most aware of – probably represents the smallest influencer in our decision-making, as consumers. It's the proverbial tip of the iceberg with so much more under the surface. Great marketers know and act on this truth intuitively. But to become consistently creative requires connecting evidence-based knowledge and creativity.

An example – appealing to DNA-based instincts

I was once approached by a friend, a smart, highly-educated consultant and enthusiastic entrepreneur whose ambition was to introduce plastic engineered fencing to the market. Clearly, his competition was wooden fencing; he was therefore competing with a long-standing tradition. I cautioned him that when you have to educate a whole market, this was not an enviable situation to be in. And I asked him what his selling proposition was, what will make the difference? Like a true engineer and financial analyst, he responded that the plastic fencing would not warp and rot, will never need painting, will always look fresh, and the added cost of the plastic fencing will be recovered within six years - so the payback was reasonable.

As a market strategy guy, I always look for the "wow". I couldn't find it in his argument. True, it was logical and rational. I figured he could probably sell the idea to a CPA quite easily. But the elusive wow factor is almost always there but often out of sight. So, I consulted "Professor" Google. I was looking for something; I would know it when I saw it. I learned a lot about plastic fence engineering and I learned a lot about wooden fences and about wood. And then I spotted a small article published by the American Association of Family Physicians (AAFP). It was a warning: "Wounds caused by wood splinters or thorns may result in sporotrichosis[66]"

In old rotting wood, including fencing material, there was a risk of having a certain fungal and pathogenic bacterial infections introduced into a child's body if they scratched themselves on an old wooden fence[67]. The article went on to say that it was not a usual thing to happen so when the child presents with fever and other symptoms, the pediatrician will likely not jump immediately to the correct diagnosis until the infection becomes very serious and potentially life threatening.

This was a WOW. It's a wow to all the mama bears out there. I can just hear the dad saying: *hey in year 6 the plastic fence might have paid the cost difference for itself but it's expensive. I'm not sure it's a practical thing for us just now.* And then I hear even more clearly and loudly what the momma bear says: *Are you kidding? I am not taking any chances that our child will be infected from splinters from our wooden fence. I want that plastic fence now and I want that old fence torn up and hauled away!*

A mother's love for her child is like nothing else in the world. It knows no law, no pity, it dares all things and crushes down remorselessly all that stands in its path.

- Agatha Christie

Ok, perhaps I am dramatizing a bit but I think you get the picture. There are battles I am willing to fight, but not that one.

Let's look at another example of the application of multiple levels of motivation – consistent with my model – that I can apply to the highly-charged and highly-invested political arena.

In the recent American elections, Mr. Trump and his communication and marketing team can be seen attempting to trigger responses. The table below summarily analyses the 2016 RNC speech whereby Mr. Trump accepts the nomination, and speaks not only to the RNC but to the entire American electorate.

Levels of motivation	**Levels and Characteristics**
Logical/rational responses	**5**: analysis, deductions
Emotional responses	**4**: emotional
Religious, cultural, ethnic norms and traditions	**3**: group/cultural needs, like patriotism, belonging
Human/Maslow-esque needs	**2**: basic human needs, jobs, safety, peace
DNA species level instincts	**1**: survival, war, territorial-ism.

LEVEL 1: TRIGGERS – survival, call to action, threats of extinction Excerpts from Trump 2016 RNC Speech
"there is a crisis for our nation, attacks on police, terrorism in our cities – **threaten our very way of life. We must defend the lives of our citizens"** "180,000 illegal immigrants with criminal records (are) **roaming free to threaten peaceful citizens**" "Iran on the **path to nuclear weapons"**

LEVEL 2: TRIGGERS – basic human needs, jobs, safety, family, self-esteem

Excerpts from Trump 2016 RNC Speech

"(I will) lead our **country back to safety, prosperity, and peace"**

"Jobs, Jobs, Jobs!"

LEVEL 3: TRIGGERS – group/cultural needs, like patriotism, and a sense of belonging

Excerpts from Trump 2016 RNC Speech

"**American** people will come **first again**"

"We are going to **build a great border wall**"

"We will make **America proud again**, great again"

LEVEL 4: TRIGGERS – Emotional responses

Excerpts from Trump 2016 RNC Speech

"Remember the images of **our sailors forced to their knees by Iranian** captors at gunpoint"

"**I am your voice**"

"My **compassion is for (our) struggling citizens**"

"We are (will be) **a country of generosity and warmth**"

LEVEL 5: TRIGGERS – (Appeals to) Rational, logical, analytical

Excerpts from Trump 2016 RNC Speech

"Homicides **increased by 17%;** killings **rose by 50%**"

"Household incomes **down by more than $40,000** since"

"**I've made billions** of dollars in business, making deals"

"I'm proposing **largest tax reduction** in history"

This communication strategy is (or should be) deliberate. The elements of the speech are designed to appeal to all or most of the levels of triggers in the human psyche. The most powerful ones are at the deeper levels and the Trump campaign deftly used this with success. We all remember how the opposition criticized the Trump campaign for sowing the seeds of fear and divisiveness. In fact, what they did was also to trigger survival instincts at the most basic level intrinsic to our species. I should note that my illustration of a motivational model for marketing and communication is not intended as a political statement or as a criticism of a political candidate or indeed of a now sitting president. Indeed, both "sides" are well aware of the power of the approach and both sides used that power in an attempt to gain competitive advantage. Ms. Clinton, for example, in that same election competition had suggested that Mr. Trump's perceived attitudes toward Muslims was being used by ISIS to recruit more terrorists to endanger

America and Americans. Whether true or not is not the issue here. However, it is an example of orchestrating a sense of fear of destruction and a triggering of survival-level responses.

Although more obvious and possibly more widely applicable in politics, commercial organizations employ a similar approach to attract the attention of consumers and to influence them at various psychological levels. Look at Ford's website.

The rational approach by Ford (Canada): *"320,000 vehicles and 425,000 engines to market"*. Ford is demonstrating its knowhow, its talent, and its scale of operations: *"Ford performance captures Daytona 500 for the 5th time in 9 years"*. Here, Ford is demonstrating its achievements in technical aspects of performance.

The emotional trigger being employed in the area of group identity, pride, and patriotism: *"Proud to be Canada's largest established automaker"* and *"Ford remains committed to building a strong future in Canada"* and *"Canadian Fords were more innovative than their American counterparts. Ford of Canada: a heritage as rich as the land itself"* A clever spin designed to counter the fact that Ford is an American company operating in Canada. Invoking almost a Canadian "magic" symbol about the richness of our Canadian land and heritage and associating that notion with the Ford product.

Human basic needs as in safety are also addressed: *"The drugged driving suit – a Ford innovation that teaches young people the dangers of driving under the influence of drugs"*. This is also a Ford attempt to attract the interest and loyalty of the influencer to the consumer (parents to their children). Having parents see Ford as a protector to their children digs deep into the protective instincts of parents.

And lastly, in attempting to leverage the deep instinctual survival/war/territorial motivators that can be released with powerful symbols and by Ford's participation in "noble" causes: (Ford is) "Proud to announce the selection of a Ford engine to power the JLTV[68] family of (combat) vehicles".

IDENTIFYING AND MOTIVATING MARKET SEGMENTS INSIDE ORGANIZATIONS

On a more granular level, several market segments often exist inside one (customer) organization. It is useful to think of an organization simply as a group of people. Different people inside organizations will have different perspectives and biases depending on their role in that organization and depending on what they are being rewarded for. Accordingly, when targeting an organization, it is productive to attempt to segment these different internal interest groups and ensure that all of these understand the value of your product and service in the context that each of these internal segments value the most. Permit me an example.

I was engaged by the CEO and his board of directors (comprised of their venture capital investors) to assess the quality of their strategic marketing plan. My client, an engineering company situated in the Pacific North-West, had developed a brilliant, miniature chemical laboratory which when connected to large step-up transformers (GSUs owned by electric utilities) measures the dissolved gases in the transformers' oil (using gas chromatography), and predicts if and when these multi-million dollar transformers will fail. The engineering innovation was brilliant. The engineers were appropriately excited. They believed that the world of utilities would beat a path to their door. But sales were weak and the investors were predictably impatient. Depending on my assessment of market success, they were going to either proceed with a second tranche of funding or possibly allow the venture to fail.

It turned out that like most humans, the engineers preferred working within their comfort zones. So, they talked to their professional colleagues within target customer utilities. This was pleasant, they talked the same technical language, the utility engineers were impressed; but it wasn't enough. The sales did not materialize.

After asking some fundamental process questions, it became apparent that a one-dimensional, one-target-segment approach was inadequate to market the technology. The message had to be developed and segmented to emphasize the related, but different advantages of the technology to different influencing groups within each of the target customer organizations. This was not complicated. The technology addressed real needs. There were about 500,000 of these transformers in the world, each valued in millions of dollars. When these beasts fail, they either stop working and a brownout or blackout occurs; or they can fail catastrophically, explode, and spill thousands of gallons of highly toxic transformer oil on to the land, into the water table, or in the case of Hydro-based utilities, into rivers.

This is fairly fundamental in principal, but often gets overlooked. One must ask what the different functions, roles, and departmental/segmented goals are - in the target organization and what each manager is being held accountable for and rewarded for; and how our product or service can make them heroes. The new marketing approach took on a different look and was successful. A very simplified, summarized version is presented in the next table:

INSIDE THE SAME CUSTOMER ORGANIZATION		
TARGET CUSTOMER DEPARTMENT	**SEGMENT MESSAGE**	**PERCEIVED BENEFIT by the CUSTOMER**
CEO and Executive	Profound consumer, shareholder, and societal value	Demonstrates **leadership**; **creates a new standard** for other to benchmark against
Financial Management	Lower operational costs due to enhanced preventive maintenance strategy Fix / maintain by exception only	**Bottom line contribution.** Increased longevity of high-value fixed assets.
Engineering Management	Breakthrough technical innovation; enhanced safety, orderly maintenance protocols.	Professionalizes, **revolutionizes transformer** quality **control**, and safety
Legal and Risk Departments	Reduction in risk of catastrophic failure, personal injury, and brownouts	Possible negotiation of **lower insurance premiums.** **Lowered risk of law suits** and legal payouts.
External relations, Consumer Relations Departments	Lowered risk of injury, oil leaks, brownouts	**Protection of Environment.** **Reliability** of Service. **Public Safety**

CHAPTER 7 TAKE-AWAYS SELLING IDEAS	
1	Know what keeps your customers up at night and talk to them about *their* needs, not yours.
2	Sell by consulting. Process skills are not enough to offer. Know the content of their business and sector and for goodness sakes, have an opinion!
3	Customers will only value you if you can solve their problems and offer great ideas and suggestions.
4	The best presentations are simple, to the point, sincere, and overflowing with a wealth of authenticity, expertise, and authority. You get one kick at this can; do not enter that room without having done your research.
5	Anticipate and prepare for at least three levels of drill-down questions from your "audience". Do not be shy to practice this with your staff; they will learn that way and so will you.
6	Do not expect your customers to spend time figuring out creative ways to merchandise and re-sell your products or services. They won't. You must do it. It will also put you in control.
7	Find out where your customers hang out, physically and virtually - and go there to market to them – even if it's in the middle of an online fantasy world mass multi-player game!

CHAPTER 7 TAKE-AWAYS SELLING IDEAS	
8	Use the Aristotle formula to create spectacular presentations.
9	Leverage the power and drama of story-telling but be totally believable. Use humor cleverly and sparingly to break the ice and make a relevant point.
10	Learn how to read and react to non-verbal communications.
11	Appeal to the full spectrum of your markets' psychological triggers. Most triggers reside below the conscious, rational tip of the iceberg.
12	Train your people to work outside of their comfort-zones.

CHAPTER 8

ORGANIZATION EFFECTIVENESS

"If u were a farmer and hired a Hand to dig 20 fence posts and he didn't care if they were crooked or not, what would you do? You might tell him that you expect them to be dug straight; but that would not likely help. The hired hand's attitude is naturally one that takes pride in his work or not. If not, you will have to stand over him and scrutiny his work and you have more valuable things to do with your time. Best to fire him. If on the other hand, he comes to you and says; look boss I would like to install these posts straight but the ground is rocky and it will take longer than 20 in a day – he is thinking. And you will have to reassess your expectations of throughput. If the new cows are scheduled in a week and the 20 per day is required to finish the containment area, then you have a decision to make and to share. You may be able to delay delivery of the cows to ensure a perfect fence, or you may put in a temporary fence or u may wish to compromise and build a slightly crooked fence[69]."

Is the above story about human resources management? Well, yes, in a way it is. And in a way it's about planning and anticipating, and in an even broader way it's about being flexible. Everything *depends* and everything is related and connected. And when you connect all the dots and see business, and indeed see life that way, then you are evolving.

CELEBRATING FAILURE

"Once you embrace unpleasant news not as a negative but as evidence of a need for change; you aren't defeated by it. You're learning from it. It's all in how you approach failures. And believe me, we know a lot about failures at Microsoft."
- Bill Gates, BUSINESS @ THE SPEED OF THOUGHT

"Success is 99% failure"
- Sochiro Honda, founder of Honda Motor Company

I mean it. You've got to believe in this principle to be believed (and trusted) by your staff and colleagues. There is a lot to be learned by discussing – in the spirit of safety – what the team has taken away from experiencing failure. The idea of this kind of post mortem is not only about what signals were present that were somehow unnoticed or ignored. Failure often stems from an organization structure issue that constrains effective and timely information-sharing between units of the company. This all too common problem relates to what I call the *black hole* of the interface. The interface between any one organizational unit and another is always an opportunity for information to be sucked into oblivion somewhere in between the two, into the interface.

There are the obvious questions to be asked and discussed in a post mortem, the usual ones' deal with the quality of the company's radar and problem identification and diagnostics systems; communication, analysis, and interpretation issues; surprises relating to the competitive landscape; and most important – the customer or the customer-of-the-customer who may have turned out to be unhappy, and no one knew. But most likely someone knew, somewhere in the organization, but that information struggled unsuccessfully to be noticed and taken seriously.

It reminds me of the principle of the so-called American Dream regarding the *pursuit of happiness.* The happiness of everyone in your universe of stakeholders is the goal, the key goal that the organization must pursue with all vigor, passion, research, energy and mostly by developing and nurturing a continuing relationship with those stakeholders at a level of quality – such that you can honestly check the state of your organizational health with them. There is no universal formula for business success other than having a clear, unbiased view of your failings and the energy and courage to make the strategic decisions necessary to fix these and prevent reoccurrence. Your stakeholders will tell you how, most of the time. Your job is to do so competitively. This done, the meaning of *we learn mostly from our failures and not from our successes,* becomes more meaningful and highly productive.

To be crystal, the kind of failure that I am referring to is not about technical incompetence. Those deficits must be dealt with in other ways. Developing a winning team requires hiring the best, rewarding them highly, and maintaining the quality by weeding out the weak performers. I for one have not subscribed to the philosophy of remedial or training environments. I don't believe in second chances. Sounds harsh? Yes, of course it does. But overly nurturing weak performance (in the context of core competence) penalizes the strong performers, dilutes the quality of the team and generates a low common denominator performance environment.

The idea here is this: while people do "grow into" a job, they should be hired on the basis of raw talent and the right personality fit. That is not to say that they all must think alike; on the contrary, but they all must work at a high level, be self-motivating, be very smart and ambitious, without being self-absorbed, and they must be capable of getting enthusiastic and committed about the shared mission. If they fail in those foundational attributes, they should be dismissed without hesitation or remorse. The fact is that they will probably be happier elsewhere. I'm also in favor of personality and other testing as a condition of hiring. I would want to know if the potential new-hire enjoys pulling the wings off flies, or has a dictatorial bent, or is inherently manipulative, dishonest, or mean-spirited. I can't fix these things nor would I wish to spend the energy trying. My guess is that if all managers owned their companies and knew that every dollar spent was coming out of their own pocket and every dollar earned was being deposited into their family bank account, then they wouldn't want to spend the energy, time, funds, and other resources trying to "fix" those failings in their staff.

And so, having dealt with that, we return to celebrating failure with a more appropriate perspective. The failure that arises from actions that involved calculated risks for the sake of achieving some potentially stunning, innovative, competitive, result – is the kind of failure that I would celebrate. The potential rewards must have been very significant and the potential risks must have been known, monitored continuously, and controlled to the extent, such that at a certain "failure" level, the organization had a strategy to extricate themselves and avoid further losses and risks. That's when a post mortem is successful and when the conversation can be open and without fear of management reprisals or blame-setting.

Further, there should be a place in most organizations for pure, crazy, unbridled experimentation. Extracting talented people for a stint in a skunk-works program may end up being the smartest initiative the organization undertakes, maybe.

When I worked in the oil and gas industry early in my career, I was tapped to head up a think-tank charged with developing ideas about a new paradigm information management vision for that Fortune 50 company. I remember my boss entering my office and asking me what I was doing standing there looking out of my window. I responded that I was thinking; and he said that the company needed more people thinking. I liked Bill. And when he asked me to head up the Information Vison team, I accepted with the caveat that I be permitted to raid the organization for the best and brightest from across multiple disciplines. I chose an eastern-European-trained PhD in theoretical mathematics, a computer software engineer whiz kid, an eccentric genius shaman Blackfoot Elder-philosopher-accountant, an HR professional, and a refinery guy.

We screwed whiteboards to the walls and cloistered ourselves for several months; we ate a lot of pizza – and outside of the world we created, the business of the corporation continued like a swiss watch, regular, and orderly, with stewardship and accounting. We were left free and exempt from all of that. And we emerged with a discussion paper that transformed the way we were to do business, capture information, and make decisions - that had an immediate return of 40 million dollars a year for starters. I am convinced that it is worthwhile for some researcher to evaluate the ROI of skunk-works initiatives. Personally, I set aside 3-5% of my operating budget for such activities in the company that I led. I was never disappointed.

I'll conclude this section on failure on a low note. For those of you who feel that you have finally reached a good place in their business where you can just coast for a while – be warned. Not only does the need for change almost always come from the outside, there is also the inevitable phenomenon of *entropy* that constantly influences the inside of the organization. In physics, the 2nd law of thermodynamics demands that any system (in all of nature) will, over time, gradually and consistently degrade from a state of order to a state of disorder or randomness. Think of a satellite whose orbit decays over time. NASA must fire its rockets from time to time to nudge the satellite back into its intended orbit. It is somewhat the same in organizations. Energy is required to simply maintain it from degrading.

COLLECTIVE INTELLIGENCE

"Listen with the intent to understand, not the intent to reply"
- Stephen Covey[70]

It is challenging to leverage the inherent potential of groups mostly because of the natural tendency for egos to prove their individual value and because the organization's motivation, recognition, and reward system is targeted mostly to individuals[71]. There are organizations that have toyed with evaluating and rewarding the effectiveness of groups or teams in addition to evaluating the individual member. This can work but the individual needs are always higher on the ego pyramid. There have been rare instances where the team is evaluated as a whole single entity. In this model, the team becomes self-policing, in a way. Since they are all in the same boat and that "boat" must perform, the team will lift up and nurture its weaker members. If the boat springs a leak, everyone drowns. More to the point, if a person at one end of the boat drills a hole, he cannot simply ask others to mind their own business since he's' drilling only on his end of the boat. And if the member, after some trial, does not respond and cannot improve and carry their own weight – then it is the team that dismisses that member, not being able to tolerate being weighed down.

A 2011 study coming out of Northwestern University's School of Education and Social Policy generally supported team-based rewards and evaluation, but on the downside they said it well: *"...team-based rewards "'may be difficult for people to accept,' says Jay Schuster[72], a partner in the Los Angeles-based compensation consulting firm. 'The notion that some of an individual's pay is at risk based on someone else's behavior or by the team overall is a hard sell'" (Garvey, 2002, p.74). Thompson (2008) also recognizes the potential for motivational loss, characterized by social loafing or free riding, when team-based rewards are used. This may be driven by feelings of inequity when other team members don't pull their weight, but rewards are still allocated based on equality. This perception of unfairness may be particularly prominent for high performers who have "a general tendency to evaluate team-based rewards as distributively unfair[73]"*

In my experience, I have used a hybrid model, where team contribution is a very highly valued component of an individual's evaluation as a critical resource to the organization. To me, this not only means how well the individual contributes within a team but even more important, how he or she enables and empowers others to contribute more effectively. As I read my own previous sentence, I say to myself: someone out there (not HR professionals) is going to think this is BS. I assure you, it is not. Read on.

In most groups, in organizations, or in our personal lives - the cream always seems to rise to the top. If I participated in a team effort as the senior-ranking executive and was able to have the team members believe that in this room at this time, I was not the boss, but just another member of the team – then I would observe some interesting things going on. The person with the best idea, who could defend his or her idea with objective evidence - becomes the leader at that moment. This is essentially a new *aristocracy of the intelligencia,* based not on their position on the organization chart but on their value during the team encounter. True leadership is not taken, it is bestowed by others who see the value of being lead by the person who displays worthy leadership abilities. It is a joy to behold. More than a joy, it is profitable.

But there is an even more dramatic scenario that can be orchestrated to identify problems and opportunities and solve them. That scenario and approach takes advantage of the team's collective IQ.

Research has suggested that groups outperform individuals on a multitude of problem-solving tasks and that there is little correlation (in those scenarios) with the average (or maximum) intelligence of individual members of the group. Instead, there were correlations (aka, superior outcomes) when the group members were seen (measured) to have worked well together (i.e. social sensitivity), when there was an equal distribution and frequency of conversational turn-taking, and where there was an equal representation of females and males in the group[74].

The call-to-action is clear and actionable. Managers have an opportunity to experiment and apply these kinds of observations coming from academe, in their day-to-day management of outcomes-biased group thinking activities - to analyze, learn from, solve problems, and identify and act upon uncovered opportunities. The construct of teams ought not to be an onerous task for enlightened managers. There is no real immediate need to re-structure formal organization design. The organization chart can be left alone. In any case, a geodesic[75] type of informal organization might be considered allowing the flexibility of pulling together a rapid-deployment force, a team that can form quickly to perform a specific task, a team containing all the right ingredients (skill, discipline area, social sensitivity, gender mix, etc.) and just as rapidly the team could disband after the task is completed.

TECHNOLOGY-ENABLED INTELLIGENCE

I have been writing about harnessing team intelligence *inside* the organization. Technology has enabled a revolution in the harnessing of the intelligence of large groups of people *external* to the organization. In so doing, it has broadened and re-defined *collective intelligence*. With the exponential growth of the internet and with it, technologies like Google, YouTube, and Wikipedia – the quantum of organized intelligence never available before – is now available. Take Wikipedia with its originally stated goal to "compile the sum of all human knowledge[76]". Wikipedia includes almost 42 million pages of information and that information has been edited 877,482,924 times by 30,355,587 users (English Wikipedia) who have registered a username. Only a minority of users contribute regularly with 141,003 who have edited in the last 30 days[77].

Pause for a moment to consider these statistics. An encyclopedia of knowledge, discussion groups, analyses – as an outcome of the collective intelligence of 30 million people. The MIT Technology Review in 2013 wrote "there is no other free information source like it, many online services rely on Wikipedia. Look something up on Google or ask Siri a question on your iPhone and you'll often get back tidbits of information pulled from the encyclopedia and delivered as straight-up facts.[78]" Wikipedia may be on a decline relative to their initial period of highest growth, but it is still a powerful presence in the world of collective intelligence. New sites appear regularly, special purpose sites are growing, and of course, sophisticated new collaborative software used inside organizations and within communities of interest, appear with regularity.

I just punched in to Google the following question: "How do I boil an egg?" In 0.54 seconds, I received 97,900,000 results. When I asked: "What are the best designs for a book cover?", in 0.83 seconds, I received 70,600,000 results. Too much information? For sure, but when I punched in "how do I boil an egg at 4,000 meters", I was immediately provided with an interactive chart where I inputted egg diameter and altitude in meters. It outputted how many minutes and seconds for soft, medium, or hard boiled-eggs. All this, ironically while sitting in my *library* at home, sipping a café latte.

As a concept, collective intelligence is not new. In the late 1960s, visionaries predicted computers would be used to facilitate collaboration among people, capable of solving specific problems, and to share ideas[79]. Collective intelligence has gained astonishing momentum since then with new tools available to support profound collaboration. The last ten years have demonstrated a paradigm shift in the generation, dissemination, and sharing of user-generated content and the creation of new, value-added services. These developments have revolutionized the way people search, find, read, gather, share, develop, and consume information, and impact on the way people communicate with each other and collaborate to create new knowledge. These developments impact not only on the behaviour and decision-making of internet users, but also on the business models that organizations need to develop and adapt in order to conduct business[80].

COLLECTIVE IGNORANCE

If darkness is the absence of light, then collective ignorance is the absence of collective intelligence. To be a little provocative, I would venture that collective ignorance is often preventable – at least in the office - by simply speaking up with evidence-based arguments. This may sound simplistic, but by "speaking up", I would include such techniques as research, analysis, audience analysis, ensuring motivating influences are understood, lobbying, and other ways to manage issues and opportunities - but that is a somewhat different conversation.

This subject reminds me of what we used to call the Abilene Scenario. Allow me to relate this old story.

There was a group of folks sitting around in their old Texas ranch house on Sunday afternoon, bored and with nothing much to do. It was a hot and dusty day and they were fidgety and uncomfortable. During the general complaining about the situation, someone suggested that for something to do, they all drive in to Abilene. So, they all piled into the old red Ford pickup and drove the 53 miles down the hot, dusty road into the town of Abilene. The truck wasn't air conditioned, and by the time they got into town, they were hot and annoyed. Sitting later in the dusty diner, one of them said: why the heck did we ever come into town? They all looked at each other, and discovered that no one really wanted to go. Everyone had agreed, thinking that everyone else wanted to go. No one expressed their own true feelings.

This simple but clever anecdote reflects what many of us experience from time to time. It is an illustration of a low-energy group and the way that non-decisions are made - that result in actions that no one really wanted. Nor did it involve any ideas that anyone was particularly committed to. It happens too frequently, in our lives and in our business. There are other examples where high-energy groups – practicing a kind of "groupthink" - also suffer from similar misfortunes. There is a rhythm that sometimes happens in groups and that rhythm takes on a life of its own, and its momentum carries its followers unwillingly but passively - to actions that are not useful. Watch for this in your organizations and always ask the process questions around who supports this, and why, and what benefit does the idea deliver, and when would be the most ideal time to execute that idea, etc.

An interesting exercise that quickly demonstrates a similar phenomenon involves group reciting and adding up the running total of a string of numbers. You can try this yourself but it's more demonstrative in a group, even a small group. The idea is to start reciting each set of numbers and work down the rows, adding them up on the go. So, for example, you would say out loud: "1,000, 1,040, 2,040, etc. – until you come to the final total. You and your group will probably be wrong. Try it.

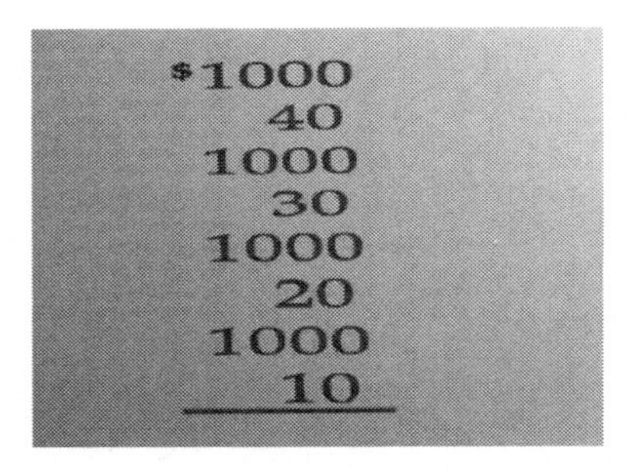

Most groups will end up with a total of 5,000. Did you? It's not uncommon. Of course, the correct total is 4,100. Most business people count by approximation from largest to smallest numbers, therefore, they might say: 4 **X** 1,000 = 4,000 plus (40+30+20+10) 100. But the point is that we get into rhythm, in this case of tens: 1000, 1040, 2040, 2070, 3070, 3090, 4090, and we "want" to say 5000. In larger groups, there will invariably be individuals that would otherwise see that the flow is misleading but they will follow the group over the cliff.

THE LEAST INTELLIGENT TEAM

"None of us is as smart as all of us." - Ken Blanchard[81]

The least intelligent team is smarter than the most intelligent individual on the team. That is quite a statement. I would not be surprised if you have a hard time believing it, but I have found it to be true, most of the time.

For those of you in a position to test this theory in your organizations, there are "games" or team exercises that demonstrate this general principle. Here is one small example that presents a challenge for a team to solve. Your spaceship crash-landed on the moon, destroying all the equipment on board except for 15 items listed below. You must leave the ship but first you must choose the most critical items to take with you; you cannot take them all. Given that it is unlikely that anyone on the team has ever been on the moon, we can assume that we start the "game" on a level-playing field.

The first stage of the exercise has each individual without any discussion with anyone else – list their own personal choice of a prioritized list of items presented in this chapter below *(Lost on the Moon, a Group Exercise)*, and rank items from most important to least important.

Some managers will also insert an additional 2nd analysis, whereby the team will simply vote to create a prioritized list and do so without any discussion or debate; a kind of Delphi technique[82]; aka: an averaging of intelligent opinion. However, the core of this exercise is to have the team[83] discuss in a democratic, participative manner, their individual ideas, debate them civilly, encouraging and drawing out the shyer members to participate fully, and manage the dynamics such that no one individual member, dominates, repeats, or overly-asserts their position. The team will then decide on the prioritization of the items presented, as a group. It is critical for the team to understand and realize that after the discussions, their collective fates will depend on the list of items that they choose. They cannot take all 15 items with them from their space craft so if they leave behind a "mission-critical" item, they will ALL die. This is an excellent metaphor for team commitment. In other words, an individual team member may not truly believe that the team has come up with the exactly correct formula but they nevertheless must commit to the group decision and "own" the outcome. Most often, they will discover that it was good that he or she did commit because the team was more correct than that individual was.

And indeed, in my experience of conducting this and other types of team exercises, the results of a high-performing team were always more correct than the individual score of the most intelligent individual. The ideal team size is 6 to 8 people. If necessary form more than one team and compete.

This is a powerful claim that I am making. The team must be trained to conduct themselves as a team but once that is accomplished, the team is capable of enormous accomplishments.

"LOST ON THE MOON[84]"

Group Exercise[85]

Your spaceship has just crash-landed on the moon. You were scheduled to rendezvous with the mother ship 200 miles away on the lighted surface of the moon, but the rough landing has ruined your ship and destroyed all the equipment on board, except for the 15 items listed below. Your crew's survival depends on reaching the mother ship, so you must choose the most critical items available for the 200-mile trip. Your task is to rank the 15 items in terms of their importance for survival. Place number 1 by the most important item, number 2 by the second most important, and so on through number 15, the least important.

INVENTORY OF ITEMS TO BE RANKED

Rank	Item
	Box of matches
	Food concentrate
	50 feet of nylon rope
	Parachute silk
	Solar-powered portable heating unit
	Two .45-caliber pistols
	One case of dehydrated milk
	Two 100-pound tanks of oxygen
	Stellar map (of the moon's constellation)
	Self-inflating life raft
	Magnetic compass
	Five gallons of water
	Signal flares
	First-aid kit containing injection needles
	Solar-powered FM receiver-transmitter

See Appendix A for answers and scoring method.

DON'T GOSSIP: NO-PASS THROUGH COMMUNICATION

"Strong minds discuss ideas, average minds discuss events, weak minds discuss people." —Socrates

Most people would agree that gossip in an organization is destructive. By gossip, I mean negative stories that are neither objective nor verified. For some reason, too many people enjoy passing negative stories forward. These "juicy" stories may temporarily give them a sense of power but there is never any percentage in sharing these, despite the temptation. Wikipedia defines gossip as "idle talk or rumor, especially about the personal or private affairs of others".

Beth Weissenberger ("Bloomberg BusinessWeek" column) notes that "For many employees, gossip in the workplace is a frequent guilty pleasure. Although it occasionally provides insight into and understanding of the nuances of office personalities and colleague relationships, it often hurts the individuals involved and damages the organization. At the very least, workplace gossip is unproductive[86]". Anthropologically speaking, gossip has been a way for us to bond with others—and sometimes a tool to isolate those who aren't supporting the group.[87] The seduction of gossip has spawned a $3 billion industry in the United States[88].

But in the workplace, studies explain that gossip is a standard currency of human connection. Research from the University of Amsterdam found that 90 percent of the conversations in the office can be characterized as gossip; and the Georgia Institute of Technology has estimated that 15% of all office email can be described as gossip[89]. These data sound unproductive. But I am not so much referring to standard gossip but to *negativity in the workplace*. I do believe that this kind of gossip is especially inappropriate, erodes trust and safety, and as such should be actively managed down.

What I espoused in my company was a "no-pass through" mental attitude. That is to say, the gossip stops with me (me is anyone), and I see it as my personal and professional duty *not* to allow it to pass from me onward. We stressed this in group meetings. We explained that negativity is destructive, unfair, and intolerable. We added this value to the organizational culture that we wished to build and maintain. It became unpopular to pass gossip forward, to participate, to become a partner in the spread of negativity in the workplace; and to do so was considered uncool. And, it worked. It felt cleaner, and everyone was (eventually) happy to comply. With the compliance, came understanding about how much better it is in the absence of negativity.

"Thou shalt not bear false witness against thy neighbour"
- the 9th of the 10 Commandments

"You shall not spread a false report. You shall not join hands with a wicked man to be a malicious witness. You shall not fall in with the many to do evil"
— Exodus 23:1-2

The bible does not *command* the reader to breathe, or eat or drink. These are natural desires. We don't require commandments that we would do ourselves without encouragement. Therefore, it is safe to assume that gossiping and lying is within the range of human activities that come, more or less, naturally to our species.

Psychologists agree. "According to renowned British psychologist Prof. Richard Wiseman, everyone is born naturally with the ability to lie and every organism knows how to lie. Findings of Wiseman's research showed that 40% of three-year old's who have just learnt to speak, lie. Therefore, lying is a very interesting topic in psychology."[90]

To gossip is certainly a bad thing, and destructive in an organization. But it is a different level of *sinister* to spread rumor and deception with the goal of sabotaging an organization or its management. I've observed organizations that are overly forgiving when dealing with such issues. The reality is that there are nasty people to be found everywhere; a tiny minority perhaps; but when found behaving at this level of destructiveness, the organization – with an appropriate zero-tolerant mindset – should immediately escort the offender to the exit door. If it costs a lot of money for that termination, I recommend that the organization eat the cost. In the words of Nike, *just do it!*

CLEARLY COMMUNICATING

"The single biggest problem in communication is the illusion that it has taken place" – George Bernard Shaw

---

Communication issues are the most traditional and pervasive of challenges within and between organizations. Whenever there is an organizational effectiveness issue, I look for what I called previously *the black hole of the interface.* Communications between work units, departments, and between other intra-organizational structures are often more complex because of different managements, priorities, goals, systems, rewards, geographies, and other reasons. However, achieving effective communications among different individuals working together in the same work environment is also challenging, but with discipline can be significantly enhanced.

For those of us who have left a meeting, still wondering whether we were (simply) *given information* or were asked to actually do something and *take action* – this communication challenge is real. Many managers and their teams are less precise than they should be when communicating. We celebrate the casual, informal, even friendly way we communicate; it tends to be a style that breaks down barriers, un-stifles the spirit of a place and encourages inclusiveness. But *casual* can go way too far when it sacrifices precision and clarity in communication. Nor is *casual* and *precise* mutually exclusive styles. As usual, I will offer an example from my personal history.

During my management days, I recall casually asking my HR guy, what our plan was regarding summer interns. To be honest, my nephew had asked me if there were any summer jobs in my company and that he would be prepared to work for free for the experience. I didn't want to appear to be trying to influence my HR department or to expect any preferential treatment, so I asked my question in the way that I did, expecting a casual response to my casual question. The response was: "I'll get back to you on that". Three days later, I was presented with a 30-page bound report, professionally titled with all the appropriate keywords, like strategy, plan, summer, internship, training, etc. What can I say? I was embarrassed. It was not my intent to generate that work. Mine was a simple question. But I was unclear. It had sounded like a request and he wanted to please me, to demonstrate his competence, even his enthusiasm. It was my responsibility to be crystal clear and I had failed. When I asked him how much effort was involved in producing the report, he confessed that it had required staff overtime at a cost of about $1000.

Sometimes management has a gilded mental model of what it takes to get things done. A report should be able to be generated by pressing a few computer keys, specifying the requested view of the data, and then view or print it; that's the typical way that senior managers often perceive it. The truth can be very different especially when what we present is used to support decision-making. After all, we are careful to ensure that relevant information is collected, checked, analyzed, reconciled, formatted and presented in the most professional manner. To be fair, the recipient of the request ought to feel empowered enough to challenge the requestor or at least to seek clarification. "Tell me what you need this for, how do you intend to use the information; this will give me an idea about the scope you require, the effort needed, the cost and time to prepare"; "How much are you willing to spend on this effort? What priority do you assign to this request; aka, what ongoing projects can be set aside while we are pursuing this one?" or "I have a quick & dirty answer to that question now, or do you require a more formal, more studied response?" These are the kinds of questions that the recipient of a request might choose to ask if the requestor failed to be clear enough – and these would be a legitimate and appropriate approach and a sign of professionalism and leadership.

A final comment: *all* management loathes *surprises*. Managers feel upended and de-stabilized when they are confronted with information that was withheld for any reason. One must avoid these scenarios. They can erode trust.

TIGHT-LOOSE

"The whole world is like a narrow bridge, and the goal is not to lose our balance"[91] - Nachman of Breslov

---

I was a tight manager and a loose manager. *Tight* in the sense of being tough and uncompromising when it came to the very few critical principles and standards; and *loose* in the sense of adaptable and accommodating once the essential standards were complied with. My team was clear on what I expected. It was also clear that management isn't a democracy; we didn't manage the business with equal votes. But we were all open to good ideas.

Ironically, some of the best ideas can arise from new hires. I normally suggest to new employees that they should continue to ask questions and that there are no dumb questions. In fact, challenging the status quo, the so-called sacred cows - can be very valuable. No matter how committed we are to continuous improvement and new courageous and even revolutionary change, it is often the "naïve" new hire who has not (yet) been lulled into the rhythm of the organization who can be a valuable source of new ideas. The key to success also includes having the right individuals, and the right team. My competitors often puzzled over how we were so successful and how scalable we were, given that in our industry that included a very creative resource, the conventional wisdom was that an agency of about 40 people was about the maximum number in order to maintain a truly creative environment. We numbered six times that population. It really was not that deep a secret. I hired the best and paid them about 25% more than the industry average. We also offered a superb professional environment, respected differences, encouraged risk-taking, and had fun. Our employee turnover was almost zero. But there was one big difference. We were extremely selective about who we took into the family. The fit had to be perfect. The interesting thing about employment law in our geography is the provision of an initial 90-day probationary period. That means that before 90 days, or on the 90th day, any new hire could be dismissed "without cause" and without the need for explanation or rationale. This allowance, in favor of the employer, is largely ignored or under-utilized by many companies. That has always puzzled me. For me, this was a gift. It provided an opportunity to truly test for the appropriate performance, attitude, native skills, and team fit – and believe me - I do not ever believe in second chances. The fact is, at least in my perception, that if an employee doesn't perform, then he or she would be happier elsewhere.

At one point, I had an employee who was under-performing. He started out well but had weakened over the past few months. I called him into my office and fired him. His immediate response? "Ira, what took you so long; I've been coasting for the past two years!"

Bottom line is that if you are doing most things right as a manager, then do not tolerate a lack of contribution. It's probably been going on longer than you think. Cut your losses, do not penalize the great performers by hanging on to the weaker ones – and clean house. I have never heard a manager express remorse for having dismissed anyone but I have heard many managers regret not having acted quickly enough.

I demanded a lot, but was fair: tight-loose. And in an organization of under 500 employees, I certainly did not want to become a remedial training center. It was sink or swim, but there were no expectations that were unreasonable. Admittedly, our standards were super high. That was what made the difference. Good versus Great.

These musings about the benefits of tight-loose are intended to deliver the message that what we should be searching for - is balance. Business like life, is often a search for balance. My term of tight-loose should not be confused with the term that has been used in management theory that relates to tight versus flexible management, arising from Douglas McGregor's[92] Theory X and Theory Y[93]. McGregor was a contemporary of Abraham Maslow and significantly contributed to the development of management and motivational theory. McGregor essentially argued that there are X managers who assume that their employees are lazy and unmotivated; and there are Y managers who assume that their employees are self-motivating and ambitious. McGregor observed that what the managers assume, they create by their assumption. What they expect, becomes their reality – by virtue of the management style that each manager type adopts, consistent with their core philosophy and assumption. This might be a quintessential example of the "self-fulfilling prophesy".

I always find it extremely interesting that there has been so much thinking on the psychology of the workplace and of management and much agreement among scholars and researchers – for many decades. I'm always interested as well, and have observed as a practitioner (not as an academic) - the skepticism that many of us who have managed large and small organizations hold, with respect to researchers and academicians. We talk about the proverbial ivory tower, about the pragmatic reality of the workplace, about the number of balls we juggle or the number of moving parts, and the vast array of random variables, and the frailty of formulaic solution, and the need for instant judgements on real-world events. And in talking about such things, we tend to go "binary" (all or nothing) and discount the theory, instead of embracing the principle and experimenting with it in our own environments. I started this book by writing that all businesses and business principles are basically the same. The search for balance and perspective, that I have talked about applies here. There is a wealth of knowledge available. The manager's role is to use it to create an environment of wisdom and insight.

ADAPTIVE MANAGEMENT[94]

"Intelligence is the ability to adapt to change"
– Stephen Hawking

I might add to Stephen Hawking's quote, that intelligence is also the ability to live and thrive in an environment of ambiguity.

Many years ago, whilst at Exxon, I had the opportunity to meet Professor of Sociology, Morris Massey. His famous theme of "What You Are Is Where You Were When" was at the time, one of the most respected commentaries and theories about values, generations, and Significant Emotional Events (SEE) – as they influence the workplace. One of his points was that we are influenced in a variety of ways from birth to about age 21. The early years to age seven are when we imprint and accept what we see and experience in particular from our parents, as the unchallenged truth. Then from age eight to about 13, we are influenced and experiment with ways of thinking about what we have seen. This is the period when we "model" behaviours. Lastly, between 14 and 20 we become socialized within our peer group and seek to develop our own unique and independent personality.

Massey's "What You Are Is Where You Were When" implies that if you are an employee today, you will behave in a way that is consistent with where you were when you were influenced the most. So, if your parents survived through the great depression (and its trauma) of 1928, you would likely view the request to work overtime hours (with overtime pay) as a reward. Whereas, if your formative years coincided with the self-absorbed and relaxed baby boomer generation, that same request to work overtime – would be viewed as a punishment. Rewards and punishments are relative, not absolute.

Each person in your employ is an individual with his or her own needs, sensitivities, and personalities. Their experiences have produced the lens through which they perceive the world. As their manager, you are an important part of their world; in fact – that is an awesome responsibility if you think about it. There is a myriad of instruments (diagnostic tests and exercises) that organizations and their HR and training folks use to help employees understand their own leadership, social, thinking and working styles. However, an effective and observant leader can pretty much identify the major personality traits and needs of their employees by simply talking and working with them. Some managers will say about themselves, that they are a person with a specific set of characteristics and a style that they call their own; and that they will be true to their style including their style of communication, regardless of with whom they are communicating and regardless of who they are managing. Anything short of that position, they would consider false, deceptive, and insincere. I understand their position but it is not a useful position. In my view, it is not an issue of integrity to practice adaptive management.

Adaptive and flexible behaviours and styles are an essential leadership quality. Psychologists have emphasized also *"that today's hyper-competitive, fast-paced, and rapidly changing global economy puts a premium on adaptable organizations and flexible leaders*[95]*"*.

As a parent of four children, my parenting philosophy has been "each, according to their own need"; that is to say that each of my children have specific needs, they digest information in different ways, are sensitive to different things, are offended easily or not, are motivated differently. Yes, I will act differently with each of them. My integrity and wholeness remain unchanged, my ethics are unchanged. My style will be flexible and adaptive. Same in management.

YOU ARE NOT AN IMPOSTER

Many have written on a psychological phenomenon known as the *imposter syndrome, or fraud syndrome*. It's usually a self-perception of inadequacy and a feeling that one doesn't deserve to have gotten to where they are in life. This is not all that terribly uncommon among high achievers who have very high personal standards and who often show signs of perfectionism. It is a deep secret often harbored by the most prominent and most senior managers. As I have advised CEOs and have at times been asked to be their coach, I was in a position to develop close, confidential, and trusting relationships with many. I was stunned to discover that so many have a nagging fear that somehow they will be “found out” as a fraud. The idea that they feel that they have been successful in “fooling” all the people all the time – is of course, irrational. High achievers do not often recognize how deep their skills and talents run because they have a sense of what they don’t know and what they would like to know – and it is a huge volume. It is said of that great author, John Steinbeck, that he wrote in his diary in 1938, “I am not a writer. I’ve been fooling myself and other people”. In 1939, he won the Pulitzer Prize for fiction.

There are advantages to a healthy modesty. It motivates one to continually learn. Overly high self-confidence may signify that you are not able to recognize your own ignorance. The bottom line is that if you think that you might be, or are an imposter, then you are not one. Real imposters don’t think that way.

CHAPTER 8 TAKE-AWAYS ORGANIZATIONAL EFFECTIVENESS	
1	Celebrate failure. I really mean it: take risks, learn, celebrate, get smart! Of course, by all means celebrate your successes also, but I don't think you needed me to tell you that.
2	Harness the collective intelligence of your organization.
3	Harness the astonishingly cheap and always-accessible technology-enabled intelligence about everything.
4	Actively avoid Abilene scenarios.
5	If you live or die together as a committed team, you'll likely live.
6	Relentlessly and deliberately manage down negativity in your workplace.
7	Keep your balance on the narrow bridge of life.
8	Always be candid, precise, and crystal clear.
9	Do not necessarily behave exactly the same way with everyone. They are motivated differently and they will digest communications differently.
10	If you are reading this book, you are not an imposter.

CHAPTER 9
BRANDING

"Your brand is what people say about you when you are not in the room"
– Jeff Bezos, Amazon

The Art and Science of Branding is an elusive subject area. Not many people would feel free and confident to talk about the challenges of designing a nuclear reactor facility – without having advanced degrees in engineering; but somehow, many of us are confident to express opinions about branding and design. I suspect that is so because engineering is driven by a very tight codified set of engineering principles and its universal language of communication is mathematics - whereas branding is not. Also, we would expect that every single bridge, roadway, and steel foundry will remain standing and will continue to function as designed. In brand development and design, we have somehow tolerated a large measure of inconsistency. We seem to accept that it is a "hit or miss" field, where some of the greatest brands have somehow been lucky in that they arose from a rare inspiration or flash of creative genius. Nothing could be farther from the truth.

People seek for years to develop their own unique brand. For many, this is not a deliberate endeavor. Others create and manage their "personal" brand in parallel to managing their careers and their future - instead of allowing themselves to be carried by the winds of fortune. Many people believe in managing reputational value and they develop and nurture their name and reputation, understanding that the only real value in life is to leave behind a good name that our families, our children can be proud of.

Organizations are the same. Some have a heightened awareness of reputational value and understand that they must "stand for something", and be true to what they stand for. They understand that their conduct and their style should authentically reflect what they stand for. These are some of the qualities that create a bond of understanding and appreciation between the creator of the brand and those who consume it. It is an emotional connection and done well, it can be very powerful.

BRAND STRUCTURES

One of the most iconic and powerful brands in America is Harley Davidson, or at least to me as a brand strategy guy. I admire the achievements of the Harley brand management folks. Their consolidated revenues for 2016 was six billion dollars (USD) and they own about 50% of the American market share[96] which is impressive given the huge competitive threats of the Japanese motorcycle market and their heavy discounting strategy - which Harley has thus far refused to match[97]. What is astonishing is the emotional attachment and resulting loyalty that Harley Davidson has achieved with its customers. Not many manufacturers have their customers tattoo the manufacturer's logo onto their skin. That level of brand equity allows for a premium to be charged. Some have called this a "brand tax" and it has allowed Harley to resist some of the competitive pressures coming from Japan and elsewhere. Harley could have been called the road warrior. Adventure and freedom (lifestyle attributes) are well represented and these concepts and the related emotion, transcend the motorcycle, allowing them to license their brand recognition. Their brand does not tie them into all of their products, though I imagine that it will be unlikely to see Harley-branded bible stands or diapers, but I could be wrong.

In Harley's case, their lifestyle brand is so strong and long-lived, that over time, like the Marlboro brand, they could not resist the temptation and the pressure of licensing their brand to others who profitably leverage that significant brand equity as long as the products were appropriate, more or less, to the brand associations and were of a quality that was consistent with the overall perception of the Harley commitment to quality. Indeed, it is profitable. Revenues on Harley brand licensing is well over 10% of their total revenues and there are few costs involved. There are dozens of examples of licencing royalties and revenues exceeding operating revenues. A perfect example is Disney where brand-generated royalties exceed revenues from its movies. Disney is essentially a merchandising company, selling products that in their words are "authentic to their story telling"[98]. Some critics have predicted "brand fatigue[99]" though the consumers do not seem to be complaining.

Leveraging brands happen in a variety of ways. The food and beverage industry lives off of this strategy. First they build respect and value for their brand, then they market other products that they develop or acquire under the known brand so that consumers will *trial* the product based on the trust they already had developed for the *master brand*.

Think Proctor and Gamble (P&G) as a master brand. Underneath that corporation are hundreds of sub-brands and distinct product (trade) names. The rationale behind sub-brands is differentiation. Why? Because differentiation conjures up in the mind of the consumer, an authority in "something". Of course, the corollary of that principle is that when a company ventures out into another category or a different (lower) quality level (as in a "value" line), then separating brands acts to protect them from being overly associated with each other and losing the brand equity that was built up. Having said that, sub-branding under a master brand is most effective when these sub-brands all deal with the same or similar category, most of the time, so that the consumer associates the master brand with the trust and confidence that the brand has earned in the consumer's heart and mind. That association of loyalty accrues to the new product appropriately positioned under the master brand. But there are many successful exceptions and examples. I recently purchased a Swiss Army winter jacket. I've always admired their pocket knives and own several types. The knives are indestructible. For every Swiss army knife that I've lost (and replaced), there is a personal adventure story that is associated with the loss. There are swiss Army knives with my initials on them at the bottom of the Epupa waterfalls in Namibia, in a ditch on the Khyber Pass, in a rice paddy in Banaue in the northern Philippines, in a creek flowing into Burnt Island Lake in Algonquin Park. I trust the company, I know their quality. I'm emotionally involved. I bought their coat.

As an aside, there is another reason why some companies choose to master-brand their products and others do not. For example, P&G has a vast array of diverse products and one will not see "P&G" anywhere on the front panel[100] of their product packaging. This approach is sometimes adopted when a company leaves open the possibility of managing a product life cycle up to some point of margin maximization or value attainment, and then "spins off" (sells) that product or product-line to a third party. The third-party buyer will value less, a product whose equity in the consumer marketplace is tied to the corporate name of the former owner who would and must take its name off the package when it sells that business. Thus, the brand equity that has been built and associated with the product's operating/market trade name is retained and the buyer retains its value and reputation in the market. So, that would make sense.

Nestle takes the opposite point of view. Its products are almost always branded with the corporate logo of the parent company, Nestle. As a result, consumers have been exposed to that name/logo/brand, and the equity that it has built is transferred to every product that they develop and take to market. The front-end investment in marketing new products is thus lessened due to the fact that the consumer may very well be willing to trial the new product, simply because it is a Nestle product, and there is a faith and trust that as a Nestle product, it will likely be well developed, of high quality, and generally trustworthy. Of course, it would likely be more difficult for Nestle to erase their name from a product, sell the product line, and expect to enjoy a premium on the sale due to the product's retained brand equity, which it had just diminished by the removal of any symbol reminding the end-user consumer about who had previously owned the product. This principle obviously does not apply across the board. Nestle for example, spun off its ophthalmic care company, Alcon, back in 2001. That company was acquired by Nestlé in 1977 but in 2001, this business was not considered part of its food and beverage core focus. But Alcon and for that matter companies like Purina (pet foods acquired by Nestle) were not branded as a member of the Nestle product family nor are they part of the core business.

SUB-BRANDS

When the company I managed (before I joined it) branded zones in the Loblaws stores, we branded the produce department: "FRESH from the FIELDS". The intent was obvious. It gave that zone an air of authority through differentiation. It also provided a landmark destination for customer navigation. The concept of "stores-in-store" was a deliberate strategy to position Loblaws as an expert in "fresh". Was it a true expert in "fresh"? Possibly not yet, but in their defence, and ours – a brand name can be aspirational. In other words, if the aspiration is sincere and meant to motivate the achievement of expertise, then it's a legitimate target.

When Costco, the Club Store phenomenon, grew in Canada and began to threaten Loblaws, with its innovative format and philosophy, the Loblaw Corporation's response was to create their mini version of a club store within their conventional store. It was about offering customers a choice. The zone featured larger, family-sized packaged products at lower retail ticket prices and signage that attacked Costco. The communications emphasized "no membership required". This was a brilliant response to a dangerous competitive threat. The Loblaw Corporation had correctly researched the one main criticism that Costco customers had: that they had to pay a membership fee, up front, essentially for the privilege of shopping the Costco store. Even so, the Loblaw counter-measure didn't really work in a sustainable way. Why? Because the fundamentals weren't there. (retail format, product assortment, no back room, economics, not really a warehouse store.)

Of course, many goals are not achieved, but that is another conversation for later. However, it's worth talking a little about branding and communications in-store. I love the retail model because we are all consumers, we have all shopped in food stores, and we can all relate to the obvious and not-so-obvious strategies and tactics that are designed to influence us to purchase. The previous examples of retailer Loblaws also demonstrates another valuable principle in communications that is directed to consumers. Every effort should be made to deliver to the customer - an idea or a suggestion – that can solve a problem and be valued.

A few years ago, I was invited to tour a prototype convenience store owned by an integrated oil and gas company. With about 3,000 g-stores (gas station retail units, like c-stores/convenience) the plan was to design and test the new prototype store before launching the new design in stages to replace their old retail formats. In the store, I was immediately faced with a long wall of refrigerated showcases within which contained a nicely planogrammed assortment of various beverages from water to carbonated soft drinks (CCDs) to juices, etc. The display case was about

6 feet high and above it, running along the entire length of about 30 feet of refrigerated glass-doored showcases - was a sign in bold red text: BEVERAGES. I reacted with a "what is *that*?". It's beverages, their CMO responded, *we are calling it what it is: clear, concise, bold. No confusion about what this offer is.* I sarcastically asked her if they ever considered putting a sign on the door, reading: DOOR; or a sign on the floor, saying: FLOOR. Of course, it's beverages; it's obvious. For heaven's sakes, the doors are glass, the section is large so they naturally achieve a "massing" effect. No customer is likely to confuse this offering with anything but beverages.

I thought this was a colossal waste of valuable communication "real estate". And when she asked me what I would suggest, and after I complained that I should not be giving my knowhow away for free, I said, that something perhaps along the lines of: ARE YOU THIRSTY?

SELL THE PROBLEM YOU SOLVE, NOT THE PRODUCT

What we try to do is to provide an idea or a suggestion. The customer responds to our question internally and will consider the idea. And the added value, essentially the contribution of that kind of communication – is that some customers will be triggered to think: *well, I wasn't thinking that way, but now that you mention it, perhaps I am a bit thirsty.* And then they will buy. This represents a psychological manipulation in a sense, but one that is decidedly legitimate and ethical. An idea is delivered, an independent choice is made, and the result will be a *lift* in beverage sales. Thirst is quenched, margins are generated; all good: win-win. The store is the package. Make it work that way.

The image of the "SNACK & POP factory" zone is an example of signage at Tesco, the UK's largest supermarket chain. The adjacency and zone-integration between soft drinks and snacks reflect an understanding of the category and applies that understanding to create a festive solution center in the store. The result: sales in both categories rose.

CONSUMERS, AND THEIR NOSES

Years ago, gas station customers got the option to pay at the pump. This is a good thing but it has its drawbacks for the gas retailer. The profit margin they enjoy when we fill up our gas tank is puny compared to the margins on chocolate bars, snacks, cigarettes, and lottery tickets. If we pay at the pump and don't enter the store, this is a problem for them. How do we induce consumers to go inside? This is typically attempted by making suggestions and delivering ideas at the pump., though they still don't really do a great job of that today.

So, technology, like pay-at-pump can be a double-edged sword for retailers. And even when they do enter the store, some things have changed. Coffee used to be brewed in open carafes and the aroma of coffee pervadied the retail space and invoked our sense of smell, inducing an impulse for coffee. The problem was that continuously applying heat to coffee oxidizes the flavor compounds in the coffee and turns it bitter, so the shelf-life in store was short, creating wastage and loss of margin.

Closed, hermetically sealed "airpots" are now being used (and coffee pod machines). They retain flavor and freshness a lot longer but there is no escape of aroma. I'm a coffee drinker. I hardly notice the coffee offering anymore when inside a G-store.

I've often wondered why someone hasn't experimented with an atomizer[101] to disseminate the aroma of coffee in convenience stores. Ethically, I would honestly explain the "manipulation" to my customers as a coffee reminder; the transparency should be appreciated and the manipulation forgiven, in my view.

Scent marketing is not that common in North America. It is easier to promote sales, especially in the food categories, by stimulating our sense of smell.

This has been going on since we barbequed meat at the entrance of our caves. The scent of freshly-baked bread, vanilla, or coffee - stimulates the sense of smell which is the most powerful of all senses. I still remember the scent of my father's after-shave lotion 60 years later. Studies demonstrate that 75% of emotions are triggered by smell and are associated with a sense of well-being and pleasure.[102]

In Europe, I have experience the scent of coconut oil diffused into beach wear retail zones, and talcum powder scent in baby and toy stores. There are companies[103] that provide this technology but it is still not commonly seen (or smelled). People in this industry claim that scent marketing[104] is growing at an annual rate of 15% with revenue at about $300 million worldwide.[105] However, when most companies talk about scent marketing, they are referring to the practice of strategically merchandising their products so that the scent will be recognized. They are not usually referring to technology that diffuses scents into the air. There is not much in the way of literature on this subject but my intuition tells me that if retailers were transparent in advising customers about the practice, customers would accept the technology[106]. Given the potential rewards, it's worth doing the research.

EPITOME OF BRAND POWER

"When you're a carpenter making a beautiful chest of drawers, you're not going to use a piece of plywood on the back, even though it faces the wall and nobody will ever see it. You'll know it's there, so you're going to use a beautiful piece of wood on the back. For you to sleep well at night, the aesthetic, the quality, has to be carried all the way through" – Steve Jobs

---

Brand Power is an overused term and an underused strategy. Yet it ought to be top of mind for all business owners and operators. The idea is to employ the meaning and attributes of the brand as a kind of filter through which management should be testing every idea and strategy. For this to work effectively, the meaning of the brand in the lives of your customers must be clearly understood. Take Harley Davidson for example (again). Name me more brands that are tattooed indelibly on the skin of customers[107]. This is rare and amazing and powerful. Brand is power.

Name me other brands that are printed on stickers and affixed conspicuously on vehicles. What is it about Harley that captures the imagination of its consumers? Harley is not really about motorcycles. Harley is about dreams and freedom. And freedom is emotional. At the heart of all great brands lay emotion - an emotional connection between the creator of the brand and the consumers of that brand.

Where Harley is about freedom, Maserati is about speed, and Volvo is about safety (though in recent years, they have receded from that ownership somewhat). These are all attributes that some identifiable segment of the market values in some way and that value has a strong emotional connection.

There are 1.2 million members of the Harley Davidson Motorcycle Club/Owners Club. This is the world's largest company/factory sponsored club. The Brand recognition is pervasive. I have visited countries where I have not seen one Harley, yet people in the smallest village recognize the name and understand the brand. By contrast, Rotary International[108], also has about 1.2 million members. That organization of dedicated volunteers has focused on one main goal; they raised one billion dollars and essentially eradicated Polio from the face of the Earth. How many people know of this enormous and stunning achievement?

Brand power is not achieved by accident nor by good works. It is a deliberate strategy executed with surgical precision and managed continuously.

THE FRAILTY OF BRANDS

Nothing lasts forever. Like all corporate assets, brands have to managed, and their value must be assessed, impaired and written off or refreshed when indicated.

Brands are a fragile resource as they really do not belong to their creators, the companies that developed them in the first place. Who then do they belong to? My answer is: they belong to the consumers of the brand, the customers, the stakeholders, suppliers, employees, the press, the public, the creditors – for these are the groups that have interpreted the meaning and the value of the brands and who make purchasing and investing and employment decisions based on their interpretation of the brand. It is not relevant if the brand's creators (the companies) intended those interpretations or not. If a brand is a promise that elicits an expectation in the minds and hearts of its stakeholders, then customers expect a promise of value, consistency, and respect; employees expect a culture; suppliers expect a valued relationship, and even the competition expect a benchmark or standard.

But brands are frail and vulnerable to their weakest links, and there are many links.

UNITED AIRLINES

In April 2017, the news focused on United, the world's third-largest airline. They have 90,000 employees, each one a link, an ambassador for their brand. Their slogans include "fly the friendly skies", "we earn trust by doing things the right way", "warm and welcoming is who we are", "we respect every voice…make decisions with facts and empathy". In their website, they say "the United brand vision is more than just words on paper". Then they had the airport police violently drag a paid customer out of his seat and off the plane. The airline had overbooked, they needed the seat for their own employee, and the legal fine print that no one reads says they can refuse service at any time. The seated customer resisted. He was heard saying "I (just) want to go home". Instead, he was dragged, bleeding off the plane. The month before at a New York gala, United's CEO had been awarded the coveted PRWeek's "Communicator of the Year Award". This award-winning communicator initially said of the incident that the customer was belligerent and uncooperative and used euphemistic corporate-speak terms like "re-accommodate" to describe violently dragging the 69-year-old passenger from his seat and off the plane. After a furious social media storm and a loss of United's share value (market cap) of 1.3 billion dollars in 24 hours, the CEO, then more contrite, promised not to again use police to enforce a business decision. Living the brand is easy to say, really hard to do.

There are many competing schools of thoughts about brands, about their fragility, and their longevity, about the factors that lead to success and power, and those that lead to decline. There is a bit of truth in most viewpoints. The secret: You and every single person in your organization would have to be sincerely passionate – in the extreme - about managing the brand. In my world, it's a condition of employment.

VERTICAL AND HORIZONTAL BRANDS

There is debate about the value of companies "sticking to their knitting", in other words, the value of focusing on the core business and becoming and maintaining a lead authority and having their brand become the indisputable symbol of that authority. This is *the vertical* philosophy. In other words: Go Deep. It's tough to be great at many things. Naturally, some critics fear this approach because the over-reliance on one market or one (great) product can carry a huge risk given the crazy velocity of the rate of change.

Think digital vs. 35 mm film – and Kodak[109]*. Think online media vs. DVDs – and Blockbuster*[110]*. Think smart phone design vs. dumb phones – and Nokia*[111]*. Think health and wellness trends – and Krispy Kreme*[112]

The equity of these and other brands have declined and in many cases have vanished, mostly because they did not or could not re-invent and introduce products or services that people wanted. It had little to do with brand management methodologies and creativity. One could argue that these companies did not adopt appropriate missions. Had Kodak believed that their mission was to enable memories; had Blockbuster committed to deliver entertainment and escapism, had Krispy Kreme's goal was to offer occasional, well-deserved indulgence – then perhaps these organizations could have been more creative about evolving with the times.

Marketers continue to assert that the brand must forge an emotional connection with customers. I have been saying this here in this book. However, these emotional connections are increasingly fragile as customer brand loyalty generally becomes weaker. Today, powerful brands know that they must continually earn loyalty by launching products and services that delight customers. That in itself demonstrates the death of customer loyalty, with some obvious exceptions. Other thinkers are more extreme in their views and believe that times have changed irreversibly and that essentially *Brands have had their run and are now dead*[113]. Given the general wisdom that the truth most often lies somewhere in the middle, I will say that product proliferation, massive product-line extensions, product cannibalism, marketing greed, increased consumer intelligence through instant access to web-based knowledge and social media / blog inputs (that analyze and scrutinize products and services), competing look-alike products, unvetted premature rushes to capture markets, as well as overall consumer cynicism and ironically, the related increase in the demands and expectations of consumers – all of these lead to a more challenging time with respect to great brand creation and growth.

Others claim that *consumers have become far more willing to experiment with products because the amount of information out there makes taking a chance far less risky*[114].

Like always, there is an ongoing shakeout with only the very best surviving and prospering. That is, net-net, a good thing.

Horizontal Brands spread risk and apply brand attributes horizontally over products that usually have commonly shared attributes. Witness: *Nike.* They began as a company marketing runners only, a vertical running brand, and they applied their brand authority to all sports and even to walkers - with the *Just Do It* call to action that inspires consumers horizontally across all activities. The strength of their brand grew because their products were of high quality. That is the bottom line that all great brands should understand and that is the risk that lay at the foundation of the brand – that it all started with a promise for the consumer and that promise generated an expectation, and heaven help the company if there is any daylight between the promise and the expectation.

As a side note, whenever I hear the Nike name, an old marketing joke comes to mind. It's probably time for a break anyway.

The marketing VP of Nike and the marketing VP of Adidas, though competitors, also happened to be friends. And they took an African safari adventure together. One morning, they awoke early to have breakfast around the camp fire before heading out on safari. Both still in their pyjamas, they heard a lion fiercely roar from behind a nearby bush. Horrified, the Adidas salesperson jumped up and started running barefoot in the opposite direction. The Nike salesperson started lacing up his Nike's. The Adidas executive shouted back to his friend: "come on now, do you really think you will be able to outrun a lion with your Nike running shoes?" The Nike VP shouted back: "The way I figure it, the only thing I have to outrun, is you!"

Jokes aside, Nike in the last 15 years shot past Adidas to dominate the US market. Their arch-rivalry (excuse the pun) has led both companies to strive for super innovation in their products and in their marketing. The consumer benefited.

EXPLOSION OF SOCIAL MEDIA

There is a ton of information available about social media platforms and their role in business. In fact, much of social media over the years has been effective in blurring the lines between *social* and *business*. What people talk about is what they talk about. The rise of social media has been astounding and revolutionary for business, lowering the cost bar to advertising and opening up and disseminating the impressions that ordinary people/consumers have about the products and services (and the companies that provide these) with which they are having experiences. It is awesome and scary and it's not going away. What is going away are the myriad of organizations in that space, that are being replaced with others at a rapid rate.

This book will not delve into social media other than to comment on these tools that deliver market and brand growth capability quickly, or diminish it, even more quickly.

Facebook[115] (FB) is currently the leading social network company with about two billion monthly active users (MAUs). 66% of those users use FB daily. Consider the potential influence people exert on others in this network. Female FB users enjoy an average of 166 friends and male FB users enjoy an average of 145 friends, and the average user spends approximately 20 minutes each day communicating on this network[116]. No organization that needs to get their message across can ignore this opportunity. Twenty years ago, if I had a fantastic dinner at a new restaurant, I may have told three friends about it and they probably would not have re-told this to anyone. Communications have become tribal.

The purchasing power of the 15 to 34 age range target segment (Millennials, who represent about 25% of the US population) is estimated to be $200 billion in 2017 and $10 trillion over their lifetime of spending[117]. Millennials do not rely on traditional advertising; many rely on blogs before they consider a purchase. They value authenticity, which supports the attention they give to other people's impressions[118], and by "other", this suggests people who are perceived to be objective and independent of the "seller". Of this significant segment, 91% of millennials use Facebook. Consider this for a moment. Since Facebook first introduced the "like, dislike" feature, 1.13 trillion[119] "likes" have been pressed; these are endorsements by peers. In addition, over 100 million hours of video[120] is being watched on FB every day.

Twitter[121], essentially a micro-blog limiting messages to 140[122] characters grew rapidly to 4,000 employees and $2 billion in 5 years. At the end of 2016, Twitter had about 320 million monthly active users[123] (MAUs). Of the

320 MAUs, about 43% use their cell phones[124] to tweet. Twitter basically asks the questions: what are you thinking? and what impresses you? Consider 43% of 320 million active users tweeting on-the-go, their impressions of your products, your services, your attention to detail and to the needs of the consumer – all to their friends, only to be (possibly) re-tweeted. To ignore these potentials would be insane. Further, to ignore the technologies that identify who on these social platforms are the key influencers in the categories of the products and services that your business lives for would be equally insane.

To be expected, concepts remain and are refined, but the players shift. Twitter has by most accounts lost ground in the news category - to Facebook. The millennial sector now tend to use Snapchat[125] with 71% of users surveyed saying they use it for chat, messaging, and imaging services[126] (5% exclusively use it for events and media content on a daily basis). Snapchat seems to have taken advantage of this popularity with their recent IPO in March 2017, which raised $3.4 billion and then rose 44% on IPO day[127]. The interesting thing here is that Snapchat lost about $515 million in 2016 on sales of about $400 million. Obviously, this is an indication on how bullish millennials (and investors who follow them) are about the continued growth of social platforms.

WhatsApp[128] has become a fabulously successful app and was acquired by Facebook in 2014[129]. It has been successful in China, India, and other countries, supplanting Twitter and other platforms. It is especially useful in geographies where cellphones are used to access web-based services cheaply, as in many developing countries that lack traditional web infrastructure. Instagram[130], also acquired by Facebook, has become a popular app for images.

Twitter has suffered from the above growth of apps, many of which were acquired by Facebook's hungry acquisition plan. That's not the important thing here. The obvious takeaway for the reluctant (traditional) business-person is that these social networks represent a very different way of selling, promoting, sharing information, and influencing markets. If you are not already proficient with these technologies, you must become proficient to survive and prosper.

CHAPTER 9 TAKE-AWAYS BRANDING	
1	Brand success is not hit or miss. It doesn't happen by accident.
2	Harley motorcycle customers tattoo the manufacturer's logo into their skin. That's the power of the emotional connection a brand can enjoy with its consumers. What would you have to do to have your customers do that?
3	Brand trust allows you to extend business lines and not start all over building loyalty.
4	Sub-brands are designed to create differentiation and authority while still being associated with your master brand – which acts as an endorser.
5	Hang out in retail stores and observe carefully how shoppers interact with products, packaging, and communications. Everything you see there is strategic.
6	Sell the problem you solve, not the product.
7	To sell, utilize all the human senses you can including smell.
8	You must be able to recognize the emotional meaning of a brand, not its literal meaning.
9	Correct brand management is maintaining at zero, the difference between the brand promise and the brand expectation.
10	Expect a shake-out and be the fittest (the most flexible) to survive.

CHAPTER 9 TAKE-AWAYS BRANDING	
11	If you are not now fully leveraging the power and economy of social media, you have probably already failed, even if you don't know it yet.

CHAPTER 10

BRANDING PLACES

PLACE BRANDING: IT'S ESSENTIALLY THE SAME AS ANY OTHER KIND OF BRANDING

Today, every country, every region and every city has to compete with every other country, region and city on the planet: for customers, for visitors, for business, for talented people, for investment, for attention, for respect. None of this happens by accident[131].

Cities, towns, regions, states, etc – can all have distinctive brands that evoke emotion and a recognition of value. Park City, Utah, USA - the home of the Sundance Film Festival boasts a population of 7,600 people and their film festival attracts over 40,000 visitors every year, injecting $80 million annually into the Utah economy. You don't need to be big to be a powerful world-renown and recognized brand. Some countries punch above their own weight in the brand recognition department; think Nepal: 540,000 visitors in 2015 generating 498 million dollars in revenue for this small country with a per capita GDP of $2400.

Singapore is small island state with no natural resources. How did it become so powerful? How did Singapore get to be famous? It only has about five million people. And what is it best known for? Probably for being a very safe environment with near ZERO crime! Causal or not, it is a world conference, financial and trade center. Tiny at 130 square kilometres, it illustrates what is possible when an organization or a place enjoys a razor-sharp focus on a success strategy.

Whether it's a world-class film festival, the experience of majestically high places, or an ultra-safe city - what binds these great branded places together is something distinctive that delivers value in the hearts and minds of their consumers. It need not be exciting nor exotic to be successful but does need to be unique in some way. A better bran muffin is all that was required to transform an otherwise non-descript diner on Toronto's College Street, The Mars, into a destination. Customers line up in front of this restaurant to purchase their bran muffins and have done so for years. What made their muffins so unique? It doesn't really matter. Perhaps they are noticeably bigger, have more real butter and more bran – but they are better by far. And having achieved the distinction of being a destination, that means that consumers were prepared to drive past the competition, to get there.

In the context of Places, the principles are essentially the same. The trick is to maintain continuity from core principles to actions to impact and to approach a "Place" as a package. It may not be so important to judge the value of a Place, based on the attributes valued by the local people of that place. On one occasion, whilst advising on Place branding for one of the Philippine provinces, the Governor of that province showed me a five-meter-high waterfall. He was so proud of his waterfall and expected me to share his enthusiasm and his confidence that people would actually travel to experience this (small) waterfall. I was not impressed and told him so. To be sure, it was pretty, but I diplomatically explained that the world had many such places and for people to spend the time, money, and effort to travel - this was not a destination that one would plan to reach. He was crestfallen. But nearby, there was an old Mangyan settlement. These were an ancient, indigenous people who settled the area and lived in a few traditional villages in the mountains.

Now this was interesting. What the locals see and take for granted – is what the world is losing every day and yearns to experience, or at least a large enough segment of the tourism market does.

Again, an understanding of the market becomes paramount. And one does not often find insight and objectivity in the client environment but beyond, in the wider consumer environment. Many clients, big and small will eventually become victim to their own propaganda. One of the greatest values of the independent consultant is actually that: *independence a*nd of course objectivity, honesty, and a passion for research, and for connecting the dots.

Here's another example from another province in the far north of the Philippines where rice paddies can be seen against the backdrop of beautiful mountains. The wide, long Cagayan River, also known as the Rio Grande de Cagayan, meanders through the fields where rural families can be seen planting, caring for, and harvesting rice through its two growing seasons. I paid a courtesy call[132] to the mayor of a local, small municipality (really a village). She was essentially a manager of a small place characterized by rice farming, water buffalo (Carabao), and sari-sari stores (small family-owned general stores). I asked her what – in her view - was special or unique about the place that she oversees. She replied: rice and an free-flowing alkaline water spring that was excellent as a health tonic, and quite valued locally. Within minutes, I was describing the value that others might see in her area's resources that she may be taking for granted. There is, I told her, some value in exploring if young people from western Europe and North America might be interested in the experience, possibly perceived as an exotic and memorable experience – in becoming guests of rural rice farming families, and working in the rice paddies for a week experiencing the life and work of these people and appreciating the hard work and the closeness to the earth that these people live all their lives. This kind of experiential tourism requires little capital; just organization and management. These qualities become important when consulting in developing world countries. It's far too easy to recommend strategies that are

complex and costly to implement. These are useless because they are not actionable or realistic. When I speculated that an experiential tourist might pay $200 for a week of working in the rice paddies, plowing with a water buffalo, and bonding with these lovely, simple people – she was flabbergasted. $200 USD translates (at time of writing) to 10,000 Philippine Pesos a week which is almost a half year's earnings for a typical small rice farming family.

As for the natural alkaline water source, this is more involved, but it was obvious that it was a resource valued locally. People would not necessarily drive to this off-the-beaten-path place for a drink of water and certainly would not come, absent of an awareness campaign. Capital intensive facilities such as spas and therapy centers are clearly beyond the grasp of poor communities. However, to begin a conversation with a bottler and to consider the market for a naturally alkaline, possibly flavoured beverage that could be marketed to consumers through retailers in nearby urban centers of the Philippines could be a viable and profitable concept. A unique beverage could carve out an interesting niche in the flavored beverage and or nutraceutical beverage marketplace. So, the technique is to ask the right probing questions, look for some level of uniqueness that consumers might value and connect the dots. A small place does have a chance to punch above their own weight and establish a market for its goods and services.

BRAND PROMISES & EXPECTATIONS

$$\sum (P - E) \geq 0$$

P= brand promise; E= brand expectation

A few years ago, I made a presentation on the future of retail at the Food Marketing Institute (FMI) at the McCormick Center in Chicago. Thousands of manufacturers and retailers attended, represented about $800 billion of sales revenues. I projected an image of a Costco gas station with more than a dozen cars waiting to fill-up, and I asked the audience if anyone could tell me what was unusual about the picture. What was unusual was that something usual was missing. There was no posted price for the gasoline! Imagine, that in a market where gas is a commodity with no or little perceived differentiation between Shell, Exxon, Chevron, Texaco, etc (except perhaps for some service attributes), and where drivers are apt to drive across town to save a few pennies on a gallon; here at Costco, they wait in line to fill up without knowing in advance what they would be asked to pay. Why? Because implicit in Costco's brand is the belief that Costco delivers best value, every time. That is Brand Power; and it's worth a lot.

Again, it's worth stressing that from the perspective of the creator of the brand - the brand is essentially a promise. And that promise triggers in the hearts and minds of the consumers of the brand, an expectation. If successful, these are one in the same. Managing the brand therefore means managing the difference between the promise and the expectation- down to zero.

CHAPTER 10 TAKE-AWAYS BRANDING PLACING	
1	There is no fundamental difference between branding a place and branding a product or a service.
2	Think of a place as a package.
3	A place can punch above its own weight. Think: Nepal.
4	A place does not need to build physical things like sports stadiums or skyscrapers to be famous. It needs to identify and offer something consumers will value. Think safety; think Singapore.
5	It's tough to be objective about your own place (country, province, region, city, or village). Get an outside-in perspective.
6	$$\sum (P - E) \geq 0$$ A positive sum would indicate you have delighted the consumer beyond their expectation.

CHAPTER 11
BRAND DEVELOPMENT MECHANICS

Brand personalities? Yes, they have personalities. It's like the ancient tradition of naming a baby and then raising that child to be true to their name.

The table below is not one of my inventions; it is a commonly used tool to help organizations (and places) come to an understanding about what their personality is or should be, and to begin to go about in a deliberate way to develop the strategy that delivers that personality to itself and to its audiences.

The five-core personality attributes are: Sincerity, Excitement, Competence, Sophistication, and Ruggedness. These personality dimensions pretty much cover the personality gamut (It's good to keep things simple). The thing to remember when trying this tool is that no one attribute is objectively more superior than another. The idea is NOT to score high marks in every attribute; nor would you if you understood this table. For example, consider Sophistication and Ruggedness. You could not have a high score in both unless you were designing a schizophrenic organization. Developing the organization's personality must be deliberate and consistent. And like all effective tools, they can be used to continuously test how serious you are in the commitment to be consistent and relevant to your stakeholders.

PERSONALITY MATTERS

BRAND PERSONALITY MATRIX	
Brand Category	Category Attributes
SINCERITY	agreeable, honest, wholesome, accepting, ethical, caring, ageless, cheerful (E.G.: THE CHURCH, NGOS, GOVERNMENTS)
EXCITEMENT	Extroverted, daring, spirited, imaginative, sociable, energy, activity, independent, innovative (E.G.: APPLE, SILICON VALLEY)

BRAND PERSONALITY MATRIX	
Brand Category	Category Attributes
COMPETENCE	Conscientious, responsible, dependable, intelligent, successful, technical, confident (E.G.: BANKS, INSURANCE COMPANIES, PHARMA)
SOPHISTICATION	Good looking, upper-class, charming, smooth (E.G.: FASHION, COSMETICS)
RUGGEDNESS	No nonsense, athletic, tough, (American) ideal of strength (E.G.: MARLBORO, LEVI, JEEP)

The use of methodologies in creative work is often what's missing in organizations and their creative agencies. A creative, inventive mindset with a disciplined process and methodology really do go well together and are complimentary.

One of the challenges in brand development exercises is that the brand development team is often exclusively a creative team, including members of a creative agency. And the client team, either internal to the client organization, or their strategy consultants (or both) – are staffed by technical, business, and in-house marketing professionals who can be quite linear in their thinking and in their approach. Accordingly, one finds different mental outlooks handing off to one another and there are often gaps in understanding and in interpretation. The brand development will therefore sometimes leave the strategy guys that were supposed to have informed the brand development phase in the first place – scratching their heads and wondering how the brand "look and feel" evolved from any part of their original strategy work. What sometimes results from this gap of understanding and synergy - is that the client organization adopts 50% of the recommendation and is left with a 100% mess. You cannot jump a canyon in two short hops.

I've written elsewhere about the *black hole of the interface.* This is an example and a reasonable argument for a multi-disciplined team, working on the whole of the lifecycle of brand development from vision, mission, strategic objectives, and roadmap – through to the brand personality, the brand messaging, and its graphical representation. I know that this is easier suggested than done and probably a costlier process; but how is it that we so often find the money and the time to do things over and over and over again, instead of spending a little more up front to get it done right once, the very first time?

Having been a CEO of a large creative agency as well as having been part of the management team of a Fortune 50 global corporation, I found that it's possible to bridge that gap and deliver to both inside and outside clients, the methodological rigor and the high-creative mindset. They deserve both and they need both to win.

The table below is an example of one template (and there are many) that we used to explain the process employed in the formulation of a brand strategy.

BRAND STRATEGY FORMULATION PROCESS			
Process	**Strategic Assessment** *Consumer centered marketing and communication objectives and strategy*	**Brand Frame** *Brand architecture and systems, strategy framework*	**Brand Identity & Positioning** *Branding strategy applied to all customer channels and experiences*
Inputs	• Internal scan • External scan • Global best practices • S.W.O.T. • Force field analysis • Ideation	• Visual brand audit • Visual language of target consumers/segments • Visual language of ideal brand positioning • Ideation	• Synthesis of markets & brand insights • Communications hierarchy • Niche branding & communications
Deliverables	• Mission congruencies • Consumer centered/Segmented ways-to-market • Brand philosophy/strategy across total enterprise	• Gap analysis and evaluation for all brands and applications through the entire enterprise offering	• Brand standards and Guidelines • Customer acquisition and retention strategies • Branding applications • Categories (e.g. for retail: stores, zones, signage, packaging)
			© Ira Teich

BRANDS CAN BE ***TOO*** SMART

Many brands are over-intellectualized and therefore not well understood. Brands are not logos and logos are not brands. The Brand can be explained as the connection that the consumer has (the consumer of the brand) with the organization/product that created the brand. In a sense, it is designed and managed because the organization (or place) wants to be understood in a certain way by its stakeholders. And the way that it wishes to be understood reflects the aspirations of the entity and its desired and unique position in its marketplace and in the lives of its stakeholders.

So, there is a lot of time, energy, and money spent on brand-related things, and on the way the image, personality and energy of the organization is delivered to its multiple audiences. This includes logos, bylines, slogans, and other visual symbols and words. Often its overdone with many brands over-intellectualizing their brand symbols and names.

Here are a few examples: The Adidas[133] logo features a slope ascending to the right to suggest that with Adidas products, one can climb mountains, whether the real geological type or indeed, the mountains and challenges in one's life.

In CISCO's logo, their place of origin, San Francisco, was a source of nostalgia and pride, so the graphic displays the shape of San Francisco's Golden Gate Bridge.

These two examples are actually conservative, and not as outlandish as many. But the point is that design intentions of brand names are often an exercise in self-indulgence and are lost on the consumer. It is understandable but should be avoided. Think about it. Marketing management confers with the design firms for hours and many concepts are discussed and developed. Renderings are pored over, presentations are given about the message behind the logo, the symbolism, the philosophy, the deliberate choice of colors, balance, scale, and typography. Countless hours of discussion follow. Meanwhile, professional fees add up. In the end, after weeks and months of discussion and work, a symbol including its intended nuance is accepted by senior management.

But the consumer wasn't in the board room. The consumer wasn't part of all the explanations, discussions, and nuances. Customers didn't spend hours poring over symbols trying to dissect their inner meaning. They never will. Perhaps the Target organization chose Target's target to be visually memorable, and very uncomplicated and simple. Clearly the amber Amazon "smile" was originally meant to suggest the unfolding vision that amazon intends to sell everything from "a" to "z". Is it that widely understood? Perhaps the simply power-red font for Exxon-Mobil and the implied supremacy regarding the 1998 Mobil merger was intended in the board room conversations. To the consumer, it likely doesn't really matter all that much.

NAMES ARE **NOT** ALL THAT IMPORTANT

The same logic applies to the corporate names themselves. Corporate names and identities are really not that important. Many are quite imaginative, clever, and even fun. Some are more instantly memorable than others. And many famous brands/names are simply simple. At the risk of being *branded* a cynic, I would suggest that many of the heavily engineered names were an unnecessary effort and expense. Miami Heat is a great name but so is The Miami scorpions, cobras, cheetahs, or sharks – if they are champions. Of course, I chose fast organisms; it's obvious that you wouldn't name a basketball team, the Miami Slow-Pokes. Harley Davidson is a great name and Harley Davidson is simply the name of two families. Wrigley's, McDonald's, Abercrombie & Fitch, Bose, Cadbury, Chrysler, Dell, Dow – are all family names. Yet when reading these names, the consumer doesn't see family names. Instead, they associate these names with the organization's reputation and more important: with the experiences that they have had with these businesses.

The important thing about a corporate name is that it should not mean anything offensive, including in a foreign language. There are numerous examples of this happening, and some are humorous. Ghana's "pee cola", means "very good" in their local language. Nokia's new smartphone translates in Spanish slang to "prostitute", not a great thing. Peugeot translates in China to Biao zhi, which unfortunately also means "prostitute." The Detergent

"Barf" which is produced in Iran, means "snow" in Farsi. And in Norway, AASS FATOL is draft beer!

Ok, enough levity – back to conventional naming and their associations. These associations grow and are reinforced with the related iconic designs and symbols over time, and can become very powerful. To my knowledge, the only occurrence ever of a public company's Annual Report to Shareholders that was published and distributed without the name of the company on its cover, was this:

The Annual Report is a formal document distributed to shareholders by law. It is truly amazing and courageous that Coca Cola published their 1994 Annual Report with (only) their iconic bottle in shadows. The caption was: "Quick. Name a soft drink". Powerful and Brilliant!

There are a number of brands and their symbols that have attained iconic stature and are widely recognized. But widely recognized does not always mean widely understood. How much do we really understand about Tide, or UNICEF or XEROX? Do we appreciate them, value them? Some are so known that they are used in a generic context; for example, to "Xerox" a document is to "copy" it. When people ask for a Kleenex, what they are mostly asking for is a "tissue". We all know this. But often, this level of recognition and awareness does not always translate into sales or brand loyalty, without the consumer knowing what the brand stands for (and valuing that) despite the high recognition value of the brand's symbols.

JEEP WRANGLER: WHY SO LOVED?

Brands that enjoy both recognition and understanding - occupy a kind of comprehension space that is more visceral than analytic and more emotional than rational. Consider Jeep. Consumer reports state that "the very essence of rugged, go-anywhere vehicles, Jeeps have a long history of customer loyalty despite lagging in reliability, fuel economy, comfort, and interior fit and finish. Nowhere has this been truer than with the rough-rider Wrangler. An archaic workhorse loved by its owners[134] [135]"

This is an easy example and one that is intuitive to most people. This iconic vehicle has been romanticized since WW2, before the first civilian version rolled out in 1945. It also hasn't visually changed all that much since then. For off-roaders it may be effective, but for most of the rest of us, I would categorize it as an outdoorsy fashion statement. For me, a notable feature of this vehicle and its image and personality is my sense that when one sees a Jeep Wrangler, one would not necessarily assume that the owner is either poor or miserly. When one sees a similarly priced Ford Escape, one would more likely conclude that the Ford owner would prefer a Range Rover or Toyota 4Runner – if they had the budget. Not so much with the

Wrangler owner. That Jeep brand somehow transcends the socio-economic associations that are so often present when relating vehicle price and the socio-economic profile of the ownership.

The above two wranglers are separated by 70 years.

There are other examples of these transcendent vehicles. Smart cars, VW beetles, Volvo station wagons are a few of these kinds of products that seem to appeal to a somewhat eccentric market that values certain specific attribute advantages such as city life, nostalgia, and safety. Thus, these products have managed to carve out market niches that tend to transcend traditional price-image considerations.

Some of these ideas are applicable to package design which I deal with elsewhere in this book. There is also a connection between brand, company personality, and ethics and honesty. If the brand makes a promise, as discussed earlier, then it stands to reason that most people do not believe promises delivered by dishonest people or dishonest organizations.

HONESTY MAKES SENSE

"Honesty is the best policy when there is money in it"
– Mark Twain

"Honesty quickly prevent a mistake from turning into a failure"
– James Altucher

"Be yourself; everyone else is already taken."
— Oscar Wilde

Morality and ethics aside, honesty is good business. Honesty is one of the basic, common ingredients for leadership. Leadership behaviour includes a reluctance to promise almost anything, but once promised, there is a passion and commitment to keep every promise. If a company agrees to pay its suppliers 30 days after the receipt of goods or services, then 31 days is a violation of a promise, a tarnishing of the company's brand. That would not be a smart way to manage the time value of money. There is no good shortcut when it comes to honesty. Even after a lifetime in business, I believe that in the interests of the longer-term success of a business, honesty pays.

In the first week after being parachuted in - to turnaround a consumer marketing consultancy and design firm, I terminated a $30,000 contract with an ethics consulting firm that my predecessor had engaged to produce an ethics policy document for the company. Instead of having a third party develop a complicated ethics policy binder to collect dust on the shelf, I gathered my teams together and announced our new zero-cost ethics policy.

It consisted of two sentences: "if what you intend to do will appear on the front page of tomorrow's newspaper in full detail, and you would be proud of that, then do it. If you would be ashamed or embarrassed, don't do it".

Honesty in leadership also suggests that the management will be open to the possibility of being wrong and therefore open to new ideas, flexible, and adaptable. Honesty is not intimidated by the truth and that attitude in senior management influences all management and employees and creates organizational culture. That culture benefits the company internally, and engenders trust, loyalty, and respect with all of the company's stakeholders. Honesty-induced trust benefits the company in obvious ways, as in enabling effective conflict resolution; and in subtle ways as well. For example, there may be a time in the life cycle of any organization, when to survive, it will need to be believed, or will need the patience of stakeholders. Lack of trust will boomerang in negative ways for that organization. In some of my work in developing countries, where corruption is pervasive in both politics and business, my message to clients (including governments) is that corruption and other forms of dishonesty does not make good business sense. There will be a reluctance, for example, on the part of large potential global partners to engage with an entity whom they cannot trust. Often, successful partnerships and other forms of alliances require a large degree of *inter-dependence*. I define that term, *inter-dependence,* as a relationship which is so close and intertwined, that the cost of disengaging can become prohibitive. All the more reason to be cautious prior to entering into that kind of fusion.

In 1990, the Harvard Business Review published an article[136] arguing that there is no objective evidence that honesty in business pays off. They claimed that "Power can be an effective substitute for trust"[137]. They make valid points, however many experienced business people, including me, have observed the phenomenon of external and internal sabotage (often anonymously) – including sabotage that was motivated by revenge, jealousy, and resistance to power. Of course, the Harvard Review article was written at a time before the powerful, revolutionary technology of social media was available. Today, a few people pursuing the truth are able to discredit a large business in the eyes of many – with little cost, and with little recourse. And if "power can be an effective substitute for trust[138]", then speaking truth to power[139], might be an effective strategy to diminish the power.

HONEST COMMUNICATIONS

"Tell a lie once and all your truths become questionable."- Ivan Junius

---

Although minor when compared with classical honesty issues, the style of communications in many large and medium-sized corporations disappoints me. What is referred to as *corporate-speak*, at times crosses a line into the area of deceit or misrepresentation. Many businesses fail to recognize that the consumer or any of their other audiences are smarter and more perceptive than they think. People generally know when they are being lied to and when the truth is obfuscated. It's like an additional animal sense that we all have to a greater or lesser degree. We seem to have some sort of internal radar for deception. But most of us pick up the signal and ignore it, sadly. Warren Buffett once said: "Either hold a rock concert, or a ballet; but don't hold a rock concert, and advertise it as a ballet".

Albert Einstein challenged us to understand deeply enough to be able to explain it simply. When a company

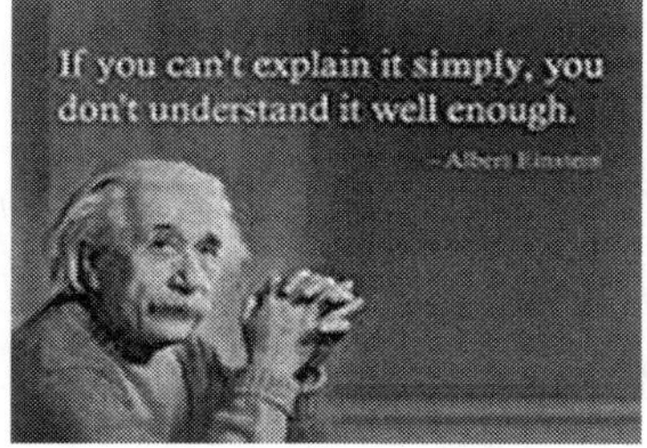

announces the good news that the *rate of decline in losses has improved,* they really mean that they lost money this month, but not as much as last month. And when a United Airlines passenger was violently dragged out of his assigned seat when he resisted a request for him to deplane because the airline had overbooked the flight, and the airline CEO called it an attempt to *"re-accommodate"* the passenger, you may ask why describe it in these terms? I don't know. Most find it dishonest, offensive, dumb, and possibly arrogant. Most everyone knows what they mean; the ones that don't know are being misinformed or misled by the awkward, unnecessary euphuisms. The ones that know just shake their heads. We are often too tolerant of the BS factor that is so pervasive in corporate communications. Have you ever been told that the part you are looking for is not available, *at this time*? What does this phrase mean? Will it be available *at another time*? Probably not; it's just something to say that somehow the pop psychology amateurs in the company's marketing communications department felt was a more diplomatic style to reduces disappointment, or to take the sting out of directly saying (as an alternative perhaps):

Sorry, but we do not carry that product anymore, or it is not being made anymore because there have been six new models of appliance since the time this part was first used. Perhaps we can look on the web or social media/buy and sell to see if someone has this part that they are selling. Or perhaps we can interest you in a new microwave with improved features?

People usually appreciate and resonate positively with the truth even if the news is disappointing.

CHAPTER 11 TAKE-AWAYS BRAND DEVELOPMENT MECHANICS	
1	To define your organization's (brand) personality, engage in an exercise that ranks the ideal relative weights of its personality attributes for: sincerity, excitement, competence, sophistication, and ruggedness.
2	If you need to jump a canyon, you cannot succeed in two short hops. Be courageous.
3	Watch out for the *black hole of the interface*. Communications and clarity get sucked into it and disappear, leaving you in the dark.
4	Brand development mechanics require a more rigorous process than simply random, brilliant, unpredictable flashes of insight.
5	It is a common mistake to over-intellectualize a brand. It should be instantly understood. Don't be obtuse. Unlike you, your stakeholders didn't spend a week philosophizing over its development.
6	Believe it or not, corporate names and identities are not (that) important. Some of the world's greatest brands are family names (McDonald's, Dell, Harley Davidson, etc.) Consumers will understand your brand names based on their experiences associated with the company and its products.

CHAPTER 11 TAKE-AWAYS BRAND DEVELOPMENT MECHANICS	
7	Make sure that your name, brand, or packaging – doesn't mean "crap" when translated into Icelandic or Urdu.
8	Wrap yourself and your organization in simple, sincere, unadulterated honesty and never let go. It will serve you well.

CHAPTER 12

PACKAGING AND DESIGN

"Design is nothing more and nothing less than the physical manifestation of a strategy" – Ira Teich

THE BLACK ART AND SCIENCE OF CONSUMER PACKAGING

Notwithstanding my earlier comments about the importance (or lack thereof) of company names, packaging is a vey different thing. In the old days, when shoppers had a relationship with their neighborhood shopkeeper, there was dialogue, advice was given, feedback was shared, and decisions to purchase were made that way.

This may still be true for environments like car showrooms, plumbing supply shops, and even some mom and pop convenient stores. But for the vast majority of stores, the environment is self-serve. In the food retail environment, the average shopping duration is about 54 minutes and in that time an average of 29.4 items are purchased[140]. About 60% of the purchases are unplanned and the shopper is open to making decisions at-shelf. The salesperson has become the package. It must sell itself.

About 70% of all consumers claim that they are not influenced by packaging. This is an unintentional lie. Intuitively, I can theorize why shoppers believe themselves immune to packaging. Consider the typical consumer who considers himself or herself as reasonably intelligent and capable of making reasonable judgements. Would these people admit that they are so shallow, so naïve, and so gullible – that they are vulnerable to the emotional manipulations of graphic designers, and buy a product based on the label attached to the container of that product? I think not. Most packaging even gets thrown out immediately. None of us would wish to consider that we are so dumb. Yet it has been convincingly shown that the package influences the purchase decision, especially for impulse purchases. Two thirds of our (food) purchases were not on our purchase list[141] when we entered the store. Retailers also use techniques to encourage the shopper to shop longer. Extending the duration of the shopping trip not only increases the dollar value of our shopping cart, but shoppers also tend to veer off their lists and buy more impulsively when they are fatigued[142] and less disciplined. They also remember what they believe should have been on their list but had forgotten to include.

At an average walking speed of 1-2[143] miles-per-hour, while shopping for an average of 54 minutes per major food shopping trip, and passing about 15,000 to 35,000 different products[144] (SKUs), you don't have to be a mathematics genius to conclude that there is huge competition among all the packages for your attention. So, packaging becomes important. With that many products competing for the attention of the shopper in the self-serve environment and with the inherent fickleness around brand loyalty – these packages must POP off the shelves, excite you, and incite you to pick them up for a closer look.

It's more impactful for manufacturers or retailers to offer a family or system of products under their brand. A solitary, orphan brand sitting alone and lonely on the shelf carries no weight, no mass, and exudes less power. The image of our design of a sub-branded premium line under Safeway's premium Safeway Select retail brand illustrates the richness of a system and a family of sub-brands that reflected the health and wellness market trend.

The example below depicts our design for Walmart's premium Sam's choice retail brand, with color sadly absent. We had branded Safeway Select because that organization was already recognized in the American market for its quality. We created Sam's Choice because we felt that the recognition wasn't there (yet) for Walmart "quality" and so we wanted to attach a kind of "personal founder's guarantee" to the brand, aka: *Sam's* Choice (Sam Walton).

It is beyond the scope of this book to get into the detail of the science and art of package design but a few core principles should be understood by all business people. I am usually a little disappointed with the quality of consumer packaging today. Much of it is pretty but not strategic, or not strategic enough. Some are brilliant but too subtle. I attribute this failing not to the design itself but to the process that begins with a strategic discussion, a design concept, and the multiple and often bureaucratic approval procedures that take place through successive layers of company management. What may have begun as a very strategic idea is often diluted by committees.

Frequently, the design tries to accommodate multiple and sometimes conflicting points of views imposed upon it by lots of different managers, each with a degree of veto power in the organization. This lack of a common shared vision is not only a failing of consumer oriented packaging design, but even more importantly, it is a failing of many organizations that do not own a shared, crisp, and well articulated vision, mission, and strategy. I comment on this challenge in the chapter on organizational and business strategy. There is also great design to be found. In my company, we were obsessed with consumer strategy, retail savvy and consumer product knowledge driving the design process. Every aspect of packaging design had to support the strategy. If we could not articulate why we chose a certain image, or illustration, or color, or message, then the design idea was considered a failure and was rejected

before we shared it with our client. Let's look at just a few examples. In the work that we did for Conagra' s Orville Redenbacher's popcorn, the audience appears in the foreground with the popcorn on-stage as the hero, on par with the film or event itself. "Theatre Style" supports the imagery. This remains one of the great examples of how the manufacturer can win the business if they truly understand the relationship that the consumer has with the product. Understanding this relationship also suggests that it can be leveraged. The not-so-obvious message here is that one needs not attend a movie theatre to consume and enjoy popcorn. It's a reminder, an idea, and a suggestion. And it worked.

Consider Kellogg's Vector Cereal. The packaging delivers the company's strategy for the product and its market. Kellogg had a challenge. The cereal category was saturated and crowded. One has only to take a walk down the cereal aisle in any supermarket. It was the knowledge of how cereals were used and by whom, and why, and when (the fundamental process questions) – that provided new thinking about how to fly above the competition, above all the crowds, and above the noise.

That insight once confirmed, identified a new market segment: the young adults out in the workforce, mostly single, mostly fitness-conscious, and who were prepared to eat a bowl of cereal for supper, or after the gym. This segment would be happy with a healthy, vitamin and mineral rich food/*meal replacement* – in the form of a familiar but different cereal. Simple and brilliant. My agency designed the package with a huge departure from tradition and convention. We put nutritional information on the front panel. We knew the customer. Also, notice the endorsing, authority-bestowing sub-brand designed and presented as The Kellogg "Institute" that recognizes a new legitimacy and value for the research and product development that delivered a new kind of scientific cereal. This product re-invented the category. The success of this product launch and subsequent sales was legendary. Eventually this product enjoyed brand extensions that included nutrition bars under the same design characteristics.

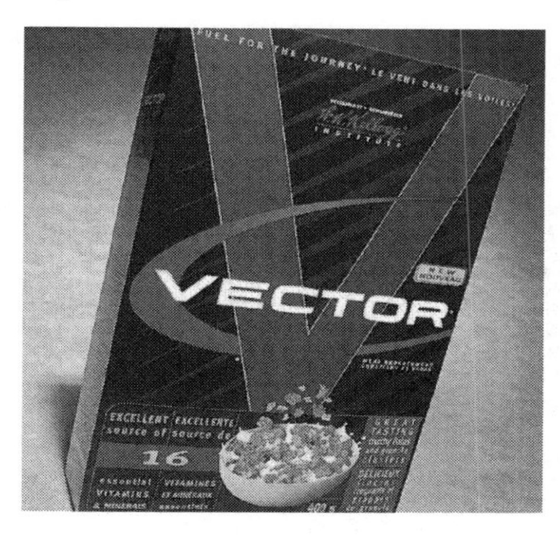

The Vector example demonstrates the value of exploring additional market segmentation to lock into alternative interest groups. Products that serve a large (combined) market segment carry the potential to be adapted and developed to provide value to narrower market clusters. If you identify a strong target, it's always best to zero in with a sniper rifle than with a shotgun. As I write this, the eye drop/eye lubricant market pops into my head. Approximately 17% of the population have blue eyes[145]. That's a big number, ergo a big market. Yet I have never seen eye drops developed specifically for this eye color despite the fact that blue eyes have different characteristics than darker color eyes, such as sensitivity to light[146]. Probably worth some research.

Another example is the work we did for Nestle. First, it is important for me to tell you that the packaging design awards that we have won are of course lovely, but these are for the most part, members of the industry congratulating each other in a kind of *love-in*. The true success of packaging design must always be measured at the cash register. I would demand of my designers to be true to the product market strategy and to strategic communication principles and not be concerned with aesthetics for the sake of aesthetics. In the boxed chocolates featured here, one of the not-too-subtle features of the design is the printed-on-box ribbon and seal that provides the impression that this box of chocolates is "wrapped" and ready to be given as a gift, "as is", directly from the store shelf. It is a very small thing that we did but at the same time it provided an idea or solved a problem in our very busy world. It saves the customer wrapping time, and Nestle was rewarded for this innovation.

The design we created for Gooderham & Worts delivered high-ticket products and so it is appropriate that the design should reflect that and ooze quality, luxury, personality and uniqueness. This was accomplished with the multi-media hand-crafted look and feel. It must be so good and precious that it can be perceived as a collector's item. That must be the standard to aim for these categories of products

It is worth mentioning that in addition to the graphical messaging strategy for product packaging, there is also strategy around *structural packaging*. Structural packaging not only protects what's inside, it can deliver a powerful statement about the manufacturer. Similarly, *secondary packaging*, such as shopping bags, shipping cartons and the like can be important. Packaging that shoppers carry out of the store serve to advertise to the larger street market. These are walking billboards.

Secondary packaging such as the above, like shipping cartons - can be designed to deliver a mass of product messaging on the retail floor. When done effectively, this "billboard effect", like the Perrier image shows how the retailer chose to merchandise the product using the Perrier shipping cartons and mass them on the retail floor. It doesn't have to cost more to design a great package than it takes to design a mediocre one.

Packaging is not only about traditional products. A deeper understanding of packaging and the environment in which packaging is merchandised leads to insight about the concept of packaging "non-products". To be clear, services can be "bundled" and "productized", that is, transformed into a product that can be packaged. For example, a set of methodologies, when used together to generate ideas, can be simply a set of tools that a consultant uses when working with a client. Alternatively, the consultant can bundle the tools together, position them into a saleable product, and package them as a branded offering, aka "Idea*ROCKET*", or *"ideaZOOM"*, or *"ideaBOOSTER"*. You get the "idea"; that's packaging also.

The Canadian Automobile Association (CAA) can sell memberships or they could create a membership "kit" whereby they could physically package the kit and merchandise the member packages on the shelves of Canadian Tire Stores, Costco, Car dealerships – with a price tag on it.

UNICEF, after having walked away from its "ownership" of Halloween donation boxes, or for that matter, any other child-based charity, could scoop up and own Valentines Day and create a physical packaging with a price tag of say $50 retail price on it. Inside the package could be information about what the $50 donation bought, aka: vaccinating 10 children against a dangerous disease or providing education for three months, or feeding a family for a month - and could include a "Friends Of ___" sweater button/pin. These packages could be sold on the shelves of drug stores, book stores, and supermarkets. For Valentines Day, it could contain on the cover and inside, a poignant note talking about how the purchaser, instead of buying flowers and chocolates, decided to help a life in despair somewhere in the world and has dedicated that gift to the recipient of the Valentine's day gift. On Mother's Day, such a package could contain one small piece of chocolate together with a note to *Mom,* saying something like this:

Mom, this year, instead of buying you the traditional big box of chocolates that are probably not that healthy anyways, I have decided – in your honor - to help a poverty-stricken child who needs medicines, food, and schooling. These are the values that you have taught me all my life, so thank you! And enjoy this small taste of chocolate too!

The point of all these remarks is to illustrate that packaging can be thought of and used strategically to create products that were not considered products before. This insight may open up for you, new opportunities and new go-to-market channels.

I believe that these gift packages would sell. Don't you? This is what marketing is about. Business starts with marketing and ends with marketing. It's marketing because it first must define a market, an audience, or a group with needs that they either recognize as needs already or have the potential to be made aware of a pent-up need. The need can be a product or a service or both. Even the way a product is manufactured has its place in marketing. Show a clean production floor, happy, fairly-remunerated employees (not underage, exploited labor - prevalent in some areas of the developing world), a high technical expertise being applied (no possibility of contaminants such as has been found in some Chinese factories), etc. – and your chances are greater that you will win a market. Of course, the product must work as promised, but these factors create an impression. People want a good reason to be loyal in our cynical world. Give it to them and they will love you for it and they will reward you for it.

CULTURAL CONSIDERATIONS IN GLOBAL MARKETING

As global marketing continues to increase, the differences in cultures and traditions become important considerations in branding and design. In the section on corporate names, I touched on a few examples of international blunders that have caused embarrassment and loss of market share, as in cases where a corporate or product name means one thing in its country of origin and carries an entirely different meaning elsewhere.

Many of us who work internationally are familiar with basic protocols and expectations. We hand out our business cards in a certain respectful manner, we shake hands, or bow, or nod at different occasions, and we respect the physical distances (personal bubble space) that are considered comfortable in various cultures - from the nose-to-nose comfort of the middle east, to the longer-than-arms-length distance in Scandinavia. Slapping a colleague or customer on the back may be friendly in Dallas or in Cairo, but not in Stockholm or Tokyo. Patting the customer's child on the head may be seen as affection in Italy, but is a terrible offence in Singapore.

Consumer product packaging, viewed by millions of people in its retail environments is also at risk of offending or misleading in different market cultures. As an example, let us look briefly at colors.

Red is considered powerful and is used around the world. Whereas it is positive and strong in India and associated with wealth and luck in China, it signifies death and mourning in South Africa; so, avoid presenting red packaging to ShopRite, Pick n' Pay, or the SPAR Group.

Yellow, akin to a golden hue, carries a royalty association in African countries and a refined sophistication in Japan, but can represent jealousy and betrayal in France[147]. In China, it is the color most associated with pornography[148]. Orange is an unhappy color in Egypt and a happy color in the Netherlands.

While Blue is generally considered a masculine color; in China, it is feminine. In the Middle East, it symbolizes protection and safety.

In many western cultures, white is associated with purity, peace, hygiene and even holiness. In China and other parts of Asia, white symbolizes death and mourning.

I have observed many cases of costly ignorance even on the part of well-respected design agencies. These problems are preventable by simply asking if there are any differences or sensitivities in the customs, linguistics, color-associations, shapes, etc. *beforehand* – between your domestic culture and the target market cultures. When professionals are presented with this question, it is reasonable to expect that if they are not sure, then they will find out. Common sense is not all than common.

STRATEGIC MARKETING AND BRANDING: UNDERSTANDING THE WALMART STORY

I have commented about Walmart in different places in this book in somewhat different contexts. I hope the reader will forgive me for that, but Walmart is interesting on many levels, and retail generally is a great model for understanding many aspects of marketing, branding and consumer response. Also, Walmart enjoys annual sales of $497 billion, or about $1.4 billion each and every day. They have 11,500 stores in 28 countries and employ 2.3 million people (1.5 million in the U.S.). 260 million shoppers visit their stores each year. They are the biggest overall retailer in the world and the largest food retailer in the world. They are worth understanding.

The marketing and design company that I led was Walmart's designer-of-record and we branded, designed, and launched thousands of products for Walmart, so I am comfortable talking about this very interesting retail model and the learnings to be gleaned from it that can be applied elsewhere.

I made several trips to Bentonville, Arkansas - the home of Walmart's headquarters, and observed first hand, the power that Walmart wielded over their "vendor-partners". CEOs from major American manufacturing corporations, with their $1500 briefcases, sat patiently on spartan wooden benches in a waiting area that looked more like a 1950's bus station than the waiting area of the planet's largest retailer. To become a supplier to Walmart meant everything.

We had a great relationship with Walmart. As with all clients, we needed to know what worried them. What worried them, worried us. We went to bed thinking about ideas that could make their goals achievable and we woke up pondering how we could increase our value to them. On a regular basis, we would confirm their level of satisfaction and delight with every aspect of our service. On one of those occasions, their VP of private label lamented to me that their suppliers in Mexico and South America had begun to complain about our prices. You see, Walmart's policy was to source locally where possible and to charge their local suppliers (to their private label program) the cost of our services, including marketing consulting, packaging design, and promotional in-store materials. Our Canadian prices were competitive in North America but not in Mexico and South America. Understandably, those suppliers did not fully appreciate Walmart's demand for consistent, high quality packaging for their products under the Walmart private label everywhere. Within 10 days, I had flown to Mexico City and contracted a local packaging and production art agency and arranged for our staff to be there to oversee the work we handed off to them. Within a month, we reduced our prices to Walmart in that market by 40%. That year, we won Walmart's most valued vendor-partner award. This is the kind of urgency and passion that every organization must embrace to win, delight and earn the privilege of keeping customers.

Let us look at Walmart through a somewhat different lens. Founder, Sam Walton had a simple idea, a simple commitment, and a clear message to his audience: American-made products at about 30% less than in other stores, every day. He invented "Everyday low prices". EDLP became a genre. And that was his brand. It meant something; namely, that the consumer did not have to cherry-pick for items on sale at different stores. They were promised value every single day. No sales, no promotions, no gimmicks. This was one man with an idea and an uncompromising execution of that idea. After his death and somewhat before, the compromising began. With a 30% discount as compared to the competition, it became challenging and obvious that Walmart would have to buy cheaper. This meant that they had to be ~~ruthless~~ tough with their manufacturer-suppliers. Suppliers would get rich on volumes, not on margins. This in turn implied that Walmart had to adopt a high volume, limited-assortment kind of strategy regarding the products they chose to sell.

It was pretty straightforward. Look at the competition in every category and follow Pareto's principle.

To illustrate, let's take toys. In Toys R Us, like most retailers there is a narrow group of products (typically 20%) that account for the majority of the profits (typically 80%), ergo Pareto's principle, otherwise known as the 80-20 rule. Walmart identified the 20% highest velocity toy products sold at Toys 'R Us and others and then ordered millions of these from the manufacturers, negotiating large, volume-related supply deals. It's not rocket science and Walmart's brilliant success was not rocket science. It was simple and like most things, the simpler the situation, the easier it is to understand and to implement, and to manage.

Over time, things changed. Like all plans - as soon as it's articulated, printed, and placed between covers – it becomes progressively obsolete. It became necessary in Walmart's case to start sourcing from China and other lower cost manufacturing geographies in order to keep true to their EDLP brand. Obviously, their preference to be "made in America" was secondary to their brand of every day low prices so that compromise was well founded. What is debatable is the pivot they took after Sam's death, when they moved to "roll-back" pricing. Roll-backs was just a euphuism for sale promotion. This countered their brand. And what essentially is a brand? It's that promise I talk about incessantly. And promises made by the owners of the brand triggers an expectation in the hearts and minds of the consumers of the brand. Managing down to zero the difference between the brand promise and the brand expectation becomes the critical challenge and objective of every well branded organization. And Walmart was weakening on that front. Of course, it can be legitimately argued that external competitive pressures like Target's general merchandise model and others, such as power centers that specialized in certain categories (Best Buy, etc.) - forced Walmart's hand. I refer to this elsewhere in this book. But this development, in my opinion, begins to explain why Walmart effectively stopped their meteoric growth in America, which had not yet been saturated by then.

Walmart has instead found its growth potential in South America and across the oceans where it has had to compete with retailers who may be smaller but some with greater international experience, like Carrefour. As this book is more of a conversation, I shall permit myself a small tangential comment about Walmart in the international space. I have had the privilege of advising a number of retailers who have faced the prospect, real or perceived, of becoming competitors to Walmart.

In 1998, I sat with the executives of Coop Konsum, one of Sweden's largest supermarkets. They were lamenting the construction of the then incomplete 8 km Oresund Bridge[149], connecting Denmark and Sweden. Konsum was sure that Walmart would be invading Scandinavia immediately once the logistical opportunities became available to them. It didn't happen, but sitting there at that time, I can tell you that the fear was palpable in the extreme. Years later in 2008, I was engaged by a Russian consortium[150] of retailers that dominated food and drug retailing in central Russia.

They had discovered that I was the former CEO of the marketing and design consultancy that advised Walmart USA and International and which had developed and launched thousands of their beverage and food SKUs. They were anxious to meet with me in Central Russia. They had heard via rumor that Carrefour (that giant international French-owned retail chain with $100+ billion of annual revenue) who already had an 8000-square meter store in Moscow's Filion Shopping Mall[151] – was planning to expand into central Russia. Further, and of greater concern, was the news that Walmart, who sometimes followed the more experienced global expansionist, Carrefour - was looking for real estate in Central Russia and was contemplating developing a retail presence there.

This common fear triggered an alliance of previously aggressive competitors. Ten tough Russian CEO/Owners were shaking in their boots at the prospect of being wiped out by two of the world's most savvy and powerful retail chains. It's not my intention to detail the response strategy I assisted them to develop but the core idea was to become stronger, better organized, focused on better customer service (an unknown in much of Russia), and in collective control of their supply chain.

Within six months, Carrefour, who was monitoring retail developments in the region, decided that these regional retailers had *somehow* become stronger and they suspended their expansion plans. Walmart followed suit. I became a hero; but the truth be told: the timing was outstanding and these foreign expansionists likely began to discover the implications of trying to grow in a rather corrupt and bloated bureaucracy. The point of course is that business niches that are based on geo-politics and geo-economics are not safe investments. Eventually, like osmosis, there will be movement from areas of higher density (read: advantage) to areas of lower density (read: opportunity).

CHAPTER 12 TAKE-AWAYS PACKAGING AND DESIGN	
1	In most (self-serve) retail environments, the package is the salesperson. It must sell itself in a split-second.
2	The true success and value of packaging design is always measured at the cash register.
3	Great packaging delivers the brand strategy and message; it's not about being independently attractive.
4	Packaging cannot make the product inside, tastier or more reliable, it can only promote "trial". Refuse to associate with a message that doesn't hold up.
5	You can package and sell an idea, literally.
6	Words, phrases, colors – mean different things in different cultural markets. Know your consumers everywhere and if necessary segment your packaging design.
7.	Secondary packaging and structural packaging telegraph your message and your brand. In fact, every single touch-point your customers encounter with your brand will either diminish you or strengthen you.
8	I have learned a great deal from Walmart. You can also. Study significant great businesses and consider what principles they use that you may be able to adapt.

CHAPTER 13
RETAIL AND CONSUMER STRATEGY

"You may not be interested in strategy,
but strategy is interested in you" – *Leon Trotsky*

RETAIL BRAND POWER

Retail has always fascinated me[152] perhaps because this sector operates at the interface with the end user-consumer. As a result, retailers must know the marketplace intimately. And they must have an uncanny understanding of both the demand side and the supply side. It is also fascinating because everyone is a consumer and has direct experience inside stores, both physical bricks and mortar stores and in the past 20 years or so, inside virtual web-based stores.

There's more to it than that. The store environment is a great laboratory for experimentation in marketing and influencing market segments and clusters - all in one place.

And that "one place" is also profoundly important. Those market strategists who are proponents of TV advertising and now web-based advertisement – often miss an important point of fact: that more people (shoppers) walk the floors of stores than the number of people combined who watch television or cruise retail-oriented websites, every day. In fact, in supermarkets alone, almost all people shop an average of 1.5 shopping trip per week[153]. More important, these shoppers, once influenced, are not in their living rooms. Instead, they are inside the store with the product in their hands or in their cart, just feet away from the cashier. So, the decision to purchase, once triggered, can be actualized immediately. This is without a doubt a terrific advantage over TV and other remote forms of advertising. Exploring smart ways to influence through store design, in-store communications, package design, and customer service – continue to be exciting and worthwhile. Success here is a function of how well the retailer (and their manufacturing partners) can understand the customer mindset.

That is not to say that online commerce and the challenges of marketing online aren't important. In fact, many of the lessons learned from in-store marketing can be imported into the online world of shopping. The virtual store would do well to emulate the dynamic, alive, 3-D, physical store. With that done, the inherent aggregational economics, operational efficiencies, product assortment, time management, and logistical advantages of online stores can be realized. The future of online stores is exciting, with 25% of online respondents saying that they order grocery products online, and with more than half (55%) who are willing to do so in the future[154]. Conventional retailers who expand into the digital format find that after a while, their customers do not distinguish between these different formats and choices. Walmart's thesis, for example, is for the digital and physical to play off each other to generate greater overall sales.

Accordingly, my model for understanding the strategic components of the totality of the retail gestalt is illustrated in the following round diagram:

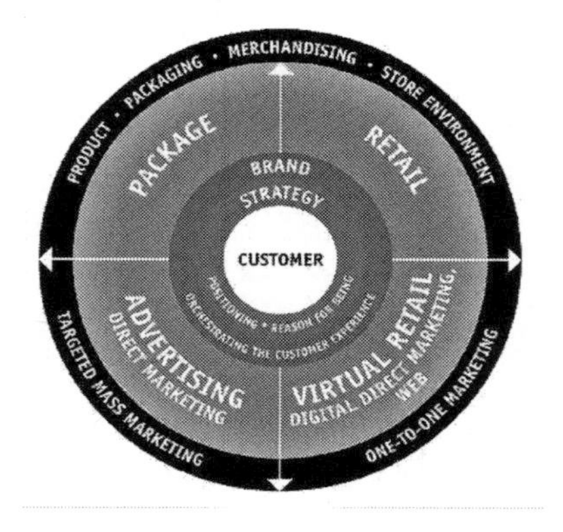

THREE GREAT RETAIL REVOLUTIONS

There have been three great revolutions in retail in the past 40 years. My first professional experience in retail was in 1974 where, as a Chartered Accountant intern, I was assigned to an operational audit of the now, long-defunct

Towers Department Store's HyperMarché (Hypermarket) in Laval, Québec. It was the first retailer in North America that introduced what they then called the "magic wand" (product UPC scanning). It was a marvellous technology which was a productivity tool for cashiers and more important for inventory management. But the really profound, transformational aspect of scanning isn't hard to understand. It shifted power away from the manufacturer to the retailer. Supermarkets immediately knew how much Lipton chicken soup they sold that day. And they could make buying and replenishment decisions quickly, confidently, and independently. Before this technology, it was the manufacturer or their rack jobber agents who advised the retailer how much to order. That all changed.

A decade later, Retail Revolution part-two arrived: the private label revolution. To be more precise, it was the rise of Retailers' Brands. Until then, retailer Marks and Spencer was the world's pioneer in "own-brand" marketing. St. Michael was their brand that they developed and used from 1928 until its discontinuation in 2000. In those earlier years, their main store in Central London recorded the highest sales per square foot[155] of any other comparable store in the world[156]. In addition, their margins on sales was one of the very highest and were sustainable. This made some sense. After all, they owned their own brand, they manufactured either directly or under contract, and they controlled everything about it. Other "private" brands at the time were mostly low quality inferior brands that catered to a bargain basement marketplace demand.

The European experience dramatically illustrated that as penetration of retailer brands increased (their introduction and usage in stores across Europe), the profitability also proportionately increased.

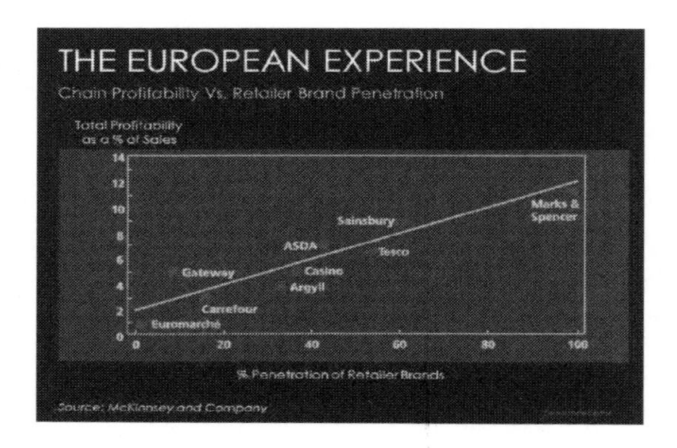

At Safeway U.K., they were so aggressive in driving their own store brand (retail brand), that they even in some cases removed the competing national brand and exclusively promoted their own. See the incredible image of their own brand, Cyclon detergent. For those readers with retail strategy experience, this image will be incredible.

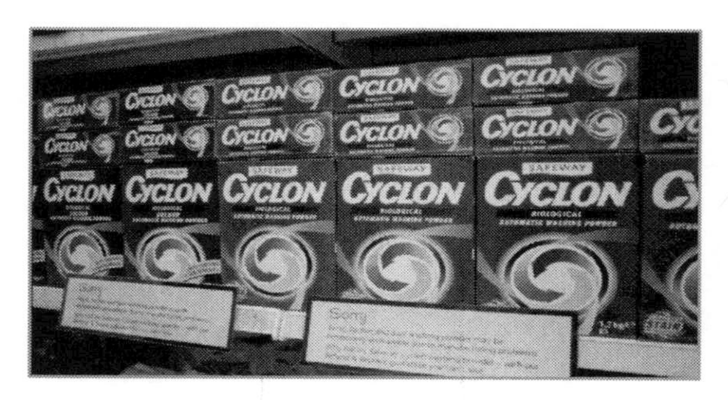

The sign ("shelf-talker") in the Cyclon image reads as follows: *"Sorry, Persil, Radon and Surf washing powder may be temporarily unavailable due to manufacturing problems. Why not try Safeway Cyclon washing powder – with our Refund & Replace guarantee you can't lose."* To sabotage these huge national brands and promote the store's own brand was a very significant new move and reflected dramatically the new power that retailers wielded with the advent of the new retail-brand revolution.

The St. Michael brand was the gold standard and competed successfully with first-tier manufacturer brands, otherwise known as National Brands. In Canada, enter the Loblaw Corporation's private label strategy and *President's Choice* was born. Books have been written on President's Choice (PC) but the key thing to know about it was that it introduced into the retail market a set of products that could compete successfully with the national brands and resulted in the second historical shift of power away from manufacturers and to the retailers.

RETAILERS WERE FREED FROM THE TYRANNY OF THE MANUFACTURERS

"...rather than serving as a guarantee of value on a product, the brand itself has increasingly become the product, a free-standing idea pasted on to innumerable surfaces. The actual product bearing the brand-name has become a medium, like radio or a billboard, to transmit the real message. The message is: It's Nike. It's Disney. It's Microsoft. It's Diesel. It's Caterpillar." – Naomi Klein *(New Statesman, January 24, 2000)*

Gold-standard brands owned by the retailers themselves had to deliver real value both in terms of quality and price. The consumer won - Teich

This changed things. A lot. Imagine the situation before the retail revolution: Coca Cola sets the retail price, and the profit margin (which they permitted the retailer) would not have been very much, if at all. There was no point in complaining. Both the retailer and their supplier, Coke knew very well that the end-consumer expected and demanded that their store carry Coke. The retailer had little choice. Coke and other powerhouse national brands had their retail customers over the proverbial barrel. So, when Loblaws and then other North American retailers introduced their Retailer Brands, everything changed.

Cott Corporation of Toronto developed a carbonated Cola beverage (and other flavours) that was indistinguishable in taste (vs. Coke) to the majority of consumers. The Loblaw Corporation merchandised their PC Cola next to Coke on shelf and boldly signed the shelf with a "compare and save" message. At launch, PC Cola was being sold at half of Coke's price per can.

Dave Nichol, the Loblaw Corporation's president at the time, made speeches about how the national brands were screwing the consumer and how the Loblaw Corporation was passing on the positive economies of their own brand to the consumer. He called the difference between the Loblaws price for a can of PC Cola and the Loblaws price for a can of Coca Cola: **The Brand Tax**. It was a spectacular revolution. Coke dug into their war chest, spending millions to mitigate the negative impact of the fallout.

Enter Walmart. Walmart followed with Toronto's Cott Corp-produced Sam's Choice Cola. It was Sam Walton's first foray into his own brand, choosing the beverage

category as the engine of that revolution. Within a year, Walmart had sold 40 million cases of Sam's Choice Cola[157].

Coke was furious. Dictators (those who dictate) hate being challenged. Consumers were delighted.

Walmart was the hero, and in the years following, they launched thousands of SKUs under their premium private brand, *Sam's Choice* and under their value brand, *Great Value* with the help of the marketing and design consultancy that I headed up. With leadership shown in Canada by the Loblaw Corporation and in the US by Walmart and others, the market for revitalized, premium, retailer brands exploded and we developed and launched Safeway U.S. brands starting with the Carbonated Soft Drink category (CSDs) which ignited the retailer brand revolution. Safeway Select was born. Many supermarket chains followed suit, Cott blossomed in the U.S., Europe and Asia, and my team became very busy.

In supermarkets, "Private Label" measured an 84% in-store decision rate indicating that shoppers were open and willing to consider non national-branded alternatives[158].

A few years later, in 2000, I was a speaker at an International Beverage Conference in New York City and when I got up to speak about retailer brands and global beverage trends, an executive VP of Coca Cola stormed out of the room. Such was the trauma that Coke experienced in those years when retailer brands usurped the margins and power of the national brands, empowering retailers and benefiting consumers. It is not surprising, given the two-part retail revolution of the 1970s and the 1980s, that the animosity between manufacturers and retailers has persisted in some form or another. Most business people in these sectors will acknowledge some degree of an adversarial dynamic in their relationship.

The retail brand revolution also may have motivated retailers to create better-designed and better-maintained stores. It's not that obvious, but to sell their own brand, the physical environment had to be attractive, look successful, modern, and clean. After all, a can of Dole pineapple slices are Dole pineapple slices everywhere, but the store's own pineapple slices will draw its credibility from the store's physical environment. A consumer might pick Dole off a dusty shelf in an old grocery store, but that store's own product would be suspect.

The third and most recent retail revolution was of course, online shopping. The virtual store has come into its own after a weak start. Pundits had forecasted its meteoric success a bit prematurely but knowing the consumer mind, it was fairly obvious that like most things, the "consumer" is too large a group to target with a single strategy. The segmentation and clustering of consumer groups is always critical to success. The younger market segments, growing up with computers and web-based activities, naturally feel comfortable with that medium. Online retail had to wait for these folks to grow up a bit more.

Of course, there were early adopters; there always are (I am one of these). And with these groups, there was still some hesitancy when it came to certain categories of products that required a more tactile experience. I am not sure that online food pickers will squeeze the tomato I ordered as well as I would. But if one is searching for the best value on a Sony TV of a certain model number and is convinced that the online retailer will complete its contract and keep credit card information secure, then that's a no-brainer. If I don't know the brand, then I would want to know the retailer. In that context, a retailer operating brick and mortar stores and complements that operation with providing their customers with an online option, wins.

There are also now many examples of hugely successful, exclusively online retailers. Amazon is the biggest book store in the world and until recently they didn't operate a single bookstore. That multinational e-commerce company's net revenue was $136 billion USD up from

$74.45 billion USD in 2013[159]. Most of you will know that there has been an ongoing conversation about companies like Amazon and Walmart having demonstrated effective disruptive strategies resulting in their becoming a logistics operation versus a retailing operation. This is somewhat semantical but important. It is also a natural and predictable consequence of their economies of scale. At their sizes, and the mission-critical need to ensure that product gets into the hands of the consumer, it's natural that they should want to bring in-house (and not outsource) high-strategic distribution capabilities. So, they own fleets of airplanes and trucks and automated warehousing and picking systems and all manner of fulfilment and delivery technology. In achieving this scale of operations, the business that they had with both UPS[160] and FedEx, for example, is in real danger (danger to UPS and FedEx) of being increasingly taken over internally by Amazon and Walmart, and others.

A key rule in business is that you should try to develop capabilities for key, core, strategic activities, and not outsource these. An additional vital ingredient is that in considering Amazon's value chain, why should they leave any money on the table if that can have it all?

What happens later, of course, is that when these giant companies realize how valuable their logistics operations are and how costly the development and set-up costs were – it is very seductive for them to grow these capabilities and harvest the benefits. The management of the distribution units (that inevitably become fiefdoms) also see themselves as legitimate, stand-alone, logistics operations with huge profit potential to sell logistics not only to their own internal retail units but to almost anyone. But don't get me started; this is not core to this book, nevertheless, it's an interesting development.

Back to online with some facts…

A National Retail Federation survey found that 43.8% of consumers shopped online during Thanksgiving 2016 with that four-day span showing a 4.2% uptick over 2015. Black Friday online sales topped $3 billion for the first time, jumping 21.6% over last year to $3.34 billion[161]. Mobile shopping saw its biggest day ever, accounting for $1.2 billion in revenue, a 33% jump compared to 2015[162].

So clearly, online is not a fad; it is here to stay and grow. Of course, it's here to stay and its fantastic. At the same time, virtual stores have both advantages and disadvantages. An online store can display millions of products, describe each one, provide video streaming about its use, provide testimonials, provide linkages to YouTube and other supporting advertising and promotion mechanics. No brick and mortar space has that much shelving, space for signage, or can do as effective a job. We are a busy society. We love the convenience, the speed, and the assortment. On the other hand, we don't get to walk out of the "store" carrying the stuff we bought and as mentioned earlier, we don't get to touch and feel and bond. Some sites now allow consumers to upload pics of themselves, view themselves virtually in the dress or sunglasses and even share with a friend and ask for their opinion - all in real time prior to a commitment to purchase. Over time, with holography and other enhanced reality technologies, other on line disadvantages will be overcome.

One of the important disadvantages of the online retail space is that whereas in a brick and mortar store it takes a few minutes to find the door and leave (and on the way out, who knows what impulses might tempt you to buy) – when online, one click of the mouse or tap of your finger (or voice command) and you can jump instantly to another site somewhere else on the planet. I have not seen any good research on this subject but my intuition suggests this is a challenge.

However, despite all the hype, e-commerce accounts for less than 10% of total retail sales[163]. Tradition does not go quietly into the night. Think vinyl records. Think paper books recently re-gaining popularity at the expense of declines in the market's enthusiasm for e-books. Amazon has begun opening physical stores. The omni-channel universe prevails.

PARTNERSHIPS

THE ADVERSARIAL DYNAMIC BETWEEN MANUFACTURERS AND RETAILERS IS SILLY

What a powerhouse scenario it would be when manufacturers and retailers really behaved as true partners. It makes so much sense because looking through to the end of the value chain, the end-user consumer is the final customer of both manufacturer and retailer. Therefore, if they have done a reasonable job at thinking through and crafting their visions and missions, both entities should have a big chunk of the same sentiments and words about satisfying consumer needs and desires, and delighting them and so forth. That being said, it is logical that there would also be important components of strategy in common.

It's been often said that sustainable partnerships must be based on enlightened, mutual, self-interest. This makes sense. However, in the manufacturer-retailer dynamic, what often stands in the way are two factors. The first is that the wrong people are negotiating the relationships. Often the manufacturer salesperson or its agent-distributor deals with a retailer's buyer. Both are motivated by a narrow set of incentives - mostly short-term, volume-related incentives. While this is understandable at a certain level, the strategic value of dealing with one manufacturer versus another is not usually considered. The set of criteria guiding the selection of manufacturer is not developed, or if developed, not well used. Those criteria ought to include the "fit" with the retailer's values, vision and mission and brand attributes, as well as where they stand in their respective maturation and growth. Retailers do not usually have a strategy function that first "vets" potential manufacturer partnerships before the details of the business arrangements, price points, planogramming, slotting fees, etc. – are worked out. The corollary is also true. Manufacturers should also be choosing their ideal retail partners based on the appropriate long-term fit. The willingness to sell to anyone is understandable but myopic. The advantages of precision targeting for partners outweigh the usual shotgun approach of accepting the first to be hit or the first who responds.

Having said that, in the case of high profile national brands (brands and their product assortment) that are expected and demanded by consumers, my comments should be taken with a grain of salt. But even under those circumstances there are relationships that are usual, and those that are special and carry special benefits. For example, a manufacturer who takes the time to step into the retailer's shoes will understand that retailers do not usually have the time or creative energy to think of new ways to sell the manufacturer's products. They will not normally propose inventive in-store merchandising strategies. Nor would the retailer normally spend the time and allocate resources to support the manufacturer's products in any special way. Essentially, retailers rent space to manufacturers, most of the time, but still control the space.

Similarly, manufacturers would not normally spend the energy or find the skills that could have their retail clients appreciate the nuances of their product brand or message. Manufacturers do not normally research well enough the retail merchandising strategies for their products, based on cogent consumer research that they can share with their retail customers. Manufacturers also tend to be more focused on building their own brands and taking credit for these exclusively instead of sharing the credit and making the retailer the hero in the eyes of their consumer. Both sides would benefit in the middle and long terms from a reduction of myopic commercial selfishness. The required collaboration is well beyond the sharing of data in real-time which is being done in many manufacturer-retailer relationships. What needs to happen is for these two potential partners to visualize and behave as if they were a single, integrated, economic enterprise serving their common customer.

If these concepts were embraced more commonly, we would probably find some very special relationships based on common interests. I would venture that this also would result in a rationalization of the proliferation of brands on store shelves. A greater trend to quasi-limited product assortment would emerge together with an emphasis of quality of choice over quantity of choice. The old (and mostly misguided) concept of carrying tons of products to gain some sort of "visual massing" effect (presumably to impress consumers about their richness of choice) would be replaced by a more careful and possibly spectacular array of successful products and compelling package designs and communications, all framed strategically to deliver lifestyle solutions within stores.

One could argue that the dynamic that I have described is somewhat naïve because retailers compete with each other in the same trading area with increasing concentration; and consumer product manufacturers are also increasingly under competitive pressures in very crowded marketplaces. Add to this reality the phenomenon of "channel blurring", the increasing situation where all retail categories and formats (food, drug, convenience, club, warehouse, c-store, g-store, large and small, etc.) all sell the same things. Nevertheless, marketing in these different channels can and should be different as they serve different needs, and although they may be serving the same consumers, all consumers behave differently under different shopping occasions that are defined by time-of-day, length of shopping trip, stock up, and convenience, etc.

HAVE YOU EVER BOUGHT A FRIDGE?

An interesting story about adversarial or unproductive relationships is the story of GE Appliances. GE sold their appliance business in 2016 to China's Haier Corporation for $5.4 billion USD. That was a pretty good price given that GE had seemed ready to sell their appliance division to Sweden's Electrolux back in 2014[164] for (only) $3.3 billion USD. As expected, GE's explanation for the sale involved the usual rationale about focusing on core business like jet engines and other big industrial stuff. GE's appliance division contributed less that 10% of the company's revenues so it all sounded logical. But there's a bit of a back story that few people know. And it has to do with the relationships between manufacturers and retailers that I have been writing about.

Back in the 1990s, GE Appliances approached us with a problem. For all their engineering research and development efforts, for all their product quality control efforts and for all of their marketing efforts - they were not present during the "last six inches" of the (retail) sale. In other words, their refrigerator would stand beside other brands and it was up to a department store appliance salesperson, earning a basic wage, to choose which brand of refrigerator to promote to the shopper standing in front of them with six other different, competing appliances. Go to The Bay today, or Home Depot, or Lowes stores. You may see GE, Samsung[165], LG, Whirlpool[166], Frigidaire[167], and Bosch[168] refrigerators, all standing next to one another. On what basis does the consumer choose? What influences them? Are they equipped to make intelligent choices? Had there been sufficient efforts on the part of GE to sustain the emotional, if not traditional connection with North American consumers? Were the fresh, aggressive marketing practices of European and Asian manufacturers being adequately countered and managed? How was retailer education about GE technology handled? How could GE influence retail sales of their products in a (retail) environment which they did not control? Did the consumer see GE appliances as part of a family of products that were connected to a lifestyle choice? There were no satisfactory answers to these kinds of questions.

And so, in an effort for GE to get closer to the consumer, to understand her better, to connect, and to understand appliance retailing better – GE asked us to design a strategic, prototype appliance store. This was somewhat of an innovative idea at the time. We designed the store and called it GE Domaine. It was to showcase the totality of the GE household and lifestyle. It was never built. GE lacked the strategic will. Ten years later, GE was actively looking for a buyer for its appliance division.

Ironically, at about the same time in Portland, Oregon, Nike opened its first Niketown store. Rumor has it that it was never intended to be profitable. After all, one bought Nike everywhere - at Nordstrom, JC Penney, Foot Locker, and Sears. Niketown was intended to be a kind of

museum to the brand. Of course, it became a roaring retail success. In Nike's case, the most brilliant partnership therefore, was to be their own supplier and their own retailer. This duality gave them the laboratory to experiment with the inter-relationships among product development, manufacturing, and retailing.

Zara[169], with $16 billion in revenues (2016) may be another shining example of a vertically integrated manufacturer-retailer; in their case as a single indivisible entity. Now considered by many as the number one clothing and fashion retailer in the world, Zara's genius is the rapidity with which it gathers and analyzes fashion trends (social media inputs are paramount here), designs, and throws them out into their retail units – all within weeks. Visit a Zara store again three weeks later and it is unlikely that you will see hardly anything that you saw three weeks before. This alone would suggest a profound customer incentive for impulse purchasing and for multiple repeat visits to a Zara store (physical or virtual) to see what's new.

Their cycle of first-to-market with continuous design creation of many recent fashion trends at affordable prices, may have led Daniel Piette[170] to say that Zara was "possibly the most innovative and devastating retailer in the world" and for CNN to report (more than 15 years ago) that:

"As it makes the clothes itself[171], it can react quickly to changing market trends. While others, including rivals Gap and H&M take up to nine months to get new lines into their shops, Zara takes just two to three weeks.[172]"

And Zara doesn't really have much of a marketing budget. They don't need one. Their marketing is mostly done by their customers, their stores are the package and the short lead-times translate to more fashionable clothing.

CHAPTER 13 TAKE-AWAYS RETAIL AND CONSUMER STRATEGY	
1	Understand retail to understand end-users. Understand end-users to understand retail.
2	Understanding the three great revolutions in retail will give you the perspective to understand future upheavals, and help you adapt and innovate.
3	Control or influence the value chain (that you are in) as much as possible. It will enable you to develop the appropriate partnerships.
4	In identifying alliances, always look deeply into what's in it for "them". You probably already understand what's in it for you.
5	E-commerce is supplanting inflexible, traditional businesses but it can be complementary if you treat it as simply another channel.
6	Everything starts and ends with the customer. 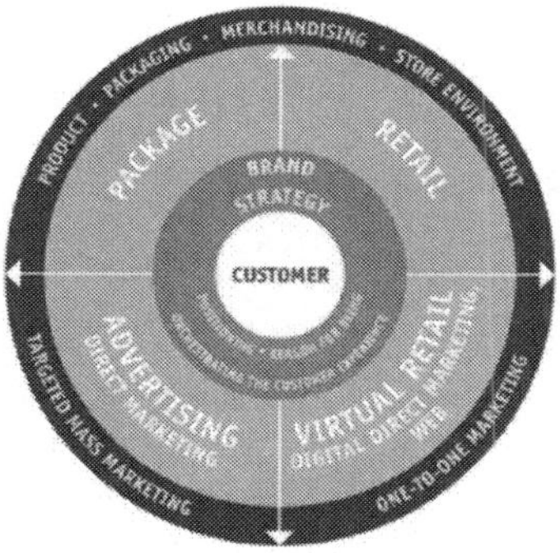

CHAPTER 14
INFORMATION, INNOVATION, INTUITION

"Intuition is reason in a hurry" – Holbrook Jackson[173]

RESULTS OF COLLABORATION

It sometimes takes a leap of faith to believe that collaboration yields results. It seems sensible. But as much as there are common goals, there are often tensions when each party to the collaboration also does business with the other party's competitors. But collaboration sometimes leads to unpredictable benefits. There are insights and truths that initially seem to defy logic and are *counter-intuitive* that arise when two organizations jointly seek ways to understand their common customer. Collaboration and its benefits are even deeper. The previous example of Zara illustrates a profound collaboration between the company and its customers. There are numerous examples. Biotherm, a skin health company collaborated with Renault, an automotive company – to develop a healthier interior car environment. UCB pharmaceuticals have collaborated with patients and opened up areas of research, so that patients anywhere can input any information they feel is relevant to UCB's pharmacological research activities. Microsoft and Toyota have worked together on how best to manage information systems for electric vehicles.

Another example is an insight referred to as the *pantry-loading effect.* This effect states that with certain categories of food and beverages (mostly CSDs[174]), the consumer will tend to consume in any given period of time, the whole of their purchases for that product. For example, if you purchase in the supermarket, a case of 24 cans of coke, you will likely consume all 24 cans in the same period of time that you would have consumed a case of 12 cans of coke. In other words, however much you load your pantry with that product, you will consume it before your next food shopping event; ergo: the *pantry loading effect.* This is somewhat counter intuitive as one might think that the consumption would be based on more human, individual, and cognitive factors. This observation and collaboration between CSD manufacturers and their retailer-customers led to the development of the 24-can case in the store. The lift in volume (and net revenues) were substantial as a result. Both benefited.

Intuition is a confusing term and a relative one. Therefore counter-intuitive must also be, by corollary, equally confusing. Consider the management of the mix[175] of products in a store. There are a few third-party vendors delivering mix management services to retailers. This entails complex software programs that are consistent with what *data mining* and then *Big Data* vendors delivered later in subsequent evolutions. The detailed analyses were amazing, though the interpretation and actionable recommendations that arose from these analyses often fell short. Yes, they were useful but they were based on the only kind of data that is available: history. That's because the future is in the future! But of course, what I mean is that the true insight is to predict what decisions consumers are likely to make in the future and then provide them, enable them, to make those decisions.

An example: Remember movie video rentals before Netflix and other online providers? Well, step back with me to the video rental days not that long ago. If you walked into a Walgreen pharmacy in America or a Shoppers Drug Mart in Canada and you had the flu, you might stagger over to the over-the-counter (OTC) medicines and purchase a cold remedy, a nasal decongestant, and some cough drops. And then, tired and disoriented, you might crawl back home and into bed.

My "intuition" tells me that if next to those medicines, the store had placed six of the top trending video movies for rent - then as a customer I may have said:

Hmm, I feel horrible, can't go to work, can't focus on a book, need some distraction from this horrible cold or flu. Perhaps I should pick up a couple of movies to watch in bed!

Am I saying that the retailer should have moved the video section to the medicine section? No, of course not. Healthy people watch movies also. Maybe put the popcorn in the regular movie section. But they could replicate a small part of the movie rental offering in a place where the consumer would see a value - in the store having delivered a good idea and a suggestion for their feeling better.

Yet, no mix management software can calculate this because it can only analyze what has happened, and not what hasn't happened but could happen if we humans used our intuition and tested that intuition. So, is intuition a magical skill that some of us are born with and some not? To some extent, perhaps in the extreme, yes – but if I had a team spending 10 minutes on product categories, asking the process questions: what, why, when, how, where, etc. – we may have come up with the potential adjacency benefits of having movies and flu medicine placed together. After all, it answers the question *when? when do people watch movies?* There would undoubtedly be a longer list than three or four, but one item on the list would probably have been: *when they are sick.*

In case I am less than clear about human intuition, it's worthwhile to write a little about data and the evolution of the value of data.

If I were to say to you: "5". You may ask what that is. And I could tell you that this is a number, a piece of data. But you will not know how to interpret and understand that data. If I then tell you that it is "5 *meters*", that becomes a degree of data that is elevated to "information"; at least you know something about that data (some people have called this "meta-data" aka: data about data; but not terribly important, so let us continue). Then I say, 5-4 was the score of the baseball game between x and y teams, and y won. That would be called: knowledge. You have data; and data in context, is information. At the next level, you now have knowledge about the winner of a competition match. You may now be able to connect that knowledge with other knowledge and come up with a whole bunch of statistics about that team that might make you quite wise about them; this is a higher form of data, evolving to information, then knowledge, and from there into wisdom. If you then are able to connect relevant other data from weather sensors to determine when the winning team is likely to win during rainy or dry game days, what happens when players are ill, which players are ill for tonight's game and so on and so on – in order to develop an understanding of the factors that can help predict the game's outcome - then you have reached the "insight" stage.

This is not rocket science, but it *is* interesting. My theory is that when we humans have insights, we do so in the same manner as "the build" that you see in my very simple data evolution model. The only difference is that all the necessary connecting-of-the-dots happens at synapse speeds of about 268[176] miles per hour; that's how Archimedes jumped out of the bathtub!

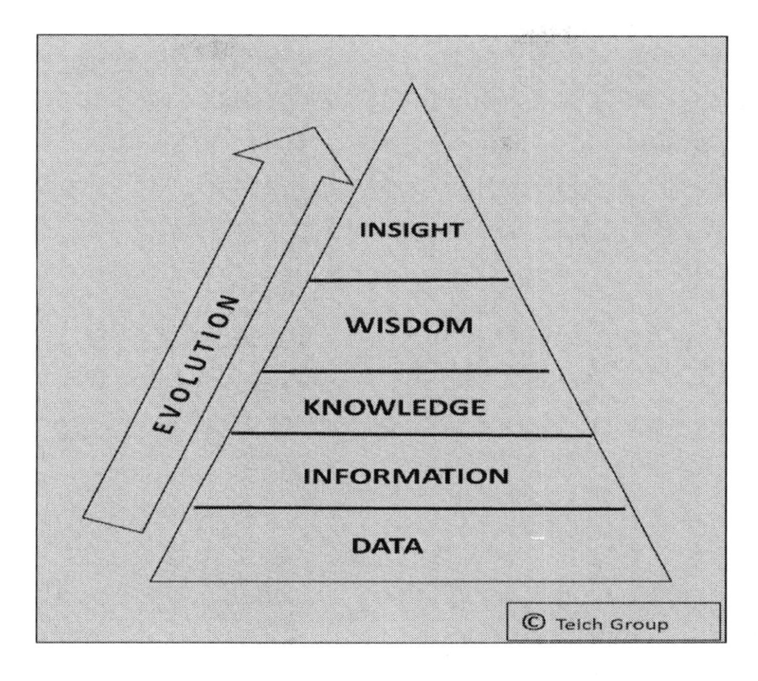

In any case, when we hear about BIG Data or Analytics as the big trend over the last few years, it is about the availability of very large computational power (really big computers) being able to take in a very large amount of data from many sources, including business transactions, environmental conditions, sensors of various kinds - and then through algorithms (smart programming) – the program can look for patterns in all that data and come up with insights and predictions.

That suggests that my intuition about flu meds and video rentals might be able to be replaced by insights from big data analytics that connected a credit card name with the purchase of flu meds at 5:15 PM followed by a video movie rental transaction at another store 20 minutes later, and so on and so on. However, that only works if there were enough sick customers who had the idea about renting a movie. My suggestion about trialing with adjacencies is all about offering ideas and suggestions to solve a consumer problem. In that sense, it may create a valid demand where no demand had existed before.

Management of business has been integrated with computing for about 50 years now. From the 1980s, the more sophisticated businesses have permitted only single source data input – that is to say that the same piece of data is inputted only once and not duplicated in multiple data bases. If the business has no redundancy of data, this ensures the integrity and quality of the data. The business, for correct management of its various activities, can call for a multitude of different reports (on paper or on screen) in multiple formats and organized in many different ways, and for many different time periods (one can call these: "views"). The concept is that although there may be multiple views, the source is common and the data, if adjusted, is adjusted in one place at one time so that all the views will have (referential) integrity with no need to reconcile among multiple views. This basic principle of data management has not changed in many years but sadly, the discipline for this has yet to be codified as a standard for all businesses.

Even today, too many employees and managers avoid using the information pyramid to manage their jobs. This is unfortunate. The effective use of information up the pyramid can be liberating and insightful. Reminds me of a personal story.

I had recently taken over the leadership of the firm and had a team of about 20 project managers whose jobs were to liaise with our clients and our design staff. Managing projects included understanding daily, how far along we were. If for example, we were 50% through the project but had consumed 60% of the time and costs budgeted for it, that 10% deficit would not be a good thing. This would suggest the need for interpretation. Were we simply being unproductive? Can we recover the 10% shortfall in time and catch up without compromising quality? Were we in the concept development stage and the creative juices simply weren't there (that happens sometimes)? Perhaps the client had asked for more (scope creep) and we hadn't incorporated the request into a revised quote. But first we had to have a system that measured all of this on a timely basis. You cannot manage what you cannot measure. And we had such a system but it wasn't used consistently. I challenged my project managers and explained that data was the abstract representation of what we do and that measuring and managing it was integral to every job. Their response? "We are creative people, visual people, we don't do well with data; it's against our natural instincts. We hate statistics and math and analysis".

I changed subjects, sort of. I turned to baseball.

It was October 23, 1996, and the world series was in full swing. the New York Yankees had played game three against the defending champions, the Atlanta Braves, the day before. Yankees won after losing the first two games. So, I asked my project managers who had watched the game. They all had watched! I asked them who won. Everyone knew that the Yankees had won 5 to 2. I asked what the secret was. They responded easily: Yankee pitcher, David Cone pitched six innings and only gave up one run. Now that I had gotten them started, the statistics were flying right and left; I couldn't keep up. They knew everything: batting averages, historical performances, runs-batted-in, who hit well against a left-handed pitcher versus a right-handed pitcher, and so on and so forth.

I stopped them and told them that they were expert statisticians. They were able to describe the game in terms of statistics and numbers and knew all the different ways to measure success in the business of baseball. They had the data and the information and the knowledge and that generated wisdom and even insight about who might win under what circumstances and how the teams were positioned for next year given the newer talent that the team had acquired and were cultivating.

So why did they embrace that skill for baseball and not apply it where it really counted - in their jobs - where they were being paid and from which they were supporting themselves and their families? How were we failing to make "measuring" our performance, valuable, interesting, and even entertaining? How could we also build upon the information pyramid and generate wisdom and insight about our business? We considered all of this and came up with workable ideas around scoring and celebrating when we reached our key metrics, and each time we caught something in time to fix. And we agreed to celebrate our learnings by identifying and harvesting and sharing insights. Our "Lunch & Learn" program was born. It was a beautiful thing.

A BIT MORE ON INTUITION

A couple of associations come to my mind when I think about intuition. The first is a mental image of Archimedes[177] jumping out of his bathtub shouting "eureka"[178] when the insight around the displacement of water flashed into his head. Archimedes suddenly understood that the volume of water displaced must be equal to the volume of the part of his body he had submerged. He then realized that this meant that the volume of irregular objects could be measured with precision, a previously intractable problem. He is said to have been so eager to share his discovery that he leapt out of his bathtub and ran through the streets of Syracuse (Greece) naked.

The second association I have deals more with the application of a discovery in one field that generates an intuition in another field. The renown physicist, Werner Karl Heisenberg[179], came up with the Heisenberg's Uncertainly Principle. It is a complex principle that is best understood through the language of mathematics but one aspect of the conversation around the principle (though not directly related to it) has been the idea that in measuring systems, the act of measuring can change the behaviour of the system that one is measuring. If one bombards an atom with subatomic particles to infer its structure, that action itself could potentially change the structure that one had intended to observe.

The applied insight is as follows: In life, there is always the "uncertainty" that by observing anything, the act of observing can skew that which is being observed – given that the observer is interacting in some way with the subject of his or her observation. This is obvious when adults observe children at play or when a manager sits in a team meeting or when a focus group is being recorded.

The above are simple examples of the generation of intuitive thinking or the application of it in real life. I hope the reader will excuse me for digressing somewhat with these examples.

Regarding intuition then, we have often heard the warning about the importance of listening to our internal intuitive voice. "Ignore your internal whispering voice, at your peril" we are told.

Intuition has been described by some scholars as a faculty of our intelligence, as the mother of wisdom, and as the power of the hidden mind[180]. Others have discussed *strategic intuition* as the mental mechanism that produces "flashes" of insight, and have investigated the relationship between intuition, insight, and sleep. There are researchers that suggest that sleep may have the potential to foster intuition by re-shuffling associations; in other words, information may be recombining in our brains during REM sleep in a way that perhaps previously overlooked connections, so associations become more obvious to us[181]. This kind of "off-line" problem solving is an interesting area of study. Most people, including me, believe that intuition comes from learning and automatic recall; often resulting in what we sometimes call: connecting-the-dots.

I have often kept a notebook and a pen by my bed, and in the morning when I awake, I have fleeting recall of some insight that had occurred to me in the wee hours of the morning. Writing these thoughts down before one forgets, can be useful.

Why discuss intuition in a business book? One of the essentials in managing a business is the ability to balance creativity and spontaneity with linear thinking and rational analysis. Many fear the intuitive leader. We have been taught that evidence-based decisions are always better, saner, and safer. On the other hand, we are being bombarded with exponentially more inputs every business day than ever before. We know that that the velocity of incoming information and the increasing need for change and flexibility will continue to increase dramatically. My argument is that intuition is not profoundly different that analysis. It looks different, but I think it is the result of quickly connecting the dots. The dots are data points which we already possessed. When Archimedes intuited his principle, there are two facts to know about his intuition: 1) that he needed to be a scientist to have come up with his intuition; it was not random, and 2) he was correct.

SCIENCE AND STORY-TELLING

This approach should be understood at the philosophical level. Business, like life, is essentially a laboratory where we conduct a series of experiments. The *scientific method* involves a series of steps that are logical and usually result in reliable conclusions. See the accompanying diagram[182]. It all starts with making an observation including thoughts that occur to you. A legitimate observation could be that when we are ill, we often stay home. The interesting questions for a retailer to ask will relate to what sick people need at home to be happy, less miserable, and distracted from their discomfort. If I was a service organization innovator, I might ask myself about the kinds of services that sick people would need, enjoy, and find useful; services they would happily pay for. At that point in the cycle, it might be appropriate to formulate an hypothesis. Non-scientific people at this point might run with their hypothesis, understanding it in their hearts as the truth. Or they might run with it because of some limited anecdotal evidence (which is not evidence at all). Life and business failures are full of these impulsive or premature conclusions.

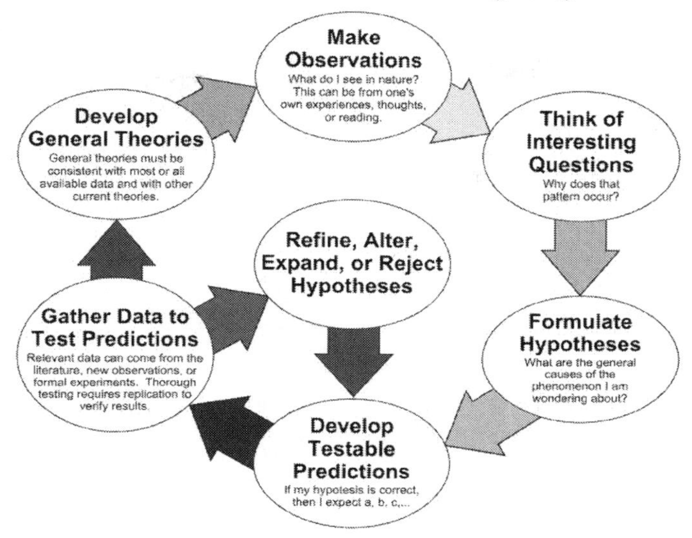

Some years ago when advising a California-based specialty food retailer, they were lamenting the low turnover (sales) of some of their more expensive produce. I stopped in at one of their stores, where they were displaying Jerusalem Artichokes. These are root vegetables, and despite their name, are native to North America and have nothing to do with Jerusalem. In fact, the early colonists from Europe sent the tubers back home to Europe where they have become popular. The French particular like this vegetable for making soup. But there, in that San Francisco store, those few Jerusalem Artichokes were languishing. I teased the chief merchandiser and told him that I could guess what their slowest moving items were without the benefit of their computer reports. He was surprised when I told him that these artichokes were probably not moving at all. He confirmed that and asked how I knew. Simple. People are not familiar with that product. And the Jerusalem Artichokes don't look all that amazing either. You see, the challenge is that not all people see life as an experiment, especially not as an experiment conducted in the dark. But give them some background and they will likely formulate an hypothesis as to whether they will enjoy or not enjoy the experience, in this case, the experience of a Jerusalem Artichoke. After the hypothesis comes the testing, and that would involve their purchase and the trial of the product. And how would we prompt the formulation of a consumer-generated hypothesis? The answer is fairly obvious: deliver information in an entertaining and compelling manner. We called that edutainment.

Information and education delivered in an entertainment way sounds like story-telling. Telling stories is effective in business communications. We are a curious species. Do not bore us and we will listen; or in this case, we will read. So, I suggested, that we give the consumer a really good excuse to experiment with this root vegetable. Let us romance it with the truth. Something generally along the following lines:

The Story of the Jerusalem Artichoke

Cultivated by native Americans. Puritans named the plant regarding the "New Jerusalem" they believed they were creating in the wilderness. Colonists brought it to Europe because it stored so well, was delicious and considered a super healthy food – but it slipped into oblivion here in America.

We are bringing it back!

How to eat it and why*. The Jerusalem artichoke was named 'best soup vegetable' at the 2002 Nice Festival. It is eaten raw as well. High in protein, low in carbs, a folk remedy for blood pressure, diabetes, and cancer.*

Try the delicious exotic Jerusalem artichoke. *Try our recipe for Jerusalem artichoke and sea scallops; white Rhone wine goes great with this vegetable, also available here!*

---

90 days later, sales had gone crazy. It didn't really take much except for the realization that people appreciate information, education, ideas and suggestions; and they will respond. And should this retail chain have invested in signage to convey the story? Of course not, not for all stores, but perhaps for one or two. The experiment should be small and controlled and when and if the hypothesis is measured and proven, then it can be rolled out. Note to reader: this of course seems to be so obvious but somehow we often permit ourselves to neglect the obvious. Success lies in the combination of innovative thinking and disciplined execution.

Therefore, intuition IS the hypothesis. In other words, intuition may be the result of a creative output, that within the scientific context, is nothing less than an hypothesis. What we then do with hypotheses is to test them. There is no conflict between creative output and rigorous analyses. They are both part of the same process, one simply follows the other.

UNDERSTAND RETAIL DESIGN AS A UNIVERSALLY APPLIED SET OF PRINCIPLES

Whether you have product, package, or a virtual or physical store, you should be mindful about what the business is trying to achieve. It is about communicating, and through the communications, bonding with the customer. In fact, the communications are not limited to the customer but to all stakeholders of the business, including suppliers, employees, investors, the media, and the public.

We often think of a "store" in terms of a retail shopping destination. But think of a bank or its cash machine (a mini store), a hotel, amusement park, museum, or a corporate head office; or for that matter - an entire country. These are all "stores" in a sense. They are selling things, products, services, entertainment, knowledge, a frame of mind or attitude, aka: their brand. They all fight for your attention and your respect. They all project touchpoints between the organization and those people and other organizations that interact with your business in some way; have an interest in your business in some way. Every time a stakeholder comes into contact with your organization for any reason, this represents an event whereby your brand will either be enhanced (will gain value/equity) or it will be diminished (lose value, and relinquish equity).

Think what happens when you purchase a $2000 laptop or a $50,000 automobile – and 90 days later you call technical support and are put on hold for 15 minutes or are rebuffed by a snooty operator, or you are placed in a conversation with a company representative (even if it's in reality a third-party call center) – who has a challenging time understanding your language. Or you may be directed to a voice recognition system whose menu does not include the selection you need.

In terms of the classical definition of a store, I have used a simple checklist and report card to evaluate just how well the "store" represents and delivers some of the important attributes to be successful. Without delving too deeply into the details surrounding effective store design, I'll simply point out that all of these categories to be evaluated (Customer, Overall Design, Operations, Wow) are important, are valid for all "places", and are somewhat interdependent. The WOW factor is both the least well-understood and the simplest to understand.

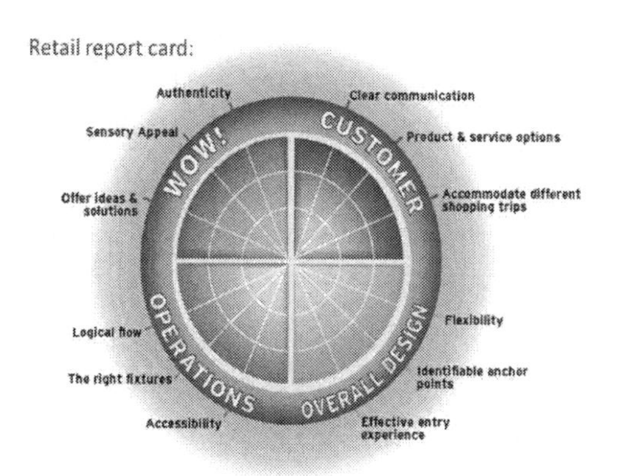

The bottom line is this: after all is said and done, after the design and its designers have shown that it has addressed all of the design imperatives, after the design brief has been (technically) satisfied; in other words, after all the technical, objective, factual information is in, and you are standing in front of a final design for the prototype (that you are about to approve) – then one word should form in your mind, and on your tongue, to the point that no matter how much you try to resist getting emotional about it, you cannot help but shout out: WOW !!!

I AM NOT JOKING ABOUT THIS…

You see, this is the problem. The company may have engaged the most famous global retail designers. Often this is to protect one's ass (language apology). If the project screws up, management can always say: *look, we hired the best, not our fault.* Second, hiring the "best" (however one defines that term) sometimes allows management to permit itself to abdicate from judging. We are unsure if this design is good, good enough, great, etc. Designers tell us, quite rightly, that we are all amateur frustrated designers. After all, any of us who has renovated a kitchen considers ourselves designers. The real "pros" tell us not to meddle. There is science involved. And we, the management, are shown the multiple focus-group inputs that we have paid $5,000 to $20,000 a pop for. We are not told that these folks who attend and participate in these sessions do so regularly for the $100 and a dry sandwich.

Teich Theory: You don't get a heck of a lot of truth for $100 and a dry sandwich.

And so, we big boys and girls can get a bit intimidated and we see the design, and no ***wow*** forms in our hearts and throats and we do what? Well, you know…we do nothing. Sad thing though – if you cannot feel the *wow*, your customers probably won't either. So, trust your instincts, send it back, demand more convincing verification of their predicted successes. Look at options.

One last clarifying comment about retail design. The "wow" that you are looking for should be about the solution that delivers the goal. It's easy to be distracted. You can design the most beautiful store exterior and carry nothing compelling inside of it. Here's an example. In the late 1990s, the Royal Ontario Museum (ROM) was having a very hard time raising funds for a major expansion and renovation. Their goal was to break through to 1 million in annual visitor attendance. They asked me to assess the possibilities and suggest a strategy for growth[183]. My recommendation was to revolutionize the visitor experience. I was not a proponent of an expensive, creative, exterior, architectural design. I was more interested in what the visitor would find on the inside. I argued that story-telling combined with high-technology to deliver real, hands-on, experiences that appeal to all the senses – would likely achieve the goal. I argued that forcing people to read those 5x7 informational cards under a glass display was work; no visitor wants to come to the museum to work. The "WOW" should be on the inside

Just as an example from the ROM - in the back bug-rooms of the ROM, the curators use flesh-eating scavenger beetles to strip the flesh off skeletons. I thought that kids would love to see how natural history specimens were created. Put a viewing window in to that room! Looking at a window display that depicts – behind glass – the city of London in the dark ages of the 1200s, was not experiential. I suggested walking through that display of a market street and experiencing the sounds, and yes, the smells of those days. My bias is not to focus as much on grandiose

public architectural spaces at the expense of ignoring the experience. My bias was the richness of the content - on the inside. However, the human ego is what it is, and what I term, the "edifice complex" (with apologies to Dr. Freud) resulted in the ROM engaging signature architects to create a very interesting structure at a cost of about $300 M. To be sure, it's a fantastic design and people take selfies next to the overhanging glass slopes, but attendance still fails to reach the million-visitor number.

ROM versus IKEA

I know that it's comparing apples and orange, but just for fun - there are 392 IKEA stores worldwide with an annual customer count of 783 million visitors, or an average of about two million visitors per year per store, compared to less than a million visitors per year to the ROM.

IKEA builds a generic steel box structure and brands it in blue and yellow. Period. The treasure hunt is on the inside. Can you imagine what the ROM could have achieved by spending $300 million on developing and bringing-to-life the stories about our world, *inside* the museum? One of the most basic business principles discussed in this book is the imperative to be defined and driven by one's customers. Though most people understand the principle, many become distracted when applying it to real decisions and investments. This may be one of those times.

CHAPTER 14 TAKE-AWAYS INFORMATION, INNOVATION, INTUITION	
1	Collaboration is the most powerful word in business English. It precedes everything worthwhile.
2	Generate and collect counter-intuitive truths; these can set you apart competitively.
3	When presented with data, always ask yourself if you can maximize its value by pushing it up through the hierarchy of information, knowledge, wisdom, and ultimately - insight.
4	Insist that all of the multiple views (reports) of your business are derived from one, single, source of data/facts.
5	Embrace uncertainty in business and in life. This is part of the physics of business.
6	Like all humans, your customers will respond to your messages - told as educational and entertaining stories.
7	Surveys do not always deliver as much value as you think. People can tell you with confidence what they did but not about what they will do.
8	Look for the "wow" in all ideas but don't work too hard at it. If it doesn't jump up and hit you over the head, it's probably not there.
9	In business, as in life, following your ego will probably not get you anywhere worthwhile.

CHAPTER 15
PARTNERSHIPS

"We're all working together: that's the secret" – Sam Walton

The Teich theory of relationships: there are only two kinds of relationships, the one that suck energy out of you, and the one that give you energy. Period.

Partnerships should first and foremost feel right, positive, and energizing. The rationale for most business partnerships involve sharing risk, sharing fixed costs, leveraging complementary strengths including knowhow, technology, talent, facilities, co-branding in the target markets, expanding/sharing customers for revenue lift, and suppliers to lower the cost of materials; and of course, pushing common competitor threats aside by the sheer size of the larger combined entity or partnership.

Those are some of the obvious reasons why two companies of any size throw in together or when one acquires another. People have different personalities and corporations also have different personalities or cultures. Failure to take full advantage of partnerships results when there is a clash of cultures. Despite all the due diligence and good intentions, and despite the congenial meetings between senior managements – the rank and file of each company that merged/partnered – are often out of synch with each other. This is tough to remedy. To avoid these issues, many such partnerships in fact do not push for organizational structural changes at all, and the acquired divisions retain much of their identity, culture, and operations. That's ok, but it leaves a lot of opportunity on the table.

There are distinctions to be made between mergers which often involve organizational restructuring, and between acquisitions which often do not merge. In my experience, both models are usually driven by the financial guys looking at theoretical predictions for lifts in shareowner value, and not being overly concerned with the myriad of organizational issues that are generated. Approximately two thirds of big mergers will disappoint on their own terms, which means they will lose value on the stock market[184].

I subscribe to the theory that market forces are driven mostly by only two factors: Fear and Greed. I like this formula because it is simple, and in pursuing truth, the simplest formula is usually the real formula. In support of this worldview, I like what Investopedia had to say:

"A merger may often have more to do with glory-seeking than business strategy. The executive ego, which is boosted by buying the competition, is a major force in M&A, especially when combined with the influences from the bankers, lawyers and other

assorted advisers who can earn big fees from clients engaged in mergers. Most CEOs get to where they are because they want to be the biggest and the best, and many top executives get a big bonus for merger deals, no matter what happens to the share price later. On the other side of the coin, mergers can be driven by generalized fear. Globalization, the arrival of new technological developments or a fast-changing economic landscape that makes the outlook uncertain are all factors that can create a strong incentive for defensive mergers. Sometimes the management team feels they have no choice and must acquire a rival before being acquired. The idea is that only big players will survive a more competitive world.[185]"

After the dust settles, companies tend to focus on cutting costs as they may be motivated to immediately demonstrate the value of synergies. Increases in revenues and margins often do not materialize. McKinsey has found that merging companies often focus on integration activities (always more complex that predicted), and cost-control and reduction, such that day-to-day operations are neglected. We all know where customers go when they see this happen. They go away. The McKinsey Study[186] determined that the loss of revenue momentum is one reason so many mergers fail to create value for shareholders.

Partnerships between very small proprietorships and other owner-operated entities are a whole different kettle of fish. They cannot pretend that they are not married. They must learn to live together. If there was a very valid reason to partner in the first place, and they went through the exercise of predicting the most troubling possible scenarios before they signed the deal, and worked out in advance what they would do in those potential future circumstances, and they can create a better combined strategy than any one of their former individual strategies – then it all may work out. Most partnerships fail to realize their potential and either break up, or simply hobble on sub-optimizing and not breaking away because they cannot afford the cost of the funeral.

Beware of partnerships. Some are great. Many are an illusion beforehand and a nightmare thereafter. Negative consequences are always unintended. Time for one of my stories…

This is one from the "old country", a story set on the platform of a train station in rural Eastern Europe of the 1800's. There was a middle-aged man standing in front and there was a young man in his early twenties, standing behind him. Both were waiting for the Friday afternoon train that travels to a small town a couple of hours away. The young man spoke to the middle-aged gentleman in front and said: "excuse me sir, do you have the time?" The gentleman did not respond. A few minutes later, the young man asked again: "sir, excuse me, do you have the time?" Again the gentleman did not answer. Irritated now at the slight, the younger man steamed, waited, and then unable to contain himself - he tapped gently on the gentleman's back and asked again. Seeing that he could not avoid the question and encounter any longer, the middle-aged gentleman turned to face the young man, took out his pocket watch, and curtly said: "it is 3:30 PM" and then quickly turned his back on him again. Well, the question was indeed answered but the young man was annoyed and felt offended. He circled around to face the gentleman and said: "look, excuse me one last time, but I think you have been discourteous to me. I asked a simple question and twice you ignored me. When I tapped you on the shoulder you felt you then had to respond, but you did so curtly, even rudely, and turned your back on me again without as much as a smile! We don't know each other, I have never wronged you, so what's going on?"

The older man sighed and shrugged and then spoke: "look, young fellow, you are right, I don't know you, but I know everyone in my village, and therefore you are a stranger there. What would have happened if I told you the time and allowed myself to engage in conversation with you? We would talk, and when the train came, we would have gone up together and likely we would have sat together. And over the next couple of hours we would have gotten to know each other a little, and because you are a stranger in town, I would have probably felt obliged to invite you to my home for the Sabbath. Now I have a beautiful daughter of marriageable age and you are a nice looking young man. You would have fallen in love with my daughter and she with you. And frankly, young fellow – ***I do not want as a son-in-law, someone who doesn't even own a watch!!!"***

Typical of these old Jewish anecdotes, there is always a moral, a wise message embedded in them. The story is a strong caution about starting something, even innocently and with all good intentions – that can lead to undesirable consequences. So, prudent people build fences to protect against these potential negative consequences. Often, in business as in our personal lives, we take small actions without fully considering the potential possible ramifications and implications of our actions. Sometimes for example, we might be tempted to associate with businesses or brands that have negative associations. The old adage comes to mind: *if you lay down next to a dog, you get fleas.*

So, I would advise you to choose your associates and your associations most carefully. Do the necessary due diligence to avoid being eventually painted by the same brush that has painted them or that they could, in the future, be painted with. It takes 10 years to build a brand and 10 seconds to lose it all.

Risk and all threats are to be managed whether as a result of alliances or not, so a few words on risk management. The Model below simply illustrates the conservative mindset in managing risk both for people as well as for organizations.

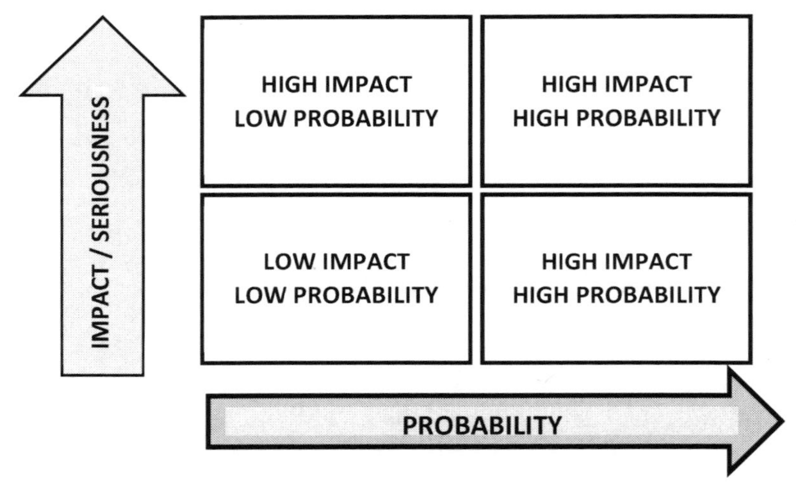

Simply stated, whether the probability of a risk materializing is low or high, doesn't matter all that much – providing that the impact or level of seriousness arising from the event – is not high. Accordingly, one doesn't have to manage significant risk avoidance strategies for those categories of risk. Conversely, even if the probability of a negative event is low, if the seriousness of the impact is high, one must manage that risk and prevent it from occurring. This simple logic is harder to mange than one may think. Some years ago, Imperial Oil's refinery in Sarnia, Ontario, Canada was very significantly damaged and put out of commission because a squirrel jumped on high-voltage lines, in the rain, and for a moment, managed unbelievably to create a conductive bridge between its front legs which were touching one set of wires and its hind legs which were touching a second set of high-voltage lines. The result was a spectacular fire. The probability of that almost-impossible event was extremely low, but the level of seriously was very high, dangerous to human life, and astronomically costly.

CHAPTER 15 TAKE-AWAYS **PARTNERSHIPS**	
1	There are only two kinds of relationships: the relationships that suck energy out of you and the ones that give you energy.
2	Naturally good partnerships usually feel right from the get go. Almost no one regrets walking away too early from something that felt wrong.
3	Before partnering, imagine even the most unlikely scenarios of potential conflict, and work out and agree (on paper) in advance how these would be managed by the partners.
4	Mergers and acquisitions are often driven by false or inappropriate motives and many fail as a result.
5	Manage risks as if the nearly impossible will befall your organization tomorrow morning. That morning will come sooner or later.

CHAPTER 16
NGOs and CHARITIES

"The smallest act of kindness is worth more than the grandest intention"
– Oscar Wilde

A PERSONAL INVITATION

My purpose in writing a bit about these forms of organization is two-fold. First, they are interesting and are often managed differently than "for profit" businesses. Second, at my stage in life, the balance that I have achieved is to spend half my time as a volunteer. It can be personally gratifying to "pay back" in these ways, and to put it mildly, many of these organizations are in need of the competencies that one has acquired during a professional career in business, either as an operator or as a consultant, or (as in my case) both. Accordingly, please take this chapter as an encouragement to get involved.

Employee of NGOs including their senior management, are a special breed. Most are extremely dedicated to the cause, which is noble. Many are challenged to perform in extraordinary ways, and most of these organizations struggle. Hate to say it but, there are often deficits in competence as well. But what is common to all of them is that the remuneration is hardly competitive and as a result these organizations are almost always constrained, operate sub-optimally, are heavy on governance and protocol, and light on innovation and genius. Many are in great need of a pool of volunteers that could bring to the table: world class strategy, decision-making, and operational and executional excellence. Many NGOs do not take full advantage of this potential resource; and many potential volunteers do not appreciate the innate value that they can offer.

Models vary, and on the revenue generation side ("funds development"), some organizations focus on high value donors, some on a high-volume of small donations, some on estates ("Planned Giving"), others on corporate and community partnerships, gifts-in-kind, and still others on Grants and bequests - both private and governmental. The competition is fierce. Except for the few larger and more sophisticated charities, most still struggle to develop a compelling business case that can deliver an understandable Social Return on Investment (SROI) and a measurable set of outcomes and impacts that are valued by objective investors (donors). As a result, they are destined to struggle with nickels and dimes, struggle to meet budgets (which are almost always optimistic), and always start a new fiscal year with no concrete idea on how they are going to "make their year". A strategy which can guarantee and predict a recurring revenue stream is often lacking and that is what often differentiates an NGO from a "for profit" business.

I have written throughout this book about the danger of relying on "hope" in business. Yet in my experience, it is hope that drives many NGOs. That is not entirely surprising given that the causes that they espouse are most often inherently causes that relate to hope; aka: poverty alleviation, food-water-health, addiction prevention and management, tolerance between peoples, youth at risk, violence in society, opportunities for disadvantaged peoples, education, others.

So, for "hope" to creep into and diffuse into the management of these organizations is not puzzling. After all, NGOs deal with many emotionally charged issues and "hope" is a word they often use to trigger sympathy about the cause and through that sympathy – donations. Yet, when it creeps into an organization's mode of managing, and replaces cold, objective diagnosis and planning - hope in that context is not productive. For example, an NGO staffer might call a donor-candidate a "prospect" (a source of expected revenue from a potential donor) even though there has been minimal or only initial contact with that person. A realistic business person would never characterize such a contact as a "prospect" but perhaps just a "suspect"; and mostly not even that. Sounds like a bit of a joke, but I am serious. I call a "suspect" a data point in a large reservoir of opportunity that requires a plan for cultivation. The hoped-for revenue from such a low-potential "suspect" should never translate to a number on a revenue projection on a budget line. Notice my realistic approach? It is often absent in most NGOs. The result of over relying on hope, is almost always disappointment.

These are all manifestations of the philosophical reliance on "hope". The selection of programs within these NGOs and other non-profit organizations can also be biased, based on the way the organization is structured and how each program manager seeks to maintain and grow "their" program, ergo: their empire. This happens in large for-profit organizations also but in those environments, there is likely a more intelligent, objective, critical, and professionally prepared strategic plan that is shared and stewarded to. And one cannot expect a $100,000/year NGO CEO to work at the same level of sophistication and with the same level of expert support as a $5 million/year Fortune 1000 corporation. There are exceptions.

Decision-making in small and medium sized NGOs is an area needing strengthening and one of the many useful contributions that professional business managers can deliver when they volunteer for boards and/or committees.

In my role in a number of such organizations, I try to keep it very simple (to start). The worst thing is to set up an organization to fail - by expecting complexity beyond their internal competences. There is also skepticism that sometimes arises with the introduction of anything new. I have found that a very simple decision methodology (first developed by Kepner-Tregoe) is the ideal first tool to help deliver rational thinking among even junior NGO staff. It goes something like as follows.

MECHANICS OF PRIORITIZING

First, we must develop a short list of criteria that must be satisfied in order for the organization to even consider a particular program of work. These are termed "musts" and there is no need to rank or weigh these "musts" since all must equally be satisfied. Examples of a short-list of "musts" might be:

1. The program must be legal and perceived to be legal.

2. The program must be consistent with the organization's vision and if it is not, then one of them must be revised. This would not normally be the vision and mission.

3. The program must not diminish the brand, image, and reputation of the organization.

Then comes the more challenging section, the section of "wants". Here, the organization develops a list of "wants" and desires; in effect, a listing of criteria with which to judge the appropriateness of working at a particular program, whether the program is proposed internally, or from the outside. Outside proposals may arise when a major potential donor comes forward with an offer to fund only a certain program and the NGO must decide whether that program fits their skills and their mission. Often, the seductive power of the offer-of-funds carries a bigger attraction than it should. And like all "businesses", we are good at adding on stuff but terrible at discarding stuff. So, instead of thinking: what does this new program replace, we often just add it, spread the organizational resources too thin, introduce too many projects and programs to focus on, and then risk moving to a mediocre implementation. But I digress, slightly; back to Kepner-Tregoe (KT).

Below is a simple illustration of a partial listing of criteria including questions such as: how fundable is this program? If in fact a specific donor is proposing to fund this program totally, then column B will be scored a "10". In other words, column A is ranked by the team without having any particular program in mind; it is program independent. A program may be a *tough* to get funded, but can be argued that in other ways, it is very important. *Tough* doesn't mean it's impossible to get funded, it means it's tough, requiring a lot more work, and perhaps more use of political capital. So, if being fundable is important, let's say that the team assigns an 8 to column A for "fundable". Now a proposal comes in with the donor committing to fund a program that happens to be of personal interest to that donor. Perhaps the donor is a wealthy Canadian of Syrian descent and wishes to have the NGO develop a program to assist new Syrian refugees into Canada. In that scenario, column B must answer the question: how close does this proposed program come to satisfying the specific criterion of being fundable. Here, the score is 10. It might be 5 if there was no source of funds but the media coverage[187] was heavy and potentially helpful in raising awareness of the need. It may be zero or 1, if there was no awareness because media attention had shifted, or the crisis had generally passed its most dramatic stages. And so, in the table below, the weighted score would be 80.

	A Ranking	**B** Project or Idea #1	Project or Idea #1 Score
"WANTS" Criteria or Filters:	How Important? Rank 1-10	How close does this project come to satisfy this criterion? Rank 1-10	**Weighted Score A X B**
-Fundable	8	10	**80**
-Marketable			
-ROI > 40%			
-Scalable			
-Replicatable			
-Technical feasibility			
-Internal competence			
-Complex alliances req'd			
-Etc.			
TOTALS	N/A	N/A	**Total weighted score for this Program**

Likewise, the exercise continues with evaluating the program against an objectively developed, pre-determined list of ranked criteria, ranked independent of any program. With multiple columns, you can evaluate and compare total weighted scores for a number of competing programs under consideration. This is not a state of art decision-making mechanism, but it is a good start, a simple model that untrained folks can easily understand. It requires no advanced statistical analysis, it is based on a series of assumptions that must be defensible but at the same time can be taught and executed in a 3-hour session. The benefit is that this can begin a path of rational analysis for a small to medium size NGO. It promotes thinking and debate. And the list of criteria assists in reminding decision-makers about what is important.

Sometimes, in the enthusiasm of the moment, important considerations are forgotten or diminished. You may have bought a house only to discover that a 3 AM train comes barrelling through the neighborhood 500 meters away every morning. Had you included that criterion on a KT list, you might have asked before you signed the deal. You may have signed the deal anyways but at least you would have done so with eyes wide open and because there were other, overwhelmingly positive, redeeming qualities to the deal. Or the information would have armed you with knowledge for a counter strategy to diminish the deleterious effects; aka: have the renovation contractor include sound insulation into his quote or pay less for the property.

I have argued about SROI[188], and perhaps it's appropriate to note that there is a lack of consistency in this area when it comes to "charitable" programs/activities in the domestic area versus in the international area. Whether right or wrong, whether an ethical-philosophical question or not – consider that if a person is lost during an avalanche in the Rocky Mountains in western Canada, our search and rescue forces will spend millions of dollars trying to find and rescue that one person. One could coldly argue that the social return on investment for such a program is low, too low. After all, those same millions of dollars employed in sub-Saharan Africa could literally save thousands of lives[189]. Should we call off a search for one Canadian and rationalize that instead, Canada might save several thousand African children – with that same amount of money? Few people would argue this. Similarly, Canadian charities focusing on domestic issues of poverty, homelessness, and addiction – would likely have an advantage with some target donor groups (including government). This does not mean that a high degree of analysis is not needed to deliver a business case. It means that many Canadians will likely have a "softer" spot for issues that plague "our own". Charities, take note. What keeps Canadian charities from gaining traction in their markets is that most fail to vigorously pursue authority and earn recognition for expertise. They will always be able to raise (some) funds from a small, loyal group of friends and business networks of their board directors, and from annual galas and events. But there is a ceiling to these kinds of funds development efforts. As a result, they struggle and often fail to attract the best, and often decline with time/entropy, and with the growing competitiveness for share-of-wallet.

The solution lay in fundamental initiatives that are hardly ever done well. The challenge is how to become thought leaders in your field, how to be recognized authorities and experts in the programs that you have adopted. How to be the "go-to" organization for the programs you operate. This is a business question that applies to all business formats that must be addressed in all organizations that wish to be successful, wish to attract the best staff, wish to attract the donors, investors, or customers, and wish to enjoy a recurring revenue model year after year.

Here are a few examples of what they should be doing; again, for illustration purposes and just a partial list:

1. Create a second board, namely a board of advisors of the "who's who" of content experts in the program category that the organization is working on.

2. Become content experts, not just process experts (a common theme that I've espoused throughout.)

3. Write articles and publish every month in one of a variety of appropriate, well-regarded professional journals and trade publications

4. Participate in speaking engagements and conferences.

5. The goal is to grow the organizational reputation to where the government, for example, will use your organization as a source of expertise and advice when formulating policy[190].

6. Align with and or commission studies that measure the economic impact and social impact of the work that you are doing.

With regard to that last point, an example is probably best. Let us assume that your organization sets out to organize multi-ethnic groups of teenagers in high schools to discuss and develop peer programs to increase tolerance, understanding, and harmony among people of different backgrounds - by seeking to focus on similarities rather than on differences and to ultimately pursue understanding and build bridges.

This is a lofty goal but at the same time, a soft goal. It is difficult to measure. It's not an objective that readily lends itself to objective measurement and as a result, the benefits of the program are open ended. You do not really know if and when you reach the objective. In other words, you cannot manage what you cannot measure.

A possible approach and strategy that delivers a more objective, compelling, and measurable goal is to re-articulate the problem in terms of a better-understood, related goal. The problem of lack of tolerance in schools leads to bullying. The problem can be expressed as one of bullying, and not of the root cause of bullying. Why? Because bullying is a manifestation of intolerance and can be measured. It is real. There are costs that are identifiable and measurable, when bullying is not managed.

We can measure the societal costs of bullying. Aside from human misery, which is always the humanistic-inspired goal, there are real, measurable economic impacts associated with, for example:

1. Welfare and social assistance costs - school absenteeism and drop out rate - leading to unemployment and social-net costs, and even loss of future employment incomes that do not attract/generate income tax inputs into the economy.

2. Health costs - Depression and other mental and emotional conditions, leading to medical support, social-net costs, prescription drugs, hospitalization, addiction treatment, suicide.

3. Judicial system costs - At risk, anti-social behaviours by bullies themselves and their victims, leading to costs of the judicial system, including costs of incarceration.

In other words, it is possible to build a fairly convincing business case for programs that your experts can throw the weight of their authority behind. The investment in your organization's program must be seen as the best use of funds with an expected social return on investment that can be measured, not only in terms of the alleviation of human misery, but in terms of dollars. Indeed, if compelling enough, government agencies may see your organization as being more competent than themselves and ideally may assign to you, the program theory and execution that they themselves might have attempted themselves with lesser effectiveness.

A business case is essential but not sufficient in order to nail down support. What is required is the same principle required of all businesses: the market demand must firmly be established. In the case of the above example, what is needed is to oversubscribe the high schools involved as partners to such a program, to have them be part of a waiting list, so to speak, and then, armed with a verifiable list of "clients" demanding service and support – approach donors, institutions, corporations, governments, boards of education – and demonstrate the extent of the unfilled demand for the specific program that your organization is "selling".

As in any competitive business, inventiveness in marketing is key, and NGOs and charities are often lacking of this quality. Too many rely on old, tired, traditional methods of fund raising. Donors are being approached all the time and there is fatigue. Corporate partnerships are normally not partnerships but a kind of begging by the NGO, and a kind of reluctant giving by corporations. There is so much competition that the trend over the last several years has been that even large corporations have shifted from large donations to a few favourite charities, to small donations to many charities. But there is little return on their investment in terms of recognition that is translatable to sales and brand equity. The bragging rights have become meager.

THE NEED FOR CREATIVITY IN NGOs

Now let us consider an example of inventiveness of a quality typical of the output of a professional business team trying to solve a problem or capture an opportunity in the world of for-profit business. The conversation around the table might go like this:

FedEx and UPS are large companies, and arguably they are generous with their charitable giving. They see it as their corporate social responsibility, but most of their donations will negatively impact their bottom line. How do we convince them to give more? Well, they already give a lot. And what's in it for them? Partnerships, to be sustainable should be based on mutual, enlightened, self-interest.

Given that a small percentage of a very big number is still a very big number, what big numbers can we leverage in the case of FedEx and UPS? UPS ships an average of 19.1 million packages every day[191] and FedEx ships an average of 12 million packages everyday[192]. Together, they handle 31 million parcels a day or 11,315,000,000 packages a year. That's a big number.

If I, as a customer, were spending $15 to send earphones to my son at College, would I mind if FedEx told me that were going to charge me $15.05 with the extra 5 cents going to save children in sub-Sahara Africa? I wouldn't have a problem with that. If my son received the package and printed on it was a FedEx "thank-you" for the donation, that might feel good. He got his luxury earphones and African children benefited. Nice.

If I were a retailer shipping a book valued at $28 to a customer and the FedEx charge was $6.05 instead of $6.00, would I mind? Probably not. If I did, could I charge the customer a charity surcharge and recover my 5 cents. Probably yes.

If you could convince these two companies to add 5 cents to their asking price for each package, the funds collected from that 5-cent charity surcharge would total about $566 million dollars USD.

Today, FedEx's worldwide charitable donations are $46 million (that includes gifts-in-kind; not real cash). UPS reports that its charitable giving in 2016 totalled $116 million USD[193] (they include in that figure, $57 million in *employee* donations to United way; not quite kosher, but ok.)

But the bottom line is that these two companies donate or cause to be donated a total of (46+116) $162 million USD. With my model that wouldn't cost them anything, they could donate $566 million USD.

In fact, they probably would not withdraw from their charitable giving; they would likely simply add the new program and enjoy the reputational value of enabling charitable giving by millions of their customers.

Let's summarize:

	FedEx $M USD	UPS $M USD	TOTAL $M USD
Traditional giving	46	116	$162
Potential: Non-traditional giving	219	347	$566
Advantage of new idea	173	231	**$404 Million**
Combined program	265	463	**$728 Million**

These are enormous numbers. We have just proposed the possibility of an additional $404 million to charity. Imagine a 10-cent charity surcharge: $808 million. Can you imagine these two companies announcing that they will raise one billion dollars a year to eradicate a major disease from the planet? What lift in brand value would arise from that plan? The bottom line is this: whether for-profit or not-for-profit, all business should operate with the same discipline, smarts, and inventiveness - to generate profits. The only difference is that the profits in charities are reinvested in programs and not distributed to owners.

FOCUS ON THE BIG NUMBERS

We sometimes hear of multi-million dollar donations to non-for-profit entities, like museums, art galleries, and universities. Often, after years of struggling with funds development, these one-time events enable major program expansion and capital investment. Normally, these kinds of donations do not come as s surprise but had been cultivated over a long period. When an individual event does come as a surprise, it is usually still the result of a concerted effort by the NGO to attract large contributions. Yet, there are many NGOs who have not chosen to focus on the area of *planned giving*. Many dream of a $500 a year donor bequeathing their $1 million-dollar home to the NGO in their will. Dreams and hope will not deliver. The NGO normally does not cultivate a network of lawyers, trustees, bank managers, investment advisors, elderly care facility managers, real estate agents - to build a pool of influencers that come into contact with potential donors in this category. There are a large number of strategies, beyond the scope of this book, such as donor-funded insurance premiums with the NGO named as beneficiary. There are many innovative marketing strategies, disciplines, and techniques that seasoned business people can offer to NGOs.

CHAPTER 16 TAKE-AWAYS **NGOs AND CHARITIES**	
1	If you have managed an organization well, you have a valuable contribution to make as a volunteer resource to a not-for-profit organization working on a noble cause. Consider volunteering and enjoy the fulfilment.
2	Most NGOs aren't good at measuring ROI. Increasingly, donors are more sophisticated and have an investor mind-set. They must be presented with a cogent business case and a proven, measurable ROI.
3	NGOs rely too much on "hope" in managing their business. Hope is not a strategy.
4	Decision-making logic, including the science and art of prioritization doesn't have to be complicated; but it has to be used. It enables focus and generates conversations that can lead to opportunity.
5	Building authority is surprisingly easy. You can (almost) schedule its attainment with a calendar of fairly routine tasks.
6	Great fund-raising (funds development) strategies do not include "begging" for donations. The deepest opportunities are corporate partnerships that leverage the vast stakeholder networks of corporations.

CHAPTER 17
THE FUTURE

"The future ain't what it used to be"
- Gary Goshgarian

Many people prognosticate about the future. It's fun and it's sexy. And it's mostly obvious or obviously wrong. The thing is, only the correct predictions get remembered years later mostly because the predictors are rendered famous, a circularity of logic. The BusinessInsider.com lists a few good ones: the 1660's prediction for organ transplants, the 1783 prediction that the U.S. population will reach 300 million by 1983, the 1840 prediction about the Cold War[194], the 1865 prediction by Jules Verne about the Apollo landing, the 1909 Tesla prediction of wireless devices, H G Wells' prediction in 1914 of the Atomic bomb, and the 1987 prediction by Robert Ebert[195] that there would be video-on-demand, like Netflix.

Futurists also tend to divide themselves into glass-half-full and glass-half-empty categories. I am the first one to assert that there is a useful role for both optimists and pessimists in our world. After all, it must have been an optimist who invented the airplane and surely a pessimist invented the parachute!

There is a slew of dark predictions that were put out by Gizmodo.com[196]. These included the return of authoritarian regimes on earth, the demise of privacy, the dominance and possible future revolt of robots, extinction-level climate change, the end of the antibiotic era, the loss of all satellites due to a massive solar storm, the flooding of coastal cities by rising ocean levels, and no chance of contacts with aliens. Each of these dark scenarios can be triggers to thinking about business opportunities.

There are also fairly bright and happy futures being predicted[197] along a now-to-year-2050 timeline. These include texting by thinking, organ generation in stem cell factories and by 3D printing, cures for all manner of diseases including heart disease and cancers, holographic technology replacing the need for international business travel, super-high-speed trains everywhere connecting rural and urban areas, a million drones patrolling all major cities, human colonies on Mars, space hotels, male birth control pills, wireless electricity, fusion reactors generating almost free energy everywhere, nanotech clothing that never needs cleaning, and the elimination of road and air accidents.

It's really quite easy to predict stuff. Most of us are amateur futurists. The best are probably science fiction writers like Gene Roddenberry, the creator of Star Trek. And there is a 50-50 chance that they are nearly correct. In my early role as head of financial reporting at a Fortune 10 Canadian corporation, I was the one who reported the earnings and the analyses of company-wide performance to the executive committee and to the board of directors every quarter. After those presentations, I then released the information to the press. I was an insider and the information was confidential. In fact, I was the very first person in the corporation of about 8,000 employees who had the whole financial picture every quarter. And every quarter, I would guess if the company's share price would go up or down. I was correct 50% of the time.

There are of course some very obvious trends, not fads – that most people extrapolate and most businesses prepare for. We see the explosion of web-based applications, collaborations, and services. These will not go away. They serve as a source of business inspiration and innovation every day. Not rocket science.

We see the population grow but not the growth of new land and we all know that urban single-family homes will continue to give way to smaller units for reasons of economy as well as due to the deterioration of the "institution of marriage", the family unit, and the tendency toward smaller families. This is already an observable fact and there is no obvious reason that the trajectory will change.

We see the explosion of access to electronic media, the growth of user-generated media including real-time, online streaming information and there is no evidence that the increasing velocity of this change will abate.

We see the developing, emerging nations like India, Brazil, Philippines, China, and others – taking a much more dominant role in world trade and consumption both as exporters (including cheaper, high technology exports) and as a new rapidly growing consumer base as their middle-class numbers explode. This suggests that the risks of investing in these continually emerging economies, grow smaller, and the investments more attractive.

We see a true global community having become a reality and we shall see peoples and systems increasingly becoming more effective in channelling capital to the right groups of start-up ventures anywhere in the world, either facilitated by web-applications, like crowdfunding, or through more traditional (concentrated) groups of investors. We shall continue to see larger companies spin-off incubators, realizing that their size and scale and culture cannot provide the agility required for early-stage innovation.

These observations are all obvious. We would come up with all of them in 30 minutes over a sandwich. We are exposed to these truisms all the time. Some businesses respond to these with their own strategies; others have not and will not.

Most of us have a reasonably good idea what to counsel our kids, if they would listen. As for growth careers, we know that data analytics will begin to deal with the enormous volumes of data inputs and sensors measuring and observing everything, everywhere.

We can predict with certainty that scientific research and engineering will continue to grow, requiring multi-disciplines to provoke innovation from science and technology.

With respect to the soft arts, and in an increasingly fast and confusing world, a world of violence and political confusion, a world of augmented reality, a world where 63% of households include online gamers spending 6.5 hours a week on average playing with others[198] [199] - we shall need more and more meaningful recreational experiences, emotional handholding, therapy and counselling, and safe places, both literally and metaphorically.

And the organizations that we spawn or work for will increasingly require talent and leadership that thrive on uncertainty and on speed and agility. We will not look back on huge bricks and mortar 9-5 edifices to business. Many of those dinosaurs will give way to virtual companies with structures that model partnerships we sometimes call internal-external: Airbnb and Uber come to mind.

In addition to internal-external, we shall also see more of inside-out innovation, the trend where more and more organizations have forsaken the traditional axiom of building on their core strengths to conquer new markets[200]. Instead, they seek collaboration and open innovation.

Lastly, we see quantum innovation[201], a neat term that basically means super ambitious goals, vision goals, and true stretch targets that represents a leap into a new dimension of scale; differences in orders of magnitude.

When Google expresses its will to organize the world's knowledge, this is quantum innovation.

When Tesla announced in 2003 that its vision is to create the most compelling car company of the 21st century by driving the world's transition to electric vehicles – that is a quantum innovation goal. No one could have imagined that it's value would have eclipsed that of Nissan in 2017 and Ford, later in that year; that is to say, no one except Mr. Musk. Its sister company, SpaceX, on their home page, announces matter-of-factly: "The company was founded in 2002 to revolutionize space technology, with the ultimate goal of enabling people to live on other planets.[202]" This is not science fiction, this is the goal of a responsible and visionary organization, inspired by a visionary leader, Elon Musk: Another *Quantum Innovation* company.

One of the more profoundly exciting and intimidating extrapolations we have all read about are those concerning *singularity*. Technological singularity often refers to the continued development, at exponential rates, of self-improving computer intelligence. In the field of memory storage and access, the advances in miniaturization now include atomic-based computer memory. Super fast, high bandwidth telecommunications allow more and more sharing of information and group collaboration. The combination of these developments, together with robotics, have triggered both excitement and alarm among futurists with respect to paradigm shifts for humanity.

Some have predicted the end of humanity as we know it, with the ascendency of what some call *bio-digital* fusion. Personally, I'm not alarmed but I am interested. I somehow believe that our emotions, to a large extent, drive our imagination and our creativity. This book is not an appropriate venue to debate the mechanics versus the humanity of the spectrum of emotional responses or whether human emotion and creativity can be chemically engineered and synthesized, or indeed whether science will ever reverse-engineer a human to a machine. After all, this is a book primarily written to enhance your business and management skills and insights.

In that context, some of the most imaginative minds are owned by science fiction writers and other futurists, many of whom are inspired by science fiction. Isaac Asimov[203] wrote about the effects of technology and risk - on cocooning 35 years before it became a prediction as Trend #1 in Faith Popcorn's, The Popcorn Report[204]. Many new product and service inventions and innovations can be found in the works of Sci-Fi writers, long before they became real. This is understandable. Most of these ideas satisfy human desires: the desire to have more time, to enjoy better health and wellness, and longevity, more happiness, more safety, better entertainment. The difference is that science fiction writers are free and unconstrained by the limitations of current realities. When these writers think about safety, they can go all the way by inventing personal force fields and super powers, and mind control. Better health demands can be satisfied with replaceable organs, cyborgs, and indeed, immortality. Entertainment needs can be met with Star Trek holo-decks. We could go on and on. Look at what we have today that was inspired by science fiction. My iPhone is charging wirelessly: wireless electricity. A robot vacuum cleaner works 24/7 and never askes for a raise, nor can it fall down the stairs. Body parts are indeed being produced. Holographic theatres and Holorooms are part of the very fast development taking place currently in the augmented reality industry. Weapons that track movement, identify hostile intentions, lock on to targets with speed-of-light lasers, and automatically fire at them – exist. Kids and adults hover on boards. The rich can buy personal car-planes and jet-packs. There are serious engineering articles about capturing asteroids and mining them. We are told that real money has been spent on tracking thousands of chunks of rocks which may collide with our planet one day, and we are designing ways to deflect or destroy them before they do. Businesses have plans for space hotels and space tourism. Some of us, including me, are anxiously looking forward to buying self-driving autonomous cars, which already exist. People have already been arrested for "printing" out a handgun on a 3-D printer at home. Most "new" product and service ideas are already out there, to be found, considered, and commercialized.

Go do it and have fun.

CHAPTER 17
TAKE-AWAYS

THE FUTURE

1	Optimism and pessimism are both useful mental outlooks. Embrace this dichotomy; but to advance, favor optimism.
2	It's easier to predict ten years out than next week. Day traders would make more money flipping burgers at McDonald's. Like slot machine gamblers, you only hear about the wins.
3	Wide sweeping trends like burgeoning middle classes in new-economy countries, crowd-funding, peer-to-peer businesses, and most internet-based economies – are obvious frameworks for enhancing traditional enterprises and developing new ones.
4	Be aware of quantum-level innovation and the lessons to be learned – for hitching on to these shooting stars.
5	Most innovations in the marketplace were written about years before in science fiction. Read science fiction for ideas to commercialize products and services.

APPENDIX

LOST ON THE MOON TEAM EXERCISE

INVENTORY OF ITEMS TO BE RANKED

Rank Items by Importance, the most important being #1, and the least important item, being #15.

Rank	Item
	Box of matches
	Food concentrate
	50 feet of nylon rope
	Parachute silk
	Solar-powered portable heating unit
	Two .45-caliber pistols
	One case of dehydrated milk
	Two 100-pound tanks of oxygen
	Stellar map (of the moon's constellation)
	Self-inflating life raft
	Magnetic compass
	Five gallons of water
	Signal flares
	First-aid kit containing injection needles
	Solar-powered FM receiver-transmitter

ANSWER SHEET

Do NOT look at these answers until the exercise is completed.

	NASA's Reasoning	NASA[205]'s Ranking
Box of Matches	No oxygen on moon to sustain flame; virtually worthless	15
Food Concentrate	Efficient means of Supplying energy requirements	4
Fifty feet of nylon rope	Useful in scaling cliffs, tying injured together	6
Parachute silk	Protection from sun's rays	8
Solar-powered portable Heating unit	Not needed unless on Dark side	13
Two .45 caliber pistols	Possible means of self-Propulsion	11
One case of dehydrated Milk	Bulkier duplication of Food concentrate	12
Two 100-pound tanks of oxygen	Most pressing survival Need	1
Stellar map (of the moon's Constellation)	Primary means of Navigation	3
Self-inflating life raft	CO2 bottle in military raft may be used for propulsion	9
Magnetic compass	Magnetic field on moon Is not polarized; Worthless for navigation	14
Five gallons of water	Replacement for Tremendous liquid loss on lighted side	2

	NASA's Reasoning	NASA[205]'s Ranking
Signal flares	Distress signal when Mother ship is sighted	10
First-aid kit injection needles	Needles for vitamins, Medicines, etc, will Fit special aperture in NASA space suits.	7
Solar powered FM-receiver transmitter	For communication with Mother ship; but FM Requires line-of-sight Transmission and short Ranges.	5
		TOTAL

Error points are the absolute difference between your ranks and NASA's ranks (disregard plus or minus signs).

Totalling the error points will provide a total score per individual, and per team that can be compared to the scoring table in order to determine if the individual or team actually survived their moon landing ordeal.

SCORE RANGE	NASA INTERPRETATION SCORE EXPLANATION
0-25	Excellent
26-32	Good
33-45	Average
46-55	Fair
56-70	Poor
71-112	Poor; suggest possible faking, or use of earth-bound logic

Any score below average likely translates that the participant individual or team – has perished on the moon

ABOUT THE AUTHOR

In a career spanning 45 years, Ira Teich advanced through executive ranks of a Fortune 50 multi-national before becoming senior partner of a renown consulting firm heading up its market strategy practice.

Ira transitioned to CEO, and chief strategist of a Harvard acclaimed consumer strategy consultancy, brand development, retail, and product packaging design firm, growing that Canadian agency globally, to the most successful in Canada and one of the five largest in the world.

Now semi-retired, and somehow busier than ever, he founded the Teich Group and continues an international practice in growth, market, brand, and communication strategies. He is also sits on a number of boards and volunteers with the Canadian Executive Service Organization as an advisor to governments in the developing world. Ira has travelled or worked in 80 countries.

"I don't want to become immortal through my work. I want to become immortal through not dying"

- Woody Allen

Index

D

E

F

G

H

I

J

K

L

M

N

O

P

Q

R

S

T

U

V

W

Y

Z

Endnotes

[1] 'USA Statistics,' *Inc. 2015*

[2] Ira Teich, 2016 Workshop on Effective mentoring for Dept. of Trade and Industry, Region 4A, Philippines

[3] Available at Bloomberg.com July 19, 2012

[4] "E-book sales represent 25% of total book sales in the U.S.," *Statistica*, available at <https://www.statista.com/topics/1453/digital-publishing/>

[5] Albert Einstein, "I am enough of an artist to draw freely upon my imagination. Imagination is more important than knowledge. For knowledge is limited, whereas imagination encircles the world"

[6] Ernest Hemingway, *The Sun Also Rises,* "How did you go bankrupt? Two ways. Gradually, then suddenly."

[7] ROI: Return on Investment

[8] Shane Parrish is founder of Farnam Street; an online intellectual hub

[9] Mahatma Gandhi, "The Truth Shall Set You Free"

[10] Malcolm Gladwell, *The Tipping Point: How Little Things Can Make a Big Difference* (2000). Available at <https://en.wikipedia.org/wiki/The_Tipping_Point>. Book sold 1.7 million copies by 2007

[11] McKinsey Quarterly February 2017

[12] Ibid.

[13] Available at <www.labelinsight.com/foodrevolution study>

[14] Available at <http://blog.labelinsight.com/study-ninety-four-percent-of-consumers-say-food-product-transparency-from-brands-and-manufacturers-is-important-impacts-purchase>

[15] Margo Chase, "It Sounds Obvious, but to Be Trusted, Brands Must Be Honest, 3 lessons from marketers who did it right", *Adweek, Jan 12, 2017*

[16] Michael Siegel, Lynne Doner Lotenberg, "Marketing Public Health: Strategies to Promote Social Change", 2007

[17] Robert Harrington, "Value Line - Philip Morris International: A Short SWOT Analysis", October 06, 2014

[18] Allan Hall, "German companies Bosch, Mercedes, Deutsche Bank, and VW get very rich using 300,000 concentration camp slaves", *Mail Online*, June 2014, Berlin. Available at <http://www.dailymail.co.uk/news/article-2663635/Revealed-How-Nazis-helped-German-companies>

[19] Available at <http://www.nytimes.com/1998/06/13/world/world-news-briefs-volkswagen-faces-suit-over-jewish-slave-labor.html>

[20] Peter Michael Senge, PhD (1947-) senior lecturer MIT Sloan School of Management

[21] Robert is currently the CEO and Chairman of Disney

[22] Available at <https://en.wikipedia.org/wiki/Pizza_Pizza>

[23]Available at <http://www.japantimes.co.jp/news/2016/01/26/business/corporate-business/despite-tpp-ford-exit-closed-japan-indonesia/>

---

[24] Available at <http://www.cultofmac.com/39789/apple-iphone-takes-72-percent-of-japan-smartphone-market/>

[25] Available at <http://www.japantimes.co.jp/news/2016/02/20/business/corporate-business/japan-iphone-shipments>

[26] Ralph Waldo Emerson (1803 – 1882) was a renown 19th century American philosopher.

[27] University of Surrey, Guildford, England "Creating Value: Between Commerce and Commons", *Background paper for a presentation at the ARC Centre for the Creative Industries and Innovation*, International Conference in Brisbane, June 2008

[28] Random House Inc., 2012

[29] Ibid.

[30] Ibid.

[31] For example, Allergan, Bausch + Lomb, Abbott, others.

[32] Available at <www.cdc.gov./contactlenses/>

[33] Joseph F. Hair, et al, "Essentials of Business research methods", (*Routledge*, Business & Economics, Mar 4, 2015

[34] Comment: Definition of 'Category Killer Large companies that put less efficient and highly specialized merchants out of business. Category killers can attain this status by being cheaper, easier, bigger, or more popular than the competition. Best examples of a category killer are Wal Mart. More information available at <http://www.ivestopedia .com /terms/c/categorykiller.asp>

[35] Lewin (1890-1947), recognized as the "founder of social psychology". He was ranked as the 18th most cited psychologist of the 20th century. Available at <https://en.wikipedia.org/wiki/Kurt_Lewin>

[36] Definition available at <http://lms.aspira.org/sites/default /files/Force%20Field%20Analysis.pdf>

[37] With thanks to change-management-coach/web

[38] FIDE, Investment and Exports, is a private non-profit organization created in 1984 to promote investment, develop exports and work closely with the government and other private organization - in Honduras. Available at <Hondurasinfo.hn>

[39] SWOT: Strengths, Weaknesses, Opportunities, Threats – a very old and sometimes useful model/quadrant for having the client think through these dimensions of their business. The insight comes with turning weaknesses into strengths and threats into opportunities, etc.

[40] Reader: please excuse the mixed metaphor.

[41] Available at <http://www.mytotalretail.com/article/walmart-rolls-back-prices/>, August 23, 2016

[42] SKU is a stock keeping unit. Each product including different packaging sizes of the same product, is considered a separate SKU

[43] May-June 1992 issue

[44] Dr. Leonard Wong, associate research professor at the U.S. Army War College's Strategic Studies Institute said the paper "Why They Fight: Combat Mo-

tivation in the Iraq" validated the popular belief that unit cohesion is a key issue in motivating soldiers to fight. Available at <https://www.the-balance.com/why-soldiers-fight-3331792>

[45] Peterson retired in 2002 as Chairman of the Board, and Chief Executive Officer of imperial Oil, Exxon's Canadian subsidiary in Canada.

[46] In earlier days, before PowerPoint - presentations were made with "transparencies' and an overhead projector.

[47] Yes, believe it or not, there many smokers around that table

[48] CESO/SACO (SACO: French acronym), formerly referred to as Canadian Executive Service Overseas. They are an NGO, funded in large part by the Government of Canada, and use a pool of Canadian experts in various fields – to assist many developing countries. An amazing organization.

[49] Women's groups, community associations, rural improvement clubs

[50] Bibinka is prepared with milled rice, coconut milk, sugar, eggs (sometimes), traditionally baked in a clay oven on banana leaves.

[51] SM Supermarket is a Filipino supermarket chain owned by SM Investments and is operated through Super Value Inc. As of May 30, 2014, SM Investments operated 42 supermarkets and 98 SaveMore branches across the Philippines. Available at <https://en.wikipedia.org/wiki/SM_Supermarket>

[52] Which happened to be Tuguegarao, technically a "2nd-class city" in the northern province of Cagayan. The SM supermarket chain has a very nice store in that town of about 160,000 people.

[53] A local neighborhood political official

[54] This could be required since the modern equipment is supposed to deliver the same taste as the old clay baking traditional techniques; this may require experimental with baking times, and other adjustments.

[55] The adage about "follow the money" holds true here. Understand how your customer/re-seller is rewarded and ensure that this motivation is directly addressed and is crystal clear in your presentation.

[56] Termed: MMOS (massively multiplayer online games) or MMO

[57] Jagex Game Studios

[58] Available at <http://www.2007runescapegold.com/archive/rs-news/How-many-runescape-players-in-total-now-in-the-year-2016>

[59] Owner: Blizzard Entertainment, Available at <https://en.wikipedia.org/wiki/World_of_Warcraft>

[60] FONA International, "Purchasing Power of Teens," Available at <https://www.fona.com/resource-center/blog/purchasing-power-teens>

[61] Aristotle (384–322 BC) was an ancient Greek philosopher and scientist. At seventeen or eighteen years of age, he joined Plato's Academy in Athens, and remained there until the age of thirty-seven (c. 347 BC). His writings cover many subjects – including physics, biology, zoology, metaphysics, logic, ethics, aesthetics, poetry, theater, music, rhetoric, linguistics, politics and government – and constitute the first comprehensive system of Western philosophy.

[62] By Malcolm Gladwell

[63] Chip and Dan Heath, Random House, 2007

---

[64] Maslow, "A Review of General Psychology survey", published 2002, ranked Maslow as the tenth most cited psychologist of the 20th century, Available at <Wikipedia>

[65] Marina Adshade, PhD, "Why Do Mothers Care More About Their Children Than Fathers?", *Psychology Today*, January 2014

[66] Michael L. O'Dell, M.D., University of Texas Medical Branch at Galveston, Galveston, Texas, "Skin and Wound Infections: An Overview"., *Am Fam Physician*, 15;57(10):2424-2432, May 1998

[67] Ibid.

[68] Acronym JLTV: Joint Light Tactical Vehicle with which the U.S. army plans to replace the Humvee.

[69] Anonymous

[70] Dr. Stephen Covey, PhD, (1932-2012), "the 7 Habits of Highly Effective People". His most popular book, sold 25 million copies.

[71] Comment: Individual evaluations always include their contribution to teamwork, but still represent an individual employee evaluation. Team only evaluations are very different.

[72] Schuster-Zingheim and Associates

[73] Cable & Judge, 1994; DeMatteo & Eby, 1997; DeMatteo et al., 1997; Duffy, Shaw & Stark, 1999; Yamagashi, 1988; as cited by Haines & Taggar, 2006, p. 202

[74] Anita Williams Woolley, Christopher F. Chabris, Alex Pentland, Nada Hashmi, Thomas W. Malone – affiliated with: Carnegie Mellon University, Union College, Massachusetts Institute of Technology (MIT) Center for Collective Intelligence, MIT Sloan School of Management, *Science,* 29 Oct 2010: Vol. 330, Issue 6004, pp. 686-688

[75] Comment: Consider the architectural structure of a geodesic dome; suggesting a 'self-supporting" structure.

[76] "The Decline of Wikipedia", *MIT Technology Review,* Oct 2013

[77] Available at <https://en.wikipedia.org/wiki/Wikipedia:Wikipedians>

[78] "The Decline of Wikipedia", *MIT Technology Review*, Oct 2013

[79] "Communications of the ACM" *Volume 53 Issue 4*, April 2010

[80] Marianna Sigala, University of the Aegean, Greece, "WEB 2.0, Social Marketing Strategies and Distribution Channels for City Destinations: Enhancing the Participatory Role of Travelers and Exploiting their Collective Intelligence", *Source Title: Social Computing: Concepts, Methodologies, Tools, and Applications,* 2010

[81] Kenneth Hartley Blanchard, PhD (Cornell 1967) (1939 -) is an American author and management expert. His writing career includes over 60 published books. His most successful book, "The One Minute Manager" has sold over 13 Million books.

[82] Comment: The Delphi method is a structured communication technique or method, originally developed as a systematic, interactive forecasting method which relies on a panel of experts. Available at <Wikipedia>

[83] Comment: I would suggest a team size of 6 to 8 people

[84] Comment: The correct answers to this exercise, which were provided by NASA, as well as a scoring sheet which measures the deltas between the correct ranking versus the individual and team ranking, and calculates if the individual or the team would have actually survived the Moon ordeal. See Appendix.
[85] Comment: The source of this exercise is unknown. There are many versions of this team exercise available on the web, and more than one claimant to its copyright. However, I was presented this exercise for the first time during leadership training at Exxon Corp. in 1985 or thereabouts, well before any claims that I am seeing on the web material. Accordingly, I assume that this material is within the public domain.
[86] *Bloomberg Business Week*
[87] Peggy Drexler Ph.D., "Why We Love to Gossip", *Psychology Today*, August 2014
[88] Ibid.
[89] Ibid.
[90] "What Psychologists Tell Us About Lying", October 2013, Available at <http://www.compulsivelyingdisorder.com/what-psychologists-tell-us-about-lying>posted>
[91] Nachman of Breslov (1772 – 1810), known as Reb Nachman of Breslov or simply as Rebbe Nachman, founder: Breslov Hasidic dynasty
[92] Douglas Murray McGregor (1906 – 1964) was a management professor at the MIT Sloan School of Management
[93] He is best known for his Theory X and Theory Y as presented in his book 'The Human Side of Enterprise' (1960), which proposed that manager's individual assumptions about human nature and behaviour determined how individual manages their employees. (Wikipedia).
[94] Comment: Not to be confused with: "Adaptive management (AM)", also known as "adaptive resource management (ARM)" or "Adaptive Environmental Assessment and Management (AEAM)", is a structured, iterative process of robust decision making in the face of uncertainty, with an aim to reducing uncertainty over time via system monitoring, Available at <https://en.wikipedia.org/wiki/Adaptive_management>
[95] Robert B. Kaiser, "Introduction to the special issue on developing flexible and adaptable leaders for an age of uncertainty", *American Psychological Association*, 2010 Volume 62, Issue 2 (Jun). Pgs.77-80
[96] *The Wall Street Journal*, July 21, 2015
[97] Harley has come up with creative financing offers, which one could interpret as a form of discounting.
[98] <http://variety.com/2014/biz/news/disney-brands-generate-record-40-9-billion-from-licensed-merchandise-in-2013>
[99] Natalie Robehmed, "The 'Frozen' Effect: When Disney's Movie Merchandising Is Too Much", *Forbes*
[100] Comment: it will of course be in the small print on a back panel, as corporate ownership information

---

[101] Technical name: aroma atomizer diffuser

[102] Available at <http://www.aromaco.co.uk/>

[103] Available at <https://aromatechsystems.com/pages/foodsales-scenting; http://us.moodmedia.com/scent-solutions/>, and <https://www.air-aroma.com/scenting; http://www.aromaco.co.uk/>

[104] Jennifer Dublino, VP-development at Scent World, a global non-profit organization

[105] "Dollars & Scents: From Clothes to Cars to Banks, Brands Seek Distinction Through Fragrance - How Marketers Are Selling with a Signature Sensory Experience", *Advertising Age,* December 09, 2014

[106] Comment: Caveat might relate to consumers that may be deleteriously affected due to asthmatic and other conditions.

[107] Source of Harley tattoo pic <https://www.google.ca/search?q=harley+tattoos+designs&biw>

[108] 33,000 clubs, in 200+ countries, available at <www.contactrotary.org/faqs/>

[109] Eastman Kodak co. turned its first annual profit despite more declines in overall revenue since emerging from bankruptcy roughly three years ago. (March 7, 2017) It began operations in 1888.

[110] At its peak in 2004, Blockbuster consisted of nearly 60,000 employees and over 8,000 stores. It filed for bankruptcy in 2010, available at <https://en.wikipedia.org/wiki/Blockbuster_LLC>

[111] James Surowiecki, "The Wisdom of Crowds", *The New Yorker.*
"In 2002, Nokia had the sixth-most-valuable brand in the world, valued by the consultancy Interbrand at $30 billion; but It didn't produce the clamshell-design cell phones that customers wanted. Customers jumped ship, and the company's sales tumbled. Nokia lost $6 billion in equity".

[112] Ibid. "In 2003, Fortune called the doughnut maker America's "hottest brand." Then came what might prove to be the hottest name of 2004: Atkins (protein diet craze)"

[113] Kevin Roberts, CEO of advertising agency Saatchi & Saatchi and author of the book Lovemarks. "Now the consumer is boss. There's nowhere for brands to hide."

[114] Ibid.

[115] Facebook was founded by Mark Zuckerberg in 2004

[116] DMR STATS, available at <expandedramblings.com>

[117] Ibid.

[118] Dan Shwabel, "10 New Findings About the Millennial Consumer" *Forbes,* January 20, 2015

[119] DMR STATS (expandedramblings.com)

[120] Ibid.

[121] Comment: Twitter was created in March 2006 by Jack Dorsey, Noah Glass, Biz Stone, and Evan Williams in California

---

[122] Comment: As of September 2016, Twitter relaxed their 140-character rule. Now, when users add a photo, GIF, video or poll to their tweet, it will not count towards the 140-character limit. A quote tweet, which displays somebody else's tweet within your own, will also not count. Available at <http://www.telegraph.co.uk/technology/>

[123] About 700 million registered Twitter users.

[124] Available at <www.statisticsbrain.com>, September 2016 data

[125] Snapchat is an image messaging and multimedia mobile application created by Evan Spiegel, Bobby Murphy, and Reggie Brown, former students at Stanford University (in 2011)

[126] Available at <Wikipedia>

[127] Ira Teich, "IPO day lifts are not terribly meaningful"

[128] Comment: WhatsApp Messenger is a freeware, cross-platform and end-to-end encrypted instant messaging application for smartphones using the Internet to make voice calls, one to one video calls; send text messages, images, GIF, videos, documents, user location, audio files, phone contacts and voice notes and are visible to all contacts; similar to Snapchat, Facebook and Instagram Stories. Available at <Wikipedia>

[129] Ibid.

[130] Comment: Instagram is a mobile photo-sharing application and service that allows users to share pictures and videos either publicly or privately on the service, as well as through a variety of other social networking platforms, such as Facebook, Twitter, Tumblr, and Flickr. Available at <Wikipedia>

[131] Adapted from <thebuzzbusiness.com>, some of the best words on this subject.

[132] Comment: This is a custom in the Philippines. When doing any kind of work or observation in an area, one pays a courtesy call to the person who is politically in charge of that area- very much like what a traveler would have to do when travelling in ancient times.

[133] Adidas AG is a German multinational corporation that designs and manufactures sports shoes, clothing and accessories headquartered in Herzogenaurach, Bavaria. It is the largest sportswear manufacturer in Europe and the second biggest in the world, <Wikipedia>

[134] Available at <consumerreports.org/cro/cars/car-brands/jeep/index>

[135] Comment: author discloses, as a Wrangler owner, he is biased.

[136] Amar Bhide, Howard H. Stevenson, "Why Be Honest If Honesty Doesn't Pay?", September–October 1990

[137] Ibid.

[138] Ibid.

[139] A popular term today that speaks to the effectiveness of popular (and courageous) stand against corrupt entities and or untruths.

[140]POPAI Consumer Buying Habits Statistics 1999

---

[141] Deloitte, "The call to re-connect with consumers" *2015 Study*. Indicated that "At-the-shelf purchases were trending upward, with 51% of consumers decided to purchase at the shelf", *The 2015 American Pantry Study, available at* < https://www2.deloitte.com>, Teich suspects that number is even higher.
[142] Gilroy, "Time on retailers' side: Impulse purchases rise the longer shoppers are in store", *University of Notre Dame,* 2015
[143] "Shopping carts are usually designed for a maximum of 2 mph (originally to protect against theft from the store" – *Food Marketing Institute <FMI>*
[144] Depending on store size, number of SKUs could reach as high as 60,000.
[145] Available at <https://en.wikipedia.org/wiki/Eye_color>
[146] Available at <https://essilorusa.com/content/essilor-usa/en/news-room/news/sensitive_to_light.html>
[147] "What Colors Mean in Other Cultures", January 26, 2016, available at <http://www.huffingtonpost.com/smartertravel/what-colors-mean-in-other_b_9078674.html>
[148] Ibid.
[149] The Bridge was completed in 2000
[150] An unlikely and temporary alliance of 10 food retailers under the name of MOST Association with the singular common goal of fighting foreign competition in their trading area of Miass, Zlatoust, and Chebarkul, and Chelyabinsk.
[151] This was the first investment for Carrefour in Russia, and probably served also as a "listening post" strategy to ascertain the value of expanding further in this challenging country.
[152] The company that I led as its CEO and chief strategy officer, was complimented by Harvard Business Review, which called us: "the world's best retail doctors".
[153] Available at <www.statista.com>
[154] *The Future of Grocery*, April 2015, available at <www.nielson>
[155] Sales/Sq. ft.: This metric was one of the most important standard metric that demonstrated a retailer's success.
[156] Comment: By the way, out of interest, the 2nd highest sales/sq. ft. store was Honest Ed's in Toronto, Canada. Honest Ed's, an icon was finally closed in January 2017.
[157] Ira Teich, "The Power of Retailer Brands", *Design Management Institute (DMI)Magazine*
[158] Available at <POPAI Consumer Buying Habits Study/Meyers research Center>
[159] Available at <https://www.statista.com/statistics/266282/annual-net-revenue-of-amazoncom>
[160] 10% of Amazon's deliveries, worth $550 million in fees to UPS and FedEx is in danger of being absorbed internally by Amazon, available at <www.trefis.com>
[161] Source: Adobe Digital Insights
[162] *USA TODAY,* Published Nov. 27, 2016 | Updated, Nov. 28, 2016

[163] Nicholas Carr, "Amazon's Next Big Move: Take over the Mall", *MIT Technology Review*, November 14, 2016

[164] Comment: The deal was scrapped by U.S. Justice depart over anti-trust concerns

[165] Comment: Samsung and LG are both south Korea conglomerates

[166] Comment: Whirlpool owns Maytag, Kitchenaide, Amana, Inglis, and many other brands

[167] Owned by Electrolux (Sweden)

[168] German multinational

[169] Founded in Spain in 1974. The clothing retailer**Error! Bookmark not defined.** has more than 2,100 stores worldwide and is the flagship brand of the Inditex Group. Zara is renowned for its ability to develop a new product and get it to stores within two weeks, while other retailers take six months.

[170] Fashion Director for Louis Vuitton (LVMH)

[171] Mostly in company-owned facilities in Spain, Portugal, and Turkey, available at <https://en.wikipedia.org/wiki/Zara**Error! Bookmark not defined.**_retailer>

[172] Available at <http://edition.cnn.com/BUSINESS/programs/yourbusiness/stories2001/zara>

[173] George Holbrook Jackson (31 December 1874 – 16 June 1948) was a British journalist, writer and publisher. He was recognised as one of the leading bibliophiles of his time. (Wikipedia)

[174] CSDs: Carbonated soft drinks

[175] Managing the Mix, is also a technical term, and is related operationally to planning where products are placed on store shelves; I.e. planogramming, and adjacencies.

[176] Valerie Ross, "Numbers: The Nervous System, from 268-MPH Signals to Trillions of Synapses", *Discover magazine*, March, 2011

[177] The ancient Greek mathematician (287-212 B.B.)

[178] Eureka" comes from the Ancient Greek word εὕρηκα heúrēka, meaning "I have found (it)" (Wikipedia)

[179] (1901 – 1976) a German theoretical physicist and one of the key pioneers of quantum mechanics. Nobel prize in physics in 1932.

[180] Daniel Cappon, "Intuition and Management: Research and Application", Greenwood Publishing, 1994

[181] Edward Elgar, "Handbook of Intuition Research"

[182] Available at <https://en.wikipedia.org/wiki/Scientific_method>

[183] Ira Teich, Teich Group, 2000. "Consumer Opportunity Assessment: Phase One: The Royal Ontario Museum", January 20, 2000, Toronto

[184] Investopedia, available at <http://www.investopedia.com/university/mergers/mergers5.asp#ixzz4ZVNIRepK>

[185] "Mergers and Acquisitions: Why They Can Fail" *Investopedia,* available at <http://www.investopedia.com/university/mergers/mergers5.asp>

[186] , Scott A. Christofferson, Robert S. McNish, and Diane L. Sias, "Where mergers go wrong", *McKinsey Quarterly*, May 2004

[187] Comment: The influence of media on the program choices of charitable organization is a reality that is sometimes unfortunate, given that there are causes that are preventable with relatively small amounts of funds per preventable deaths (such as Malaria), that are simply not sexy in the media. This is an example where the charity itself could do a better job, by transforming their static web presence – into more of a TV channel. But beyond the scope of this book.
[188] SROI: Social Return on Investment
[189] The highest (most conservatively estimated) cost of saving a child's life is about $3,000 according to Business Insider July 29, 2015, available at <http://www.businessinsider.com/the-worlds-best-charity-can-save-a-life>. Most Charities argue that smaller donations will do the same.
[190] Example: the government of Canada will routinely call upon the CEO of UNICEF Canada – to participate on policy formulation with regards to the Rights of the Child.
[191] 2016, available at <Pressroom.ups.com>
[192] 2016, available at <About.van.fedex.com>
[193] Availability at <https://sustainability.ups.com/the-ups-foundation>
[194] Predicted by Alexis de Tocqeville in 1840
[195]Roger Joseph Ebert (1942 – 2013) American film critic and historian, and author. In 1975, Ebert became the first film critic to win the Pulitzer Prize for Criticism.
[196] 2016, July, available at <Gizmodo.com>
[197] Available at <Futuretimeline.net>
[198] Consumers spent $23.5 billion on the gaming industry in 2015. $16.5 billion was spent on gaming content alone, available at <http://www.polygon.com/2016/4/29/11539102/gaming-stats-2016-esa-essential-facts>
[199] Allegra Frank, "Take a look at the average American gamer in new survey findings: 1.7 gamers in every house and two hands on every controller", Apr 29, 2016
[200] 2015, available at <Inc.com>
[201] Ibid.
[202] Available at <http://www.spacex.com/about>
[203] Asimov: His book, "The Naked Sun" was published in 1956
[204] The Popcorn Report, by Faith Popcorn, was published by Harper Business in 1991.
[205] The answers were provided by NASA in the 1980s, and should be considered as irrefutable.

Made in the USA
Columbia, SC
19 September 2017